Production Bible Series

Volume 1 (Enraptured)

Production Bible Series

Volume 1 (Enraptured)

Stephen Makoge Enongene

King's Word Publishing

© 2016 by Stephen Makoge Enongene

Publication by King's Word Publication, 2016

For your questions and publishing needs, write to:

    E.C. Nakeli
    40 S Church st
    Westminster, MD 21157
    E-mail: *ecnakeli@yahoo.com*

Printed in the United States of America

All rights reserved. No part of this publication may be reproduced, stored in a retrieval systems, or transmitted in ay form or by any means— for example, electronic, photocopy, recording—without the prior written permission of the publisher. The only exception is brief quotations in printed reviews.

To contact the author, write to:

    Stephen Makoge Enongene
    Hackenstrasße 1
    80331, Munich, Germany
    E-mail: stephen_enongene@yahoo.com

Production Bible Series Volume 1 (Enraptured) / Stephen Makoge Enongene
ISBN: 978-1-945055-03-4

    All Scripture is taken from the Authorized King James Version of the Bible unless otherwise noted.

Cover and Interior Design: Zach Essama

Table of Contents

Dedication vii
General Preface to Volume 1 1
Face to Face With Jesus (A Testimony) 9

Book The First: The Mystery of Christ as You 21
Introduction 23
Chapter 1: The Secrets of God Are Glorious 29
Chapter 2: Attaining the Secret Place of Divine Love 41
Chapter 3: The Fundamental Mysteries of the Secret Place 67

Book the Second: The Four Pillar of Salvation 89
Introduction 91
Chapter 1: You Need Deliverance 95
Chapter 2: You Cannot Save Yourself 107
Chapter 3: Jesus Has Already Obtained Eternal Redemption For You ... 119
Chapter 4: There Is No Hope For Eternal Life Without Jesus Christ 131

Book the Third: The Holy Spirit and Our Restitution and Restoration 149
Introduction 151
Chapter 1: Lessons on the Holy Spirit 155
Chapter 2: The Holy Spirit Is the Power
of God's Might, and the Might of His Power 167
Chapter 3: Presentation of the Gifts (I Corinthians Chapter 12) 221
Chapter 4: How The Gifts Are Categorised 229
An Epilogue To The Trilogy: Toward A Christian Communion 231

DEDICATION

This volume is dedicated to all lovers of Jesus Christ.

GENERAL PREFACE TO VOLUME 1

The Gospel of Jesus Christ is a revelation (Deuteronomy 29:29; Matthew 11:25; 13, I Corinthians 2:6-8, II Timothy 3:15-17). This is because the Bible is not a book, but a book of books: a book of wisdom, general knowledge, history, science, mystery, arts, divine love, and supreme power which is why it has to be ordained through a supreme vessel from on high (John 15:16; Romans 10:14-17). This means that certain aspects may be revealed to certain people at certain times for specific purposes. Often, the anointing gets doled out through the Holy Spirit in order to edify, and leverage the authority and performance of the recipient in a clearly designated area of operation. God is sovereign, and no respecter of persons (Exodus 1:17; 16:19; 33:19; IISamuel 14:14; II Chronicles 19:7; Acts 10:34; Romans 2:11; Ephesians 6:9; James 2:9). Perhaps we should highlight our Mighty God by drawing inspiration from king David's prayer of praise:

> *"Thine O Lord, is the greatness, and the power, and the glory, and the victory, and the majesty: for all that is in the heaven and in the earth is thine; thine is the kingdom, O Lord, and thou art exalted as head above all. Both riches and honour come of thee, and thou reignest over all; and in thine hand is power and might; and in thine hand it is to make great, and to give strength unto all. Now therefore, our God, we thank thee, and praise thy glorious name. But who am I, and what is my people, that we should be able*

to offer so willingly after this sort? for all things come from thee, and of thine own have we given thee. For we are strangers before thee, and sojourners, as were all our fathers: our days on earth are as a shadow, and there is none abiding" (I Chronicles 29:11-15)

Spiritual gifts are distributed according to the judgment of the Holy Spirit (I Corinthians 12:11). Even so, just as the sun, the rain and time happen to all unconditionally, and without any regard to persons, positions, culture or material consideration, the Lord establishes a level playing field for everyone. In fact, no single person (apart from Jesus Christ, who is Lord of all) can claim a monopoly of all the pieces of the jigsaw. Paul teaches that we all know in part (I Corinthians 13:9). Moreover, we all are blessed with different kinds and levels of anointing for various purposes as enunciated in the Holy Scriptures (Romans 12; Ephesians 4:7-16). Hence we tend to need each others' perspectives in fellowship to avoid unnecessary pitfalls in this race, and also to be able to evolve in the realm of the Spirit, becoming more consistent in our daily strive toward perfection (Proverbs 4:18; James 1:2-4).

In essence the purpose of a devout Christian believer in Christ hinges not on duration, but rather on donation (Matthew 10:8; Luke 6:38). In other words, Christian growth, advancement and/or maturity in the Spirit does not depend on longevity, but rather on character, commitment and faithfulness to the Perfect Law. That is to say, before God sent you to earth He had completed every preparatory work on your entire being, congruent with the imperatives marking the entire duration of your life cycle. Take the automotive industry as a case in point. Beloved, to all intents and purposes, the car companies would never consign to market any unfinished product, bereft of the requisite due diligence in performance! Friend, come to think of it, these are just human concerns that are liable to errors, but still they aspire for excellence. Now imagine, if those man-made enterprises can show such discipline, then it goes without saying that with God diligence should not only be expected but guaranteed. Friend, the Lord God never launches an incomplete human being to earth (Philipians 4:13). Thus He has your present, past and future trapped in temporal time, as your soul and spirit which both encompass temporariness are mysteriously encapsulated in your earthly body (Psalm 139:14-16; Jeremiah 1:5-10). Hence within the inevitable medium of exchange, even in tandem with the supreme power of the Holy Ghost, the natural and the supernatural are yoked together to perform supernatural feats of valour (Daniel 11:32; John 14:12, 15:1-14; Romans 8:14-27; Ephesians 2:10). Never you ever risk putting yourself in the situation in future where you entertain any doubts about your capabilities as an accomplished full-blown human being, deserving of self-esteem, and self-determination. Never ruminate on, or express regrets because you failed to do what you know you should or ought to have done. Be patient with yourself. treat your body with the utmost care—it is holy ground! You alone are the sole master of the decisions that can make a difference to your life.

We Are Ordained To Lead With Our Hearts As Servant-kings

Beloved, life is made up of leaders and followers. Leaders must serve others to earn respect from followers. To this end, it is incumbent upon all leaders to understand that leadership means more than just pursuing a pursuing a career or a profession. It is a vocation, even a calling. The Bible states that the powers that be are ordained of God. Jesus Himself was a proponent of the loyalty that subjects owe to their leaders. In fact, the king of kings teaches that His disciples should give onto Caesar what is his, and onto God what is His. But for leaders to get to this level they will have to stay humble in their development. God should be the Originator of all growth. The tussle for position is a clear hindrance to progress in most churches. Not all men of God are good leaders. The testimony of Jesus must be the standard for all Christians: "And the child grew and waxed strong in spirit, filled with wisdom: and the grace of God was upon him (Luke 2:40). Jesus knew His mission inside out, and worked tirelessly to achieve His purpose *"And he said unto them, How is it that ye sought me? Wist ye not that I must be about my Father's business?"* (Luke 2:49). He knew exactly what He was going to become from childhood on, and never looked back. Brethren, as a leader or one in-the-making, knowing your mission means that you should proceed backwards from your target. The target is visionary. An introspective, inner look into your ethical values and judgments will help give a sense of originality and authenticity as to how you can accomplish your purpose in the vineyard of God. Remember God is perfectly organised. Everything has its place (Genesis 1:1-31; 8:15-19,22).

Everyone has their position (Matthew 10:24-25). Everything has its time (Ecclesiastes 3:1-8). The Spirit will reveal yours in the fulness of time, even as you keep a willing, humble and loving heart (I Peter 2:5-11; John 16:12-15):

> *"Keep thy heart with all diligence; for out of it are the issues of life"* (Proverbs 4:23).

Working backwards from your target also presupposes sound understanding of your followers—getting to know them, learning about their needs and listening to understand and, assimilate, or internalise their wishes and concerns, to see how best to address those. That is why it took Jesus thirty years to set His ministry afoot—literally, after mastering the culture and people; their politics and economy. Followers, on their part, benefit from the vision, protection, and wise guidance provided by God through His servant-kings. A Scriptural paradigm of this versatile model is discernible in the ministry of Jesus. During His three-and-a-half–year reign Jesus had the following number of disciples: Our Lord had the 3 (Matthew 17:1), He had the 12 (Matthew 10:2), and He also had the 70 (Luke 10:17). While all of them were equally important in terms of kingdom values, yet still they were appreciated and assigned variously. Jesus engaged them differently, and at different times with clear instructions as to the range and scope of their mission:

> *"These twelve Jesus sent forth, and commanded them, saying, Go not into the way of the Gentiles, and into any city of the Samaritans enter ye not: But go rather to the lost sheep of the house of Israel"* (Matthew 10:56).

Thus, the first mission field was limited to the Jews. But after they were granted power their theatre of operation was extended beyond the borders of Israel:

> *"And Jesus came and spake unto them, saying, All power is given unto me in heaven and in earth. Go ye therefore, and teach all nations, baptizing them in the name of the Father, and of the Son, and of the Holy Ghost: Teaching them to observe all things whatsoever I have commanded you: and, lo, I am with you always, even unto the end of the world"* (Matthew 28:18-20).

> *"But ye shall receive power, after that the Holy Ghost is come upon you; and ye shall be witnesses unto me both in Jerusalem, and in all Judaea, and in Samaria, and unto the uttermost part of the earth"* (Acts 1:8)

The talents were granted to each and everyone according to their individual ability (Matthew 25:15; I Corinthians 12). Beloved, everyone is called according to their anointing (Romans 12:3-8).

Thus I was called by Jesus to join the ranks of this erudite race of glory because many others out there need the courage and heavenly initiative I am made to deliver, chiefly by setting the pace thanks to the anointing I received from Jesus. On that score I was not surprised as the Master Himself had declared that the harvest is plenty, but the workers are few (John 4:35-38). Few, in the sense that leaders and apostles are chosen by God Himself. Brethren, the silent, decent majority are crying out to be led. It was Edmund Burke who remarked so famously 300 years ago:

> *"Bad things happen when good people do nothing."*

A Christian rendition of this remark would ascribe the good people to be followers of Christ, in the Spirit. It is bad enough for well meant, Christ-like, born again folks to stay neutral which creates a vacuum for bullies, and psychopathic grabbers to hold sway! It is most awful when we, the elect of God, recoil to passive criticism and insincere murmuring (Numbers 11:1). On the flip side, the Bible teaches that it is more honourable to give than to receive, and those who have been meek enough to make the right choice: operating from the giving end, should have the boldness to stick their necks out and be counted among the brave (Isaiah 53:12). After all it was from the mountain top, and not from the valley that Jesus Christ stood when He declared to His disciples that a candle that purveys light is not placed under the table (Matthew 5:14-16). Ideally, and in order to better maximise its impact it is placed on the table. Brethren, I write to encourage all true believers to embrace the Grand Commission of Jesus Christ readily available to everyone who believes in Him (Matthew 28:18-20; 10:5-8; Mark 16:15-18; Acts 1:8). *"Arise, shine, for thy light is come, and the glory of the Lord is risen upon thee."* (Isaiah 60:1). So, like Jesus, I declare onto you, friend: rise and shine, for you are the light of the world. But don't indulge in vainglory (Jeremiah 9:23-24). Understand and acknowledge the source of your strength and stay humble to your God who has called you to a battle you have already been guaranteed victorious. Hence, endeavour to be diligent in the operational strategy of your life mission.

Understandably sometimes the experiences of life can be so stuffed up with challenges that a heart would pray for death. In other words negativity has become so searing and corrosive lately—and the bad news is, there is hardly anyone who is free from its guilt! Which unequivocally lends credence to the ubiquitous phrase in Scripture, *fear not!* In both the Old and the New Testaments of the Bible we Christians are constantly apprised of the collective range of the spectre of evil among humans (Genesis 8:21; Psalm 14:1-3). Across the globe, this scourge is pervasive. From culture to culture; nation to nation; person to person the atrocities we keep throwing at each other to flatter our selfish egos and preposterous greed are abysmal. Malachi Other clergymen take advantage of their privileged positions on the pulpit to meddle with divine judgment. Too often, in a thinly disguised campaign of self-promotion which is in flagrant contravention of scriptural doctrine preachers indulge in insincere self-hallelujahs. Church leaders scheme to arrogate onto themselves all the praises derived from the wisdom and righteousness of God, almost without qualms. Indeed, the legacy of Geoffrey Chaucer's satirical corpus on the modern church is on and well in virtually all the denominations today! Consequently, it is obvious: the clergy, once again, have chosen to blaspheme, and in fact, inadvertently contrived to nibble on the sanctity of God's inalienable glory (I Corinthians 9:16). In so doing, they are counting on God's infinite mercy and grace. But God's Word is God's Word! We only deceive ourselves by tinkering with it, and in this contest we are bound to learn the hard way, (mark Jonah's wise words after his punitive expedition: *"They that observe lying vanities forsake their own mercy. But I will sacrifice unto thee with the voice of thanksgiving; I will pay that I have vowed. Salvation is of the Lord."* (Jonah 2:8-9). Apostle Paul also had to shed more light on the syndrome, apparently targeting the meek and repentant servants, in his famous epistle to the Galatians:

"Be not deceived; God is not mocked: for whatsoever a man soweth, that shall he also reap. For he that soweth to his flesh shall of the flesh reap corruption; but he that soweth to the Spirit shall of the Spirit reap life everlasting. And let us not be weary in well being doing: for in due season we shall reap, if we faint not. As we have therefore opportunity, let us do good unto all men, especially unto them who are of the household of faith. Ye see how large a letter I have written unto you with mine own hand" (Galatians 6:7-11).

FACE TO FACE WITH JESUS
(A TESTIMONY)

"It is not expedient for me doubtless to glory, I will come to visions and revelations of the Lord. I knew a man in Christ above fourteen years ago, (whether in the body, I cannot tell; or whether out of the body, I cannot tell: God knoweth;) such an one caught up to the third heaven. And I knew such a man, (whether in the body, or out of the body, I cannot tell: God knoweth;) How that he was caught up into paradise, and heard unspeakable words, which it is not lawful for a man to utter. Of such an one will I glory: yet of myself I will not glory, but in mine infirmities. For though I would desire to glory, I shall not be a fool; for I will say the truth: but now I forbear, lest any man should think of me above that which he seeth me to be, or that he heareth of me" (II Corinthians 12:1-6).

Like the Apostle Paul, I hereby posit that it is not appropriate for me to boast, but since it would not be wise of me to ignore all the apostolic gifts so bountifully bestowed upon me in the house of God, in Christ Jesus, I do deem it worthwhile to carry on rejoicing boldly about visions and revelations from the Spirit. Unlike Paul, however, my maiden vision dates back almost ten years ago, just before the birth of my son, Marlon, of the same age. The scene was my office room in the centre of Munich. I had not even started going to church at all by then, but just happened to be the lucky recipient of a Bible from my younger sister, Helen, living in Karlsruhe at the time. Helen, was a born again Christian who was hell-bent on converting me as well. Henceforth, each and every one of our routine marathon telephone conversations was the scene of a heated debate in which we would end up agreeing to disagree, leaving us both exhausted, utterly stretched out of our wits, having literally more questions than answers going forward. Week-in, week-out, we would hypothesize on a wide range of issues concerning our spirituality, and I must confess, I was several times baffled by the sharpness of Helen's arguments as well as the coolness of her resolve. She definitely came to me with the wisdom and power of the Holy Spirit, while my hackneyed tirades were premised on the rudiments of men's wisdom. If there is one thing I tend to credit my sister for, is her persistence. As I always came off totally exhausted, and feeling inadequate, it became increasingly clearer and clearer, at least to myself, that I was the one who needed to make amends in my life, and not her. Brethren, it might sound rather nonchalant now, expressing these deep thoughts in a more or less casual way, but back then it was not, by any means, an easy decision to take. To cut a long story short, it turned out, this whole humdrum was an uphill task as I became embroiled in an internal war with my very self. I had read Shakespeare at school, and have always been a man of letters. Given my literary background therefore, it proved a handful for me to rid myself of all the bunches of earthly, sensual and devilish notions to satisfy the flesh. I reckoned I had to break free from all the selfishly churned parochial fixation on, and blind allegiance to worldly paradigms and time-honoured man-made, traditional dogmas. Eventually she managed to link me up with the works of such great men of God as Dereck Prince, Myles Munroe and many other famous authors and evangelists of the Gospel, and expectedly, through the workings of the Holy Spirit I ended up putting up a standing order on my bank account to subsidise my church offerings on a more consistent basis. I then became a de facto member of a Pentacostal church in Oberdedingen, a town near Karlsruhe (Southern Germany).

When my son was born, I became even more introspective in my transition to parenthood. Gradually, I began to recall the good old days back in Cameroon when my parents would take me and the other siblings to church, every Sunday. Furthermore, as the Holy Spirit urged me forth into reading the Scriptures, almost on a weekly basis, I grew fond of the charisma of Jesus: namely through the uncanny wisdom embedded in the parables which informed His sermons, as well as the quiet dignity that marked His graceful personality. I was also thrilled by the elevated style which adorned all the byways and highways of the Pauline letters. But this was later bound to become second nature to me, and eventually a life style when I called my sister to complain about my son's nightly restlessness for which my wife and I had no remedy, as the child would cry every late night for days on end–and this is what has strengthened my faith so far.–beloved, at my sister's advice I was told to read specially designated sections of the Gospel (in the toilet ha! ha!) after everyone else had gone to bed. Being shy of betraying my new life style before my unbelieving wife, Nora, I never wanted to rock the boat by y appearing, so to speak, *"fundamentally"* religious in her presence. But then, guess what happened: each time I managed to read and pray before going to bed there was a marked difference in my little boy's condition—he slept like a log! And the habitual spooky movements and other strange noises increasingly faded into oblivion. As a matter of fact his situation so improved that we scarcely were even able to imagine the awkwardness that had blighted the previous nights.

Having achieved my purpose I thought it would be reasonable to common sense, and especially expedient for me, should I continue in my meditative nightly chore. Beloved in Christ, such was the state I was in when one fine morning on a certain week day something happened to me that I will never live to forget! It was just before the break of dawn, once I had decided to pass the night in the office so as to avoid being caught in the early morning rush-hour traffic woes the Munich commuter system was then prone to. Lying in bed, on my office couch, all of a sudden it felt like in a trance: brethren I perceived a light so bright like I had never, ever experienced in my life. Sure enough, it was the true Light! So, lying there all alone I felt rather listless and could barely move my body parts about in self-defence, as it were, lying spiritually enraptured! Once beads of extreme joy began streaming down my cheeks I knew it was unmistakable; there was no question. It was Jesus, the Lamb of God that took away the sins of the world. All I can remember at that point in time of what transpired during the mysterious moments of that initial divine encounter, were the simple questions He put across to me: namely, *"Will you build me a church?"* This, He asked twice and in my exalted state I could only acquiesce.

First thing in the morning, having regained consciousness and strength I tried to touch my *"wet cheeks"* just to discover they were as dry as ever; not even the faintest trace of a tear would be found anywhere on my face! That is when I felt for the first time in my life I must have been caught up in the third heaven, and like Enoch, Elijah, Paul and John (Genesis 5:24; II Kings 2; Revelation 4:1) the testimony was spot on. The fact I was in a trance proves the possibility of a natural body going to heaven. Hence like Paul I corroborate my belief in the consciousness of souls after leaving the body (II Corinthians 5:8; Philippians 1:21-24; Hebrews 12:23).

> *"And they overcame him by the blood of the Lamb, and by the word of their testimony"* (Revelation 12:11).

Brethren, the next testimony goes out to those of you out there who have been praying for healing to come to your physical bodies or your loved ones, and for the restoration and restitution of your families and financial well being, but have just not had any answers to your prayers yet.

It is also for those of you out there, who feel that God is a respecter of persons, as you hear testimonies of others who seem to have had every single one of their prayers answered immediately and have been instantaneously, even miraculously healed.

Perhaps you are like some people I have come across walking dejectedly out of a victory, miracle crusade where the power of God performed miracles: healing broken bodies, eradicating cancer and stamping out arthritis; delivering hundreds from the scourge of drug addiction, and alcoholism, while your own needs are yet to be met. Your troubles linger, and your days get long. But if you can connect to the power of my message, and believe in my good report in spirit and in truth, then this testimony is for you! The Spirit of God has made it available to you for a good purpose, in order to give you a new headway through the renewing of your mind by faith—in giving you the awareness of God's will to grant your healing, threshold to the attainment of eternal salvation (Jeremiah 29:11-13; Matthew 19:29; Luke 18:28; Mark 10:29-30):

> *"He that receiveth you receiveth me, and he that receiveth me receiveth him that sent me. He that receiveth a prophet in the name of a prophet shall receive a prophet's reward; and he that receiveth a righteous man in the name of a righteous man shall receive a righteous man's reward. And whosoever shall give to drink unto one of these little ones a cup of cold water only in the name of a disciple, verily I say unto you, he shall in no wise lose his reward"* (Matthew 10:40-42)

Beloved, you may not know this, but the truth is I have sought the face of God for you. I have fasted and interceded before God on your behalf: for the answer to your unanswered prayers and for your healing and deliverance is at hand. I have pleaded your case from the secret place and petitioned God for your total absolution (Isaiah 43:26). I have summoned the Most High to intervene in your situation in order to enable you grow in stature and wisdom; in love with God and man.

> *"If ye then be risen with Christ, seek those things which are above, where Christ sitteth on the right hand of God. Set your affection on things above, not on things on the earth. For ye are dead, and your life is hid with Christ in God"* (Colossians 3:1-3).

The second encounter with Jesus of Nazareth, therefore, was at my current home in Pasing near Munich, Germany. It was on the morning of Good Friday 2010. By that time I was fully involved in the activities of my present church, *Holy Ghost Fire Revival Ministry ev*, whose Munich branch was to be launched in October of the same year. The inauguration of the church was the culmination of a prophecy dated back in 1996. Since then, Pastor Joe Boadi Danquah, (then assistant Pastor at Body of Christ for All Nations, another Pentecostal church in Munich) had been running a weekly prayer group at his private flat in Perlach, a Munich suburb.

Having been commissioned and anointed by the Holy Spirit to join this august forum, I was also assigned in my calling to publish the Word of God, as a scribe of the Most High. Consequently I was confronted with the task of not only following the lengthy sermons, but most especially selecting suitable themes from the Scripture to write on, which proved tricky given I was only a baby Christian back then. Having said that, I vouch right here, even through intuition and spiritual insight for the doctrine which holds that the Lord does not give us what we can handle. On the contrary, He teaches us to handle what we have been given (Psalm 8:2). Therefore my initiation was rather precipitated through various media, including the now famous Christian channel, God TV where I was made to listen to an army of God's generals drawn from different countries around the globe who were travelling to, and exploring opportunities from every nook and cranny on the face of the earth for souls; healing, delivering, teaching, interpreting and preaching the Gospel of Jesus Christ through the entire length and breath of the world as they went.

However like many Christians today, I was caught in the dilemma between the cravings of the valley (my old habits), and the high calling of God in Christ Jesus on the mountain (Philippians 3:13-14). Old habits die hard, they say, and for me it was this nasty old habit of always trying to prove my mettle in aspect of football: making commentaries and analysis to all who would have the simple courtesy and patience to listen to my monologues! Now, back in my native Cameroon the situation kind of took care of itself as my talkative behaviour was limited to the narrow student circles on campus. It was small talk, cum idle talk! And nothing more. But in Europe, it turned out, football is big business—a situation which rendered my silly habit of killing time mostly lacklustre, if not nonsensical. As a matter of fact I managed to alienate many of my professional and social contacts inadvertently due to my callous gibberish.

That is why on that Thursday night, having spent the better part of the evening on the phone with a friend of mine: apparently our nocturnal conversation was centred on weighing our country's chances of making it through to the final stages of the World Cup that was to be held in that year for the first time on African soil—South Africa. Sure enough, after many hours of processing and trading platitudes with each other, and choking ourselves on the phone with tedious arguments of insidious intents, I was so drained and sapped of every ounce of energy that I esteemed myself not quite fit to focus on anything mentally demanding; I didn't really fathom I could actually meet my routine writing task on the night. In fact, one of the reasons behind my lackadaisical attitude on that night toward my nightly assignment was the fact that Friday was supposed to be a bridge holiday, so I worked out it would make more sense to call off my evening duty, and chose to shift everything to the next day, which would be the commencement of the weekend.

Brethren, lest I forget, suffices to mention that this was not the first instance of my recalcitrant attitude towards the Holy Spirit. It is worthwhile recalling that there had been a couple of similar incidents in the past when my apparent lack of commitment toward my work would force the Comforter to put my personal ego to the test by reminding me of friends of mine who had already obtained their doctorate degrees from renown universities in the United States and England. He did this knowing I loathe the taste of intellectual bluntness in relation to my peers. Still there was a night I decided to go to bed without having invested enough time on my Biblical research work, and lo, and behold, what I saw on that night when I tried to close my eyes lying in bed will never leave my memory. Friend, my bedroom's rooftop and ceiling seemed to had been violently ripped off, and like the scenes in Maurice Sendak's famous kindergarten picture book *Where the Wild Things Are*, to my mind I felt like someone had me seated by the window of a supersonic aircraft in high altitude! As the plane's momentum left behind the layers of cloud at terrific speed, I was instantly reminded in all transcience and frivolity of the usefulness of the passage of time on earth. Of course I first took it for some kind of hallucination so I opened my eyes and closed them three times, but the harsh reality persisted, and then suddenly I knew it was the Holy Spirit who was warning me of the need to get down to work, and to desist from passively whiling off precious time on trivialities in a transient world.

Hence the Lion of Judah's arrival which left me utterly flabbergasted was seldom uncalled for, and to all intents and purposes it was a welcome comeuppance. Indeed at the end of my phone call the night before, I knew I had transgressed once again, but somehow I managed to soothe my distressed conscience in the hypothesis suffered from the Prufrockian Paralysis. As earlier mentioned, brethren, this second episode with Jesus occurred between the hours of 4 a.m. and 5:30 a.m. on Good Friday Morning, 2010. As I lay in bed my son had left his piano standing next to my study table, just about two metres away.

All of a sudden I woke up having been aroused by the sound of the piano. It was as though He had run His fingers across the keyboard at one go, to announce His arrival! And once I saw Him it was as compelling as ever! There was no mistake. Beloved, there is no gainsaying of His stature as Prince of Peace. The graceful aura around Him speaks volumes of the love and holiness so effusively extolled in Scripture. But what surprised me the most was that He appeared in the image of the Lion of Judah! A Huge Lion!!! Brethren I was in my room, playing host to my Maker, The Maker of heaven and earth, Preserver of mankind, and I was not by any means scared! Instead, being enraptured, I attempted to approach Jesus, but He would not have me. He motioned at me to stay put and listen to His Sermon. The preaching was anchored on the rectitude and power of the Almighty, His Father—Jehovah Elohim, and His great works. Beloved Jesus preaches from the very bottom of His guts! There is no comparison. As He went on I had the perception I was listening to some musical symphony or of something akin to a rapping slow-jam which gradually lulled me to sleep. Hence, as I slowly gave in to the lullaby produced by this melodious outpouring, Jesus was cross: *"You dare sleep while I preach? Are you a child to be fed with milk?"*, He bellowed! The tone was serious without being threatening in any aspect. Again, I felt really drowsy with my eyes drenched in tears from the mountains of impressions gleaned at that singular instant.

In the end He departed, sanctifying my house, even likening it to the isles of Japan. This last encounter has left an indelible memory of the Prince of Life on me which means that the awe of His overwhelming presence enhances the Spirit of the fear of the Lord in me. And as a consequence of this, whenever I find myself preaching the Gospel I bend over backwards to reach out to the congregation in a way that serves to checkmate any excesses of personal emotions from intruding into my sermons. I strive to avoid my preaching running awry. Brethren, I must see to it that my speech does not wander off target. I stress what is written in Scripture, rather than spuriously suggesting how it ought to have been written! Too often, preachers I have observed so far tend to unconsciously (or by design?) obfuscate their message through a preposterous blend of their personal opinion and/or their subjective interpretation of the Scriptures:

Here is an excerpt from one of Saint Paul's letters that has always caught my attention in view of the discipline preachers have got to maintain through their arduous task of teaching the Gospel of Jesus Christ:

> *"As ye have therefore received Christ Jesus the Lord, so walk ye in him: Rooted and built up in him, and stablished in the faith, as ye have been taught, abounding therein with thanksgiving. Beware lest any spoil you through philosophy and vain deceit, after the tradition of men, after the rudiments of the world, and not after Christ. For in him dwelleth all the fulness of the Godhead bodily. And ye are complete in him, which is the head of all principality and power: in whom also ye are circumcised with the circumcision made without hands, in puttin off the body of the sins of the flesh by the circumcision of Christ: Buried with him in baptism, wherein also ye are risen with him through the faith of the operation of God, who hath raised him from the dead. And you, being dead in your sins and the uncircumcision of your flesh, hath he quickened together with him, having forgiven you all trespasses; Blotting out the handwriting of ordinances that was against us, which was contrary to us, and took it out of the way, nailing it to his cross; And having spoiled principalities and power, he made a show of them openly, triumphing over them in it. Let no man therefore judge you in meat, or in drink, or in respect of an holyday, or of the new moon, or of the sabbath days; Which are a shadow of things to come; but the body is of Christ. Let no man beguile you of your reward in a voluntary humility and worshipping of angels, intruding into those things which he hath not seen, vainly puffed up by his fleshly mind, And not holding the Head, from which all the body by joints and bands having nourishment ministered, and knit together, increaseth with the increase of God. Wherefore, if ye be dead with Christ from the rudiments of the world, why, as though living in the world, are ye subject to ordinances, (Touch not; taste not; handle not; Which all are to perish with the using;) after the commandments and doctrines of men? Which things have indeed a shew of wisdom in will worship, and humility, and neglecting of the body; not in any honour to the satisfying of the flesh"* (Colossians 2:6-23).

Brethren, needless for me to stress finally that The Secret Place where our Saviour is seated on the right hand of His Father is the source of all power

(Matthew 28:18, Mark 14:62, Romans 13:1, Colossians 1:16-19; I Timothy 6:16). This presents us as Christian believers in Christ with the spiritual obligation to observe by faith, and respond in reverent awe to the love and grace granted freely onto us in plenteous store. Thanks to various razor-sharp examples drawn from both the Old and the New Testaments of the Bible, I have been able to substantiate this view so as to put across the essential message that Christian life without a meditative and consistent prayer regime is as good as going to battle without the requisite strategy, equipment and supplies. While the Old Testament could be described as the covenant of the law or letter which was limited to the children of Israel, the New Testament is all-embracing, and operates in the Spirit. Brethren ,the dispensation of grace is about those who worship God in spirit and in truth; it is about those who have been born again in water and in the Spirit; it is about those whose righteousness must exceed that of the first century Scribes and Pharisees. In short, it is the Tabernacle that is not made by the hands of men—it is the dispensation of the Messiah Himself.

Once again, however, it should be noted that old habits die hard, and one of the keenest challenges we face today as true followers of Christ is the task of accepting change in our system of worship—departing from the defunct dogmatic ordinances of Old Testament Scribes and Pharisees, while embracing the ministry of the Holy Spirit that has come to inaugurate Christ's kingdom in us—friend, the Holy Spirit has restored the heaven atmosphere on earth (Matthew 3:16-17; John 3:3-12). This is the dispensation of the individual church where we fulfil the multiple roles of being the temple of God, His living stones, and people chosen from his heart whom He has made kings serving as priests. The new church is epitomised in the practices of the early Christians, and especially as duplicated in the ministry of Saint Paul, who did not only author most of the books of the New Testament, but was, indeed, an institution in his own right in most of the ancient cities where he went preaching and teaching the Gospel as recorded in the Book of Acts. Paul managed to establish a parallel system based on God's precepts which existed as an alternative government, different to the reigning monarchies at the time.

Consequently, the vision of Production Bible is about putting the practices in local churches in the spotlight. In due course, I will be undertaking to project an appraisal which will serve to question the kingdom values obtained in the modern church in general, presuming many of these splinter congregations are nothing but micro-macrocosms of the more established ministries. The various ecclesiastical denominations that embody the church of Jesus Christ today: whether Catholics, Protestants, Pentecostals, Charismatics or Methodists are led by personalities, who, sooner or later, are bound to face the daunting task of justifying their calling (John 12:44-50; 8:14-18; John 15:16). They will be tested by their fruit: every branch that is grafted onto Jesus bears good fruit (John 15:5; Galatians 5:22). Conversely, any fruit that stinks is not from the true vine, and is rooted in sin. Such a tree must be uprooted and destroyed (John 15:6; Galatians 5:19-21). Ministers will have to evolve a spiritually wholesome lifestyle which encompasses all the allure, mirage, fragrances and other puffed-up philosophies of vain pursuit (Romans 8:14-17; II Corinthians 5:17) They must labour to target the bull's eye of success which encapsulates the mark for the prize of the high calling of God in Christ Jesus. Brethren, instead of going round the same mount over and over again; to inadvertently prolong a journey of eleven days into that which could only be achieved after forty years of wandering in the wilderness, Jesus has come to help us shoot straight (Hebrews 9:11-14)!

Please come along and enjoy being chaperoned by the Holy Spirit who has ordained me to present this material in a way that He deemed fit for your perusal. God bless you as you read on:

> *"Then said they unto him, What shall we do, that we might work the works of God? Jesus answered and said unto them, This is the work of God, that ye believe on him whom he hath sent"* (John 6:28-29).

Book The First

THE MYSTERY OF CHRIST AS YOU

INTRODUCTION

The Concise Oxford English Dictionary defines *"mystery"* as something that is difficult or impossible to understand or explain, such as a secret, a puzzle, a code or a password which leads to private sites or grounds. The term private itself seems like a misnomer here given that we are actually talking about the Gospel of Jesus Christ, Creator of the whole universe and everything that is in it (Genesis 1:1; Psalm 24:1; Isaiah 54:5). Access to all secret places are in the firm hands of our Lord Jesus who is the true gate to all righteousness as well as the Kingdom of His Father:

> *"That in blessing I will bless thee, and in multiplying I will multiply thy seed as the stars of the heaven, and as the sand which is upon the sea shore; AND THY SEED SHALL POSSESS THE GATE OF HIS ENEMIES; and in thy seed shall all the nations of the earth be blessed"* (Genesis 22:17-18).

This is the promise that was made to the patriarch, Abraham four hundred and thirty years before the laws of Moses (which were added because of sin). The *seed* here is Jesus of Nazareth who is the Messiah. God remembers His covenant forever, even as it was commanded to Abraham, (Genesis 12:1; 17:6-8), and the oath He made with Isaac (Genesis 26:1-5), and confirmed it with Jacob, and which bacame an evalastic law to the children of Israel (Genesis 28:10-19). Dearly beloved in Christ, nobody can deviate the purpose of

God, which is sealed in the love God bears us in Christ Jesus, according to Saint Paul:

> *"Christ hath redeemed us from the curse of the law, being made a curse for us: for it is written, Cursed is every one that hangeth on a tree: That the blessing of Abraham might come on the Gentiles through Jesus Christ; that we might receive the promise of the Spirit through faith. Brethren, I speak after the manner of men; Though it be but a man's covenant, yet if it be confirmed, no man disannulleth, or addeth thereto. Now to Abraham and his seed were the promises made. He SAITH NOT, AND TO SEEDS, AS OF MANY; BUT AS OF ONE, AND TO THY SEED, WHICH IS CHRIST. And this I say, that the covenant, that was confirmed before of God in Christ, the law, which was four hundred and thirty years after, cannot disannul, that it should make the promise of none effect. For if the inheritance be of the law, it is no more of promise: but God gave it to Abraham by promise"* (Galatians 3:15-18).

God executes His leadership on us through our ordained authority and leadership. For the Scripture says, whatsoever we bind on earth, shall be bound in heaven (Matthew 18:18). However, our leaders command such power and authority, not due to earthly influence, but rather because it is ordained of God (John 19:11). Hence, God's everlasting covenant (for life in Christ is everlasting—eternal life: Philippians 1:21is on condition that we stay subject to Christian, civilised, governing authority (Matthew 22:1; I Peter 2:13-17; Romans 14):

> *"Thus saith the Lord to his anointed, to Cyrus, whose right hand I have holden, to subdue nations before him; and I will loose the loins of kings,* TO OPEN BEFORE HIM THE TWO LEAVED GATES; AND THE GATES SHALL NOT BE SHUT; *I will go before thee, and make the crooked places straight:* I WILL BREAK IN PIECES THE GATES OF BRASS, AND CUT IN SUNDER THE BARS OF IRON: AND I WILL GIVE THEE THE TREASURES OF DARKNESS, AND HIDDEN RICHES OF SECRET PLACES, *that thou mayest know that I, the Lord, which call thee by thy name, am the God of Israel"* (Isaiah 45:1-3).

All the above scriptural references point to the existence of the superior power of a Supreme Being that cannot be questioned or gainsaid, and Who is firmly in control of things both in heaven and on earth: Jehovah Elohim is His name. The Most High God, who sent His only begotten Son to deliver us from our self-imposed bondage, is the Originator of all mysteries for a good and excellent cause. Mysteries exist to perfect the saints, edify the body of Christ and therefore further the cause of God's holy calling as well as serve to advance the good fortunes of His graceful purpose in Christ through the Holy Ghost, who shares the love abroad in our hearts. Above all, mysteries, are there to project our understanding of the multiple dimensions of God's ways through prophecies and parables; signs and wonders; fulfilled plans which are backed up by miracles, addressed to the senses of all faithful believers in Christ.

Nevertheless, our thesis is about celebrating this privilege status without necessarily exaggerating the nature and purpose of the mysteries involved; we seek the face of God to enable us establish this truth by making the difference between the godly and ungodly ostensibly clear for all to see that it is hopeless to try to compare what is spiritual to what is material. According to Jesus, what is earthly is earthly, and what is heavenly is heavenly (John 3:3-13). We cannot compare the Providential with the mundane; the devout with the heathen; the sublime with the banal, anymore than we can dare to compare more succulent fruits with coarse ones, without confusing them; in other words before we proceed to pass judgment on either: appreciating and/or depreciating the one or the other, we must strive to understand their differences and usefulness. Beloved in Christ, peaches are peaches and coconuts are coconuts.

Friend, we are going to set the ball rolling by submitting some key Biblical citations to buttress our argument on the meaning and content of the great mysteries in the Gospel of Jesus Christ who has ordained strength in the mouths of babes and sucklings because of the enemy; in order to keep the enemy at bay, thereby using the weak things of the universe to confound the strong; using the Davids of this world to humble the Goliaths; using the foolish things of this world to humble the wise: in other words, Jehovah would use the nonesense of faith to confound the wisdom of unbelief—Take the case of Naaman, Commander-in-Chief of the Syrian Army! Brethren, I am talking about a man through whom the Lord had achieved great deeds of valour in the region, but who was compelled to follow the advice of his housemaid, and later had to submit to the wise counsel of his servants before ultimately yielding to the authority of Elisher, the prophet of God in Samaria. Beloved, then and only then, was he eligible for absolution; only then was he humble enough to be granted deliverance from the Lord. Hence, his deliverance was locked up in mystery.

As you would appreciate dear reader, the working of miracles, such as Moses' parting of the Red sea to secure the deliverance of Israel through a heavily initiative in the Bible indexes God's creative genius and highlights the preponderance of mysteries, locked up in signs, wonders and miracles, in the Scripture as celebrated by the psalmist below:

> "The sea saw it, and fled: Jordan was driven back. The mountains skipped like rams, and the little hills like lambs. What ailed thee, O thou sea, that thou fleddest? thou Jordan, that thou wast driven back? Ye mountains, that ye skipped like rams; and ye little hills, like lambs? Tremble, thou earth, at the presence of the Lord, at the presence of the God of Jacob; Which turned the rock into a standing water, the flint into a fountain of water"
> (Psalm 114).

That is why we must admit that the battle is not ours, but the Lord's, and the weapons of our warfare are not carnal, but spiritual. In fact, we fight not against flesh and blood, but against principalities and powers; against spiritual wickedness in high places (Ephesians 6:10-12). Thus, whether it is about subduing the enemy who is our offender so as to achieve our deliverance, using the word of wisdom, knowledge, understanding, counsel and might (like He did through Esther and Mordecai), to subsidise the freedom of His people, Judah, the chosen tribe through which the Messiah was to come, or even obtaining the restoration, safety, health and security of His great and faithful servants like Daniel, Shadrach, Meshach and Abednego in whom the Lord performed miracles of hitherto unprecedented proportions, these mysteries all have one thing in common: they have all served a great and sound cause for humanity on earth, in terms of strengthening our faith and belief as well as curbing the trend of apostasy the world over, especially in these end times. But that is not what we plan to celebrate here. Ours is of a higher order: invoking all the seven Spirits of God—the Spirit of God; the Spirit of the fear of the Lord; the Spirit of understanding; the Spirit of knowledge; the Spirit of wisdom; and that of counsel and might to apprehend the unfathomable depths of the hidden truth in the volumes of the Gospel of Jesus Christ, even as Saint Paul's letter to Timothy does let us know:

> *"And without controversy great is the mystery of godliness: God was manifest in the flesh, justified in the Spirit, seen of angels, preached unto the Gentiles, believed on in the world, received up into glory"* (I Timothy 3:16).

Chapter 1

THE SECRETS OF GOD ARE GLORIOUS

What makes the mysteries of God special? Does God simply intend to hide things from His creatures to make life tougher for us? God forbid! How could the Almighty who spared not His own Son, but delivered Him up for us all, turn around and scheme to hurt our feelings? Therefore, the love of God for us has been put beyond doubt through the sufferings, death and resurrection of our Lord Jesus Christ, the only begotten Son of the Father. Now, are there any benefits derived from this strategy of keeping things out of reach for the recipient in particular, and out of public gaze in general until such a time that He deems it fit to make it known to all to behold and absorb? Yes, of course. After all, the Bible says, in the book of Ecclesiastes 3, there is time for everything on the face of this earth. The ultimate Planner He is, God knows exactly when to release our blessings, as stated in the book of Habakkuk:

> *"And the Lord answered me, and said, Write the vision, and make it plain upon tables, that he may run that readeth it. For the vision is yet for an appointed time, but at the end it shall speak, and not lie: though it tarry, wait for it; because it will surely come, it will not tarry"* (Habakkuk 2:2-3).

Hence, the vision of our Saviour's second coming, as proved in Hebrews 10:37 is yet for an appointed time, but in the end it shall speak and not lie. Friend,

God is not a man that he should lie, nor the son of man, that he should repent (Numbers 23:19). Though the vision tarries, exercise patience, and longsuffering—the rapture of Christ will not tarry, and neither will your vision or God's promise for your life. Beloved, God's verdict to your petition will be yours sooner that later, but remember one thing, God is sovereign:

> *"The secret things belong unto the Lord our God: but those things which are revealed belong unto us and to our children for ever, that we may do all the words of this law"* (Deuteronomy 29:29).

Thus, the things that have not yet been revealed, belong to God and it is wise and righteous in the sight of God for us not to have access to them as yet; but the revealed things of Scripture are ours forever, that we may know, understand and do the will of God with willingness and enthusiasm, like obedient children of the Most High

> *"And he said unto them, It is not for you to know the times or the seasons, which the Father hath put in his own power. But ye shall receive power, after that the Holy Ghost is come upon you: and ye shall be witnesses unto me both in Jerusalem, and in Judaea, and in Samaria, and unto the uttermost part of the earth"* (Acts 1:7-8).

Brethren, you may not be in any position to change or influence God's plans for your life because it is secret. But it is secret because you are special to God whose plans for you are of good and not of evil, to give you an expected end (Jeremiah 29:11). You see, brethren, when the disciples got a bit restive about their deliverance, as Jesus was about to ascend onto heaven to be glorified by His Father, so He bade them take life easy, obey simple instructions and see the glory of God upon their lives in due season. This, they did, and the rest is history.

> *"What man is he that feareth the Lord? him shall he teach in the way that he shall choose. His soul shall dwell at ease; and his seed shall inherit the earth. The secret of the Lord is with them that fear him; and he will shew them his covenant"* (Psalm 25:12-14).

Friend, just imagine the blessings included in the package of those who elect to fear the Lord, as enunciated in the verses above:

First off, he or she will be taught by God—a priest of the Spirit, capable of decoding the mysteries of the Gospel of Jesus Christ. Secondly, s/he will be safe and at peace—for s/he that dwells in the secret place of the Most High shall abide under the shadow of the Almighty (Psalm 91:1). Thirdly, Their children will be blessed—children are a heritage of the Lord (Psalm 127:3-5). Hence the fruitfulness involved in fearing God. Fourthly, s/he will know God's secret, which is the will of God. You will become a friend of God (Genesis 18:17-19; Psalm 84:11; John 15:15; James 2:23)—s/he will become an apostle and/or a prophet of the Most High God! Lastly, they will know God's covenant, even the Perfect Law which is the ultimate key to salvation and eternal life.

Beloved in Christ, those things that have been revealed can only be apprehended, understood or fully captured, and known by the initiated as is revealed onto and into the spirit of the initiated:

> *"It is the glory of God to conceal a thing: but the honour of kings is to search out a matter"* (Proverbs 25:2).

First of all, the knowledge referred to here is not ordinary, mundane or carnal—earthly, sensual, devilish knowledge—but rather the subliminal type that descendeth from above: *"But the wisdom that is from above is first pure, then peaceable, gentle, and easy to be intreated, full of mercy and good fruits, without partiality, and without hypocrisy. And the fruit of righteousness is sown in peace of them that make peace."* (James 3:14-18). The knowledge implied in God's lament through His servant, the prophet Hosea is therefore not the perverse knowledge derived from man's wisdom, but that of Christ:

> *"He shall see of the travail of his soul, and shall be satisfied: by his knowledge shall my righteous servant justify many; for he shall bear their iniquities"* (Isaiah 53:11).

Therefore, the mystery of Christ as you is about your knowledge and awareness and consciousness that Christ is in you as you! Hence the Christ as you is the Gospel of Jesus Christ. Brethren, the Gospel of Jesus Christ is not in word, but in power; it is the Gospel of power:

> *"Call unto me, and I will answer thee, and shew thee great and mighty things, which thou knowest not"* (Jeremiah 33:3).

We have seen in the verses above how the apostles of the early church had had to be empowered by the Holy Ghost before they were ordained to carry on the works of God in Christ Jesus. We also do know by faith (for our knowledge of Christ is exclusively in the Spirit—II Corinthians 5:14-19—and nobody calls Jesus Lord but by the Spirit—I Corinthians 12:1-3) that our Lord Jesus Christ, as a man, also had to benefit from the anointing of His Father in the Holy Ghost and power in order to accomplish His mission on earth (Acts 10:38). Consequently, as you read this book, brethren, I pray that Christ may fill and full your spirit as you. I pray the Lord God that the Christ, the Crystal and the Charisma of God now manifest in your spirit in Jesus' mighty name!

Brethren, power must manifest when the Gospel of Christ is read: Therefore, I declare—Receive power! Let the Revealer of all truths both floodlight into the mind of your understanding and unveil all truths: especially the deep truth behind this powerful secret of our God which is Christ as you. No wonder Christ Himself taught with the utmost vehemence, as He evoked the mysterious principles and divine ethics of the kingdom of heaven on earth to His disciples:

> *"I will open my mouth in a parable: I will utter dark sayings of old"*
> (Psalm 78:2).

Thus, by Matthew 13, Jesus had begun using an elaborate array of scintillating parables which baffles His adversaries and has gone on to mesmerised even the savviest theologians over the ages. The reasons for His novel approach to teaching were many and varied:

1. These will include the unction to fulfil a prophecy, as stated above. The Messiah anchored His doctrine based on the prophet Isaiah who is quoted as having prophesied as follows:

"And in them is fulfilled the prophecy of Esaias (Greek), which saith, By hearing ye shall hear, and shall not understand; and seeing ye shall see, and shall not perceive: For this people's heart is waxed gross, and their ears are dull of hearing, and their eyes they have closed; lest at any time they should see with their eyes, and hear with their ears, and should understand with their heart, and should be converted, and I should heal them. But blessed are your eyes, for they see: and your ears, for they hear. For verily I say unto you, That many prophets and righteous men have desired to see those things which ye see, and have not seen them; and to hear those which which ye hear, and have not heard them" (Matthew 13:14-17).

Brethren, the deepest secrets of the Gospel of Jesus Christ are only made available to those whose hearts have been prepared by the Holy Spirit to perform the will of God:

"The Lord is my shepherd; I shall not want. He maketh me to lie down in green pastures: he leadeth me beside the still waters. He restoreth my soul: he leadeth me in the paths of righteousness for his name's sake. Yea, though I walk through the valley of the shadow of death, I will fear no evil: for thou art with me; thy rod and thy staff they comfort me. Thou preparest a table before me in the presence of mine enemies: thou anointest my head with oil; my cup running over. Surely goodness and mercy shall follow me all the days of my life: and I will dwell in the house of the Lord for ever" (Psalm 23).

In other words, those who believe in the righteousness of Christ have caught the vision on how to overcome the world. They are being shepherded by the Lord; they shall have no want; they shall rest and walk in well worked out, well ploughed, and well irrigated green pastures and later to be guided to still, deeper, waters of peace and re-invigoration; they shall obtain restoration of their soul and also benefit from the guidance of the Most High in the paths of righteousness for His name's sake, which eschews the fear of stumbling, falling or going off course; guaranteed safe passage through the risky valleys of death; no fear of evil as they reside under the watchful eyes of the Conscientious Shepherd's careful watch and protection; the comfort of the Shepherd's rod and staff (club and crook, the most common tools used by shepherds for self-defence and help—the club for the sheep's enemies and the crook for their protection; the abundance of full, prepared food to feast on in the presence of enemies. They can afford the luxury to feast in safety while the Shepherd watches, fights, and protects; their heads are anointed with perfumed oil, which always come before feasts in ancient times; their cups running over to symbolise their inheritance of the anointing of Christ (John 3:34): plenty of leftovers in terms of power, wisdom, knowledge, honour, strength and wealth which is indicated in substances and drinks; there is every confidence that such goodness and mercy will follow them throughout eternity; through faith in God, they will dwell in God's house in the next life and forever. Jesus vindicates king David's prophecy:

"For whosoever hath, to him shall be given, and he shall have more abundance: but whosoever hath not, from him shall be taken away even that he hath" (Matthew 13:12).

"The thief cometh not, but to steal, and to kill, and to destroy: I am come that they might have life, and that they might have it more abundantly" (John 10:10).

What prescience! What an illuminating and dramatic peom! Hence, the utmost relevance of the mysteries of God to our purpose. Through the mysteries the fundamental difference between the mission of Jesus and that of Lucifer is laid bare. In other words, the mysteries serve to foreground the gracefulness and truth in Jesus as opposed to the cynical adveturism of the devil. Brethren, our secret in God's will remains our power, for it is nothing else, but our divinity.

2. The other reason is that of love. The Bible says God is love. Every member of the Godhead demonstrates a measure of love for us: *"That Christ may dwell in your hearts by faith; that ye, being rooted and grounded in love, May be able to comprehend with all saints what is the breadth, and length, and depth, and height; And to know the love of Christ, which passeth knowledge, that ye might be filled with all the fulness of God"* (Ephesians 3:17-19). Hence, His love is boundless, endless, fathomless—inexhaustible, and measureless. It encompasses the universe, and time and eternity. The immensity of His love comprehends all that is above, below, and past, present and future. God's love reaches to the depth of sin and infamy, to the height of the infinite divinity. It surpasses every knowledge and wisdom. The Father gave us His Son, as a measure of His love; the Son gave us His life, as a measure of His love, and finally the Spirit condescends to help transform our lives, as measure of His love for all mankind. Love pervades the first two greatest commandments of the Most High: *"Jesus said unto them, Thou shalt love the Lord your God with all thy heart with all thy soul, and with all thy mind. This is the first and great commandment. And the second is like unto it, Thou shalt love thy neighbour as thyself. On these two commandments hang all the law and the prophets"* (Matthew 22:37-40). It is a contest on degrees of love. In fact, those who possess the true *agape* love for the Gospel are filled, while those who simply pay lip service to it are found out and discarded. According to the beatitudes, therefore: *"Blessed are they which do hunger and thirst after righteousness: for they shall be filled"* (Matthew 5:6). On the contrary, those who lack this brand of love find themselves ensnared, coming under the spell of the mantle of darkness:

"But if our gospel is hid, it is hid to them that are lost: In whom the god of this world hath blinded the minds of them which believe not, lest the light of the glorious gospel of Christ, who is the image of God, should shine unto them. For we preach not ourselves, but Christ Jesus the Lord; and ourselves your servants for Jesus' sake. For God, who commanded the light to shine out

of darkness, hath shined in our hearts, to give the light of the knowledge of the glory of God in the face of Jesus Christ" (II Corinthians 4:3-6).

God Himself earlier warned the children of Israel against selling themselves cheap to the enemy:

"Thou shalt not make unto thee any graven images, or any likeness of any thing that is in heaven above, or thatis in the earth beneath, or that is in the water under the earth: Thou shalt not bow down thyself to them, nor serve them: for I the Lord thy God am a jealous God, visiting the iniquity of the fathers upon the children unto the third and fourth generation of them that hate me; And shewing mercy unto thousands of them that love me, and keep my commandments" (Exodus 20:4-6).

Now, all revelations in the parables are directed at those who are passionately engaged, pretty much as the Apostle Paul also commands us in his letter to the Colossians (Colossians 3:1-3). Finally, in this love parade which is also a truth contest, the goal of Jesus is to add to those who love it and want more: pretty much like the obedient servants of (Matthew 25:14-30) who made use of their opportunities; invested their talents in faith and multiplied their gains, which they used in turn, to endear themselves to their master upon his return, and were entrusted with even greater responsibility; as opposed to their counterpart whose contempt for his master caused him to develop a toxic mindset, accused his master of extortion; refused to acknowledge his kindness and therefore failed to spot the clear opportunity to invest, and was eventually dispossessed, disinherited, and even dismissed in scorn to the effect of being cast away into outer darkness by his angry lord. Thus, the parables can also be said to have been used by the master (Christ) in order to conceal the truth (the power of the Gospel) from those who are wicked at heart, especially against God:

"Because it is given to you to know the mysteries of the kingdom of heaven, but to them it is not given " (Matthew 13:11).

3. One other reason for the Messiah's resort to using parables resides undoubtedly in the strategic wisdom which implied making known to mankind the mysteries by juxtaposing them with things that are already known.

To illustrate this point, take *the parable of the tares*: At the current time the realm of profession, for tares and wheat and good and bad are now mixed together in the same kingdom. However by the end of this present age the two classes will become separated by the power of the Holy Spirit. The professors will be sent to hell and the possessors of the kingdom will go on to inherit it literally forever. On the other hand, *the parable of the sower* is made fully explicit to the believer, and covers the entire range of the dispensation of grace, showing the reception and/or resistance of the Word of God in different hearts and the consequences thereof.

Therefore, the mysteries, (previously hidden secrets or future prophecies) just like the divine unction to interpret and understand them are a divine prerogative. God is no respecter of persons: Brethren, whether you are called or not is only God's choice, not yours. The choice is divine, not earthly. It is sublime, not banal. In fact, there is nothing flesh and blood can do in the presence of God Almighty:

"And we know that all things work together for good to them that love God, to them that are the called according to his purpose. For whom he did foreknow, he also did predestinate to be conformed to the image of his Son, that he might be the firstborn among many brethren. Moreover whom he did predestinate, them he also called: and whom he called, them he also justified: and whom he justified, them he also glorified" (Romans 8:28-30).

It was Moses, the law-giver of Israel who sought His favour in the wilderness, wanting to behold His presence in all glory, and the Lord obliged, albeit, with a caveat:

"And he said, I beseech thee, shew me thy glory. And he said, I will make all my goodness pass before thee, and I will proclaim the name of the Lord before thee; and will be gracious to whom I will be gracious, and will shew mercy on whom I will shew mercy...And the Lord said, Behold, there is a place by me, and thou shalt stand upon a rock" (Exodus 33:18-21).

Beloved, the New Testament serves as a the manual designed by God to help interpret the Old Testament. This is because in those days Jesus, who is the Word, the Messiah, the Light and the Seed in the Father's vineyard had not yet been made manifest to the world by the Holy Ghost. Anyway, the bottom line of all this is that without Jesus in your life, there is no way you can hear the echoes of mercy; there is no way you can partake in the whispers of joy; there is no way you can behold the glory of God which is mantled in mysteries in the Gospel of Jesus Christ. Moses would be exposed to greater revelation only if, and on condition that, he agreed to stand on God's appointed place; the Word of God which is the Rock of ages—Jesus Christ of Nazareth, the resurrected Son of the living God. The truth, the revelation does not come to you by conjecture; it is pre-ordained and planned, well before the beginning of the world, and hence the purpose of the mysteries.

4. Lastly, the parables were meant to expose the truth to interested parties in a form designed to generate greater interest. A renown philosopher, Antoine de Saint-Exupery, in his seminal work—The Little Prince—is often quoted as having said something to the effect that, if you ever should desire to have people build a ship, don't provide them with sticks and other construction material; rather teach them to yearn for the sea. On the same score, therefore, it is obvious: Jesus invented the parable to serve his purpose as the rhetorical device par excellence to evoke the beauty and splendour of the secret place that all true believers must crave.

All in all, this stylistic device subsidises His purpose in the following multifarious ways:

The similarity between the points illustrated and the illustration cannot be missed by the observer or listener; the parables give Jesus total authority over the realm of meaning and understanding in the whole narrative. Hence the principles of interpretation are given by Himself, and any false interpretation is easily noticed; their words and details are defined literally, not not paradoxically or spiritually; they embellish His teaching and render His sermons less dogmatic, by way of sharp contrast (Mark 4:30); vivid illustration (Matthew 13:3, 10, 13, 18, 24, 31-36, 53, 15:15; 21:33, 45; 22:1; 24:32). Thus parables are intended similes. They may also serve as proverbs (Luke 4:23). Finally, they cut through time and space, as the historical background and the socio-cultural context and occasion when narrated is defined, and therefore, makes for easy comprehension. The other interesting reasons could be summarised as follows:

a. They help raise the interest and hunger of the listener, urging them to yearn for further details (Matthew 13:10-17)
b. They are especially effective in imparting instruction and rebuke without appearing to be judgmental or condescending from the listener's viewpoint.
c. Parables put truth in perspective; illustrating it through comparison with something that is already familiar.
d. The stories are always true and the points at stake must be seen as plain truth, and without any controversy.
e. The points highlighted in the examples are always stated with the parable or are easily deduced from within the defined context.

Chapter 2

ATTAINING THE SECRET PLACE OF DIVINE LOVE

"But ye are come unto mount Sion, and unto the city of the living God, the heavenly Jerusalem, and to an innumerable company of angels, To the general assembly and church of the firstborn, which are written in heaven, and to God the Judge of all, and to the spirits of righteous men made perfect, And to Jesus the mediator of the new covenant, and to the blood of sprinkling, that speaketh better things than that of Abel" (Hebrews 12:22-24).

Brethren, according to the above piece of Scripture, with Christ as you, you have definitely come into an eightfold package of blessing in grace. Remember, eight is the biblical number that symbolises a brand new beginning—so you are taking off now on a whole new level in spiritual maturity and prowess. Get on board, and let's hit the road:

1. The hub of deliverance—the heavenly Mount Sion as described in the following verses (Joel 2:30-32; Romans 11:26; Revelation 14:1).

2. You have been honoured as a bonafide citizen of the capital city of God (Hebrews 11:10, 16; 13:14; Revelation 3:12; 21:1-27; 22:1-5; John 14).

3. There are innumerable angels that are put at your disposal (Hebrews 1:5-14; Revelation 5:11-14).

4. You are made floor member of the general assembly and church of the firstborn (Colossians 1:18).

5. God is your righteous Judge (v 23).

6. You mingle with and get acquainted to the spirits of just men made perfect (Revelation 6:9-11)

7. You socialise with Jesus, Mediator of the new covenant (Matthew 26:28; Hebrews 9:15).

8. You are cleansed by the blood of the Lamb (Matthew 26:28; Colossians 1:20; I Peter 1:18-23; Revelation 7:14).

Beloved in Christ, welcome to that place! It is an amazing place, reflecting the beauty and splendour of God's awesome majesty that prophets, kings and righteous men have died without having a glimpse of—Christ as you: Christ is all, and in all. Christ now pervades all. Welcome to Christ as you. What a powerful mystery—to be captured , grasped and kept in your spirit. It's available only for mature Christians:

> *"And have put on the new man, which is renewed in knowledge after the image of him that created him: Where there is neither Greek nor Jew, circumcision nor uncircumcision, Barbarian, Scythian, bond nor free: but Christ is all, and in all. Put on therefore, as the elect of God, holy and beloved, bowels of mercies, kindness, humbleness of mind, meekness, longsuffering; Forbearing one another, and forgiving one another, if any man have quarrel against any: even as Christ forgave you, so also do ye. And above all these things put on charity, which is the bond of perfectness"* (Colossians 3:10-14).

Based on a deeper reading of the above Scriptures the new man is the Spirit and nature of God in the renewed man (Ephesians 4:23-24; II Peter 1:4;

Romans 8:9, 14-16). This means the whole life itinerary has changed orientation, and is now headed in a different direction (II Cor 5:17-18). The Greek word for renewed is ananeoo—Conversely, the phrase put on means enduo in Greek—literally to be clothed with: brethren, you are clothed with the garment of salvation like a bride who adorneth herself with jewelry, and like a bridegroom who decketh himself with ornaments (Isaiah 61:10; Luke 24:49; I Th. 5:8). Thus, the new nature must be put on, and will have to manifest righteousness and true holiness. Furthermore, being renewed in knowledge is vital here. The Greek word for knowledge is epignosis—meaning full and true knowledge (I Timothy 1:4; II Timothy 3:7; Hebrews 10:26; Ephesians 1:17; 4:13; Philippians 1:9; II Peter 1:2, 3, 8, 2:20) and acknowledge (Colossians 2:2; II Timothy 2:25; Titus 1:1; Ph'm 6). On the flip side, ignorance is the lot of the average heathen who can barely afford to glean a few facts about the natural environment. Christianity teaches mankind the true and full nature of God with regards to our whole spirituality as well as our authentic natural ecology, and of the origin and destiny of all things (Acts 15:18; Ephesians 2:7; 3:9-11).

Brethren, as our days get long on earth, we tend to forget completely about the truth of our origin. The job of the *old man* we have put off is the satanic spirit that wroughts evil in the heathen, causing us to forget the richness and worthiness of our divine heritage. In this place, the phrase *the image of him that created him* (v10) implies the pattern or moral and spiritual likeness of God, in which we were created (Romans 8:29; II Corinthians 3:18). The idea here is that God's original plan for mankind is to bequeath him with full knowledge, like Adam when he named the entire universe single-handedly, and without having been attending any formalised educational training programme. Being in this place, therefore, He has renewed you, re-designed you after His original blueprint or model and has granted you power, a sound mind and true knowledge (Timothy 1:7; II Peter 1:3-13).

In the new creation, there is no segregation in terms of rights or privileges: no *haves* and *have nots*; no class or caste system—namely the separation of people along sexual lines, racial lines, colour lines or along different stations in life. In fact, the theme of equitable dispensation or a level playing field ranks paramount and is highlighted by the allusion to lowly tribes like Barbarians, even Scythians, regarded by many at the time as coming from the most inferior echelon of the barbarian hierarchy. Bond slaves are also elevated and empowered to rub shoulders with all other members within the normal rung of society (Colossians 12:13; Galatians 3:28). Christ is all things to all believers, and is in all believers (Romans 8:9-16). Beloved, all classes, races, sexes, and types of people who are in Christ constitute His body—the elect, not only the Jews. All who are called by God—whether an individual or nation—represent the elect of God. Brethren, you are a chosen generation; a royal priesthood; a peculiar people who have been chosen to be used of God (Luke 18:7).

Finally, after adding the following ingredients to your Christian stew: the new man, oceans of mercies, kindness, humbleness of mind, meekness, longsuffering, forbearance, and forgiveness, as a supreme vessel, brethren, needless to say you will ultimately have to add on divine love as the outer dressing and icing on the cake to spice up and complete the Christian stew. Love is the outer-cloak as the bond of perfection (Matthew 5:43-48; I Corinthians 13).

Friend, the Gospel of Christ and its mysteries are the heritage of God's elect in Christ: *"For whatsoever is born of God overcometh the world: and this is the victory that overcometh the world, even our faith. Who is he that overcometh the world, but he that believeth that Jesus is the Son of God?"* (I John 5:4-5). That is why there is a lot of mysteries involved in the Gospel, just in case corruption tries to inherit incorruption. As Jesus told the old gentleman called Nicodemus: What is earthly is earthly, and what is spiritual is spiritual. You should be able to distinguish between the tares and wheat without mixing them up—God is organised! Take a look at the opening chapter of the book of all origins, Genesis, and you will be able to understand His viewpoint with regards to a sense of organisation that commands due diligence and perfection. He set up the structures and patterns of all things that have so far stood the test of time. And in spite of all the unfounded evolutionary theories here and there about monkey-men, thousands of years after Gensis, no species have been able to mutate into another: birds are still birds and not fish; apes can look like men, but are not men, period! The toad is still the toad that it

Chapter 2: Attaining the Secret Place of Divine Love

was meant to be, and not a turtle or a dinosaur; a cat is still a cat, and not a leopard. Apes might look like men, but are not. Brethren, resemblance is only resemblance and not sameness. Therefore be weary of false prophets. Their acts and words are an aberration to our spiritual essence, for they are not true prophets. Peter put in a better way: false preachers are like wells without water and clouds without rain. Fortunately, God's purpose cannot be contaminated. This is primarily because God is a true Perfectionist who dislikes chaos:

> *"For by him were all things created, that are in heaven, and that are in earth, visible and invisible, whether they be thrones, or dominions, or principalities, or powers: all things were created by him, and for him: And he is before all things, and by him all things consist. And he is the head of the body, the church: who is the beginning, the firstborn from the dead; that in all things he might have the preeminence. For it pleased the Father that in him should all fulness dwell"* (Colossians 1:16-19).

Beloved in Christ, blessed are you if you have put on Christ; blessed are you if Christ is in you and for you. Oh greatly beloved in the Lord, blessed are you if Christ is with you, and moreover, blessed are you if Christ is as you, for He is the incarnation of God's diligence, perfection, wisdom and mystery. Come to think of it friend, if your faith, hope and love is prescribed by, and circumscribed to the cravings of this world, then you are planning on temporal time, for anything that has a beginning also has an end. The tragedy in life is this bitter truism that many people unwittingly let the world dictate their course and purpose. What these tragic folks fail to understand is that they were not created by the world. They came to the world on assignment, and as free, spiritual agents of God Almighty (Jeremiah 1:4-10; 17-19; Isaiah 43:21; 45:13; Romans 12:1-2). They existed before they arrived here (Psalm 139:13-16; Jeremiah 1:4-5). They fail to realise that they are in the world, but not necessarily of the world . They are not like all the material things that are being manufactured here, year after year, and that nobody can manufacture even a strand of their hair. Ultimately, they fail to realise that they are joint-heirs with the Firstborn of the First Family (Romans 8:14-17, 28-39). They unwittingly reject the precious gift, and stubbornly refuse to acknowledge the supremacy of their divine heritage in Christ *"Who is the image of the invisible God, the firstborn of every creature."* They ultimately fall short of grabbing the vision that their Brother, Jesus Christ, along side His Father, is the Creator of heaven and earth, including all that is in them: whether visible or invisible (John 1:1; 5:17-47). In other words, the person who became known as Jesus Christ, the only begotten Son of the living God, had existed as an equal member of the Godhead from all eternity (Micah 5:2; Isaiah 7:14; 9:6-7; John 1:1-2; Hebrews 1:8; Revelation 1:8-11).

Brethren, we fail in our lives because we deliberately ignore our spiritually, which is of a higher substance. Spirit beings are of a higher substance than flesh and blood. In other words, the things that are visible are inferior to those that are invisible. For example, according to his thesis to the Corinthians (I Corinthians 12), Saint Paul argues that saints should desire spiritual gifts that are superior, but we on earth, alas, would content ourselves with whatever the world presents us with, and which is of no value. Paul compares the members that are invisible and protected by the outer members to come to the conclusion that they are superior. Although we use our legs to walk, it is our minds and hearts that are responsible for the overall design and programming of our mobility and purpose.

Similarly, the material substance that are visible by sight, cannot penetrate walls and other material objects, but the spiritual body of Christ after His resurrection as well as those of other spiritual beings like angels, cherubim, seraphim, etc, are not limited to ordinary substances. Jesus enlightens Nicodemus, the Pharisee: *"The wind bloweth where it listeth, and thou hearest the sound thereof, but canst not tell whence it cometh, and whither it goeth: so is every one that is born of the Spirit"* (John 3:8).

Brethren, Christ lived on earth and in heaven simultaneously, as proven by what is recorded in Scripture, even what the Messiah told his nocturnal guest in the person of Nicodemus: *"And no man hath ascended up to heaven, but he that came down from heaven, even the Son of man which is in heaven. If I have told you earthly things, and ye believe not, how shall ye believe, if I tell you of heavenly things?"* (John 3:11-12)

Precious one in Christ, many priests, like Nicodemus believe that spiritual things operate solely after death, or when you will have ascended onto heaven. But Jesus made it abundantly clear to him that spiritual operations are also an earthly reality. All born again Christians possess unquestionable divine powers that can move mountains and change the world (Matthew 10:7-8; Mark 16:15-18; Luke 10:19; Acts 1:8). New Testament Christianity is a ministry of the Spirit: it is ordained in the Spirit, and not in carnality. That is why we are made priests of the Spirit, and not of the letter: for the letter *killeth*, but the Spirit *giveth* life (II Corinthians 3) Brethren, make no mistake: all that we have come from God, including our ideas, emotions, egos, instinct, intuition, insight , perception, hopes, talents, wishes and plans. Now let us dissect each of the aforementioned traits, beginning with our emotions. Beloved, our emotions are an index to our divinity. God is love, according to the Bible. His Majesty is associated with an emotional epithet—Love! Love pervades every strata of godliness. It is the very substance of faith. In fact, here is the litmus test of the born again experience: *"Beloved, let us love one another: for love is of God: and every one that loveth is born of God, and knoweth God. He that loveth not knoweth not God; for God is love."* (I John 4:7-8). God is our origin and ultimate source; the Alpha and Omega. His name—**I AM THAT I AM** is indicative of our very being, and personal identity as it precedes our own names in each context of self-introduction: I am Stephen Enongene. *I am* comes before both my first and surnames. Both the personal pronoun *I* and the indicative auxiliary verb form *am* represent our personality and character. Therefore, I depart from the truth that our emotions predate our present experience on earth. This is an interesting revelation, since the Bible hints at several instances of life before birth (Jeremiah I:5; Psalm 139:13-16; Galatians 1:15), we cannot readily manipulate or suppress our emotions since they are God-given, and for a higher purpose, when used at the right time, for the right reason, in the right degree and context. Again, emotions cannot be entirely suppressed, but they can be managed to good effect when brought up to consciousness, and validated through the Gospel of Jesus Christ. Even our Lord Jesus Christ Himself could not overcome the powerful force that emotions carry, but gave in and expressed His humanity, as He wept to portray the deep empathy and sympathy he felt for His friends, in what constitutes the shortest verse in the Bible (John 11:35). As you would appreciate, His was a negative emotion. This means that as you battle with life out there, you are more likely to come across more negative than postive emotions. Even the sage, Aristotle once remarked: *"Anybody can be angry—that's easy, but to be angry with the right person and to the right degree and at the right time and for the right purpose, and in the right way—that is not within everybody's power and is not easy."* Beloved in Christ, there are things that are spiritual and those that are scientifically attestable. Namely, that our emotions are too sublime and superior to be subject to mundane rational, analytical misunderstanding, misjudgment or prevarication. In fact, even for the finest brains in the arcane world of neuroscience, optimum emotional self-management or awareness is, at best, a handful, and at worst, an anathema. The supernatural, subliminal transformation of our minds is the exclusive preserve of our God:

> *"He that rejecteth me, and receiveth not my words, hath one that judgeth him: the word that I have spoken, the same shall judge him in the last day. For I have not spoken of myself; but the Father which sent me, he gave me a commandment, what I should say, and what I should speak. And I know that his commandment is life everlasting: whatsoever I speak therefore, even as the Father said unto me, so I speak"* (John 12:48-50).

Thus, we keep our emotions in check through the Spirit of the fear of God, which is one of the seven Spirits of God granted onto the Messiah (Isaiah 11:2). The next is ideas: Ideas come from the mind. The mind is sublime. It is our spiritual essence, from the Spirit of God. Our mind is the showroom for the future. God communicates with us through the mind—from whence comes our dreams, ethical values, visions, aspirations as well as other pristine thoughts that manifest in images, hunches, shapes and symbols we can only ill afford to verbalise. The mind is our memory bank, and centre of our cognitive activity. It is therefore related to our soul, the immortal part of ourselves; it churns up ideas because it is the part of our brain which is mostly preoccupied with intellectual matters, and hence a spiritual battle ground between the good forces of God, and the evil purpose of the devil. Our egos are also an important factor in the galactic warfare between good and evil. Each and every one of us is or at least does have the potential of becoming egoistic. That is to say, the propensity to live below the ego line. The forces that keep pulling us down are usually our cravings for power, prestige, recognition and reward. Most of the demonic, bitter trials we experience are usually connected to the devil teasing us by pulling the ego trigger. Jesus Christ, for example was driven by a strong divine ego, as He undertook the campaign to bring about ther first purification of the temple:

> "And the Jews' passover was at hand, and Jesus went up to Jerusalem, And found in the temple those that sold oxen and sheep and doves, and the changers of money sitting: And when he had made a scourge of small corsds, he drove them all out of the temple, and the sheep, and the oxen; and poured out the changers' money, and overthrew the tables; And said unto them that sold doves, Take these things hence; make not my Father's house an house of merchandise. And his disciples remembered that it was written, The zeal of thine house hath eaten me up" (John 2:13-17).

The King of kings was doubtless obsessed with the desire to declare the glory of God, and to make known to the congregation, the beauty and splendour of His Father's majesty before the great congregation. It was His ultimate drive: that which consumed His human ego. This was also the source of His power, as He always sought to align His desires to those of His Father. On the contrary, we often take severe punches trying to protect our natural egos which are often carnally-minded, utterly banal and downright evil. We are plagued by our selfish desires because we opt to sacrifice God's goodwill upon the altar of bigoted self-will and self-preservation. On His part, though, Jesus was fully conscious of the source of energy that drove Him. Even so, beloved, each time you are called upon to make a decision, try to see to it that none of the above human subconscious forces are influencing you, otherwise there is a good chance you might be partial in your judgment. But God gave us our egos for a good purpose—to enhance our drive, focus and determination for achieving what we truly desire, in accordance to the will of God. The instinct factor is also vital for survival, especially at a much more primitive stage of our existence. The fight or flight syndrome is also closely related to our instinct, which is a development of our genetic make-up. If left unattended, or deliberately neglected, our instinct may resurface at the most inopportune moment to sabotage our plans and betray our strategies to the opposing party. Therefore, every serious debate or deep contemplative session in Christian circles must be preceded by the invocation of the Holy Spirit in prayer and meditation (Romans 12:1-3; Ephesians 6:10-17). The same goes for our intuition which is nothing else but the strong awareness that comes with past experiences. Sometimes our judgments are grossly inflated and influenced by our past, which is regularly misinterpreted under present circumstances—hence, deceptive. In a finite world, however hard you try in your natural self, you cannot afford to be everywhere, and at every time. Only those led by the Spirit can afford this extraordinary feat. Jesus compares them to the wind (John 3:5-8). God the Father Himself made His ministers flames of fire (Hebrews 1:7).

The last of these innate forces is insight. Insight is a glimmer of light, revealing the truth about something you have been pondering about. It too, can never be said to be perfect without God, as the natural man is a finite being. Without our spiritual essence, we are pathetically limited. According to Paul, Christian revelation is divine wisdom and spiritual might:

> *"For I determined not to know any thing among you, save Jesus Christ, and him crucified. And I was with you in weakness, and in fear, and in much trembling. And my speech and my preaching was not with the enticing words of man's wisdom, but in the demonstration of the Spirit and of power: That your faith should not stand in the wisdom of men, but in the power of God. Howbeit we speak wisdom among them that are perfect: yet not the wisdom of this world, nor of the princes of this world, that come to nought: But we speak the wisdom of God in a mystery, even the hidden wisdom, which God ordained before the world unto our glory: Which none of the princes of this world knew: for had they known it, they would not have crucified the Lord of glory"* (I Corinthians 2:2-8).

The Bible warns of the dire consequences that may ensue, should we fail to keep these innate forces in check, while letting the irrational mind to overtake cognitive control in every aspect of our lives:

Chapter 2: Attaining the Secret Place of Divine Love

> "But if ye have bitter envying and strife in your hearts, glory not, and lie not against the truth. This wisdom descendeth not from above, but is earthly, sensual, devilish. For where envying and strife is, there is confusion and every evil work" (James 3:14-16).

In short, whether it is our instinct, intuition or insight, they can all be inadequate, misleading and ultimately unreliable, as tools for making great choices in life (Proverbs 3:5-6; Psalm 37:3-5, 23; 119:99-100; Isaiah 40:27-30; Jeremiah 10:23-24; James 1:22-25). Furthermore, your talents may tend to dilute your ethical values and cognition to undermine your best intentions, except we consent to walk by the promptings of the the Spirit of truth (Psalm 37:23-24; Proverbs 3:5-6; Romans 8:1-15). That is why Paul, the blessed apostle of Jesus Christ, was able to command so much self-control which enabled him to wield such great influence and power in every city-state or metropole where he plied and undertook his highly successful and quintessential apostolic mission. In fact, Paul, in his evangelical campaigns across the length and breadth of first century Europe, evinced a high sense of rapport, emotional and social intelligence, which he also taught, as he interacted and empathised joyfully with members of the various early Christian communities and congregations:

> "Those things, which ye have both learned, and received, and heard, and seen in me, do: and the God of peace shall be with you. But I rejoice in the Lord greatly, that now at the last your care of me hath flourished agains; wherein ye were also careful, but ye lacked opportunit. Not that I speak in respect of want: for I have learned, in whatsoever state I am, therewith to be content. I know both how to be abased, and I know how to abound: every where and in all things I am instructed both to be full and to be hungry, both to abound and to suffer need. I can do all things through Christ which strengtheth me. Notwithstanding ye have well done, that ye did communicate with my affliction. Now ye Philippians know also, that in the beginning of the gospel, when I departed from Macedonia, no church communicated with me but ye only. For even in Thessalonica ye sent once and again unto my necessity. Not because I desire a gift: but I desire fruit that may abound to your account. But I have all, and abound: I am full, having received of Epaphroditus the things which were sent from you, an odour of sweet smell,

a sacrifice acceptable, well-pleasing to God. But my God shall supply all your need according to his riches in glory by Christ Jesus" (Philippians 4:9-19).

Friend, Christianity is a very wholesom religion. Not only are Christians to be bona-fide mediators (Philippians 4:8); ministers of reconciliation (II Corinthians 5:14-20), but they are to practise and enjoy certain things: learn Christian practices, receive Christian blessings, hear the testimonies of Christian blessings, and see Christian miracles. Hence, as a religion, I must say that Christianity is quite spot on. It is far from being a dead, dry, formalised set of ecclesiastical edicts dusted off the shelves of some old time derelict priest or scribe. Nor is it merely a human religion of rituals, outward form, and show, but rather a divine, vibrant, vital, dynamic, liberating religion. In actual fact, to the effect that Christianity is a religion with the potential and power to deliver mankind from sin, sickness, poverty, and want, now and hereafter, it is truly and absolutely of God (Matthew 7:7-11; 17:20; 21:22; Mark 9:23; 11:22-24; 16:17-18; John 14:12-15; 15:7, 16; 16:23-26; Hebrews 11; James 1).

Thus, when, for a time the Philippians were unable to procure supplies for the Apostle Paul, he did not grow bitter, angry or desperately resort to uttering remonstrances at them. Instead, he apologises for them as lacking in opportunity to support his upkeep (v 10). Paul demonstrated the requisite Christian virtue in showing the utmost sense of benignity and gratitude for any help extended to him by fellow Christians. However, he would never make any demands upon his converts to feel duty-bound to procure any such acts of benevolent aspect so typical of Christian values. In the above verses he does not speak of it to extort or get from them, but to praise them for their help (v 11-19). Here are the ten great lessons to learn from the resilience that underpinned Paul's graceful social demeanour: to be content under all circumstances, how to be abased, how to abound, how to adapt in all places, and to thrive in all things, to be full, to be hungry, to abound, to suffer need, and above all, to have the conviction that nothing is impossible through Jesus Christ (v 13; Matthew 17:20; Mark 9:23; 11:22-24; John 14:12-15; 15:7, 16).

Brethren, Paul was a busy minister. He did not rely entirely on church collections, but picked up a part-time job to support himself financially while starting the

Chapter 2: Attaining the Secret Place of Divine Love 53

Thessalonian church, while also receiving support from Philippians. In verse 17 above, he made it clear that praises were not intended to get them feel compelled to extend further help, but to state the facts, wanting them to bear fruit which were to be credited to their accounts in heaven, so as to be rewarded in the day of Christ. In Christianity what goes around comes around! Brethren, we all do have an account in heaven for each and every act of ours on earth. Many are the references in Scripture which go to foreground this truth (Psalm 144:3; Hebrews 13:17; I Peter 4:5). We are implored at several instances in Scripture to watch our words and actions. Hence, we are either storing up wrath by our deeds or misdeeds on record in heaven (Romans 2:5), or we are storing up reward (Romans 14:1-12; I Corinthians 3:11-15; II Corinthians 5:10; Galatians 3:6). Moreover, Chritians are warned that even every idle (useless or cynical) word men will allow sleep carelessly out of their mouth, unsanctioned will have to be accounted for (Matthew 12:36). Every cup of cold water given or refused and the minutest details of life as well as the major acts will be judged (Matthew 6:1-18; 10:41-42; 16:27; Luke 6:23, 35; I Corinthians 3:8-15; 9:17). Ministers of today's church are called upon to model their ministries around the solid standards left on the sands of time by the abstemious apostles of Jesus Christ of the early church. Thus, Paul goes ahead to commend the generousity of his converts: You have sent me so much by Epaphroditus that I have all I need. Your gift is an odour of a sweet smell, a sacrifice acceptable, and well-pleasing to God (Genesis 8:20-22; Ephesians 5:2). The promise of God being the El Shadai, par excellence remains true to all who are in Christ and who are faithful to God as exemplified by these devout Philippians.

Beloved in Christ, the Apostle Paul, like all the other apostles felt divinely obliged to preach the Gospel. Let us take a keen look together, at their selfless, even empathetic policy of service, as outlined by Paul, the humble servant of Jesus Christ. First of all, the man of God claims the divine right of support from the Gospel: That is to say, to live of the largesse off the Gospel like other ministers, but single-handedly decided to waiver any such rights—he declined to exercise it:

> *"For it is written in the law of Moses, Thou shalt not muzzle the mouth of the ox that treadeth out the corn. Doth God take care for oxen? Or saith he it altogether for our sakes? For our sakes, no doubt, this is written: that he that*

> *ploweth should plow in hope; and that he that thresheth in hope should be partaker of his hope. If we have sown unto you spiritual things, is it a great thing if we shall reap your carnal things? If others be partakers of this power over you, are not we rather? Nevertheless we have not used this power; but suffer all things, lest we should hinder the gospel of Christ. Do ye not know that they which minister about holy things live of the things of the temple? and they which wait at the altar are partakers with the altar? Even so hath the Lord ordained that they which preach the gospel should live of the gospel. But I have used none of these things: neither have I written these things, that it should be so done unto me: for it were better for me to die, than that any man should make my glory void"* (I Corinthians 9:9-15).

Brethren, an appraisal of the above piece of Scripture would reveal three over-arching truths: namely, that it is scripturally ordained and legitimate for apostles like Paul and Barnabas to live off the proceeds of the altar. In fact, Barnabas adopted Paul's policy of supporting himself financially(Acts 4:36-37). Secondly, it is worthy of note that it is the church that is officially responsible for the daily upkeep of its minister, and not secular labour. Paul's method was, however, that of self-reliance, and he and Barnabas had a trade by which they were able to support themselves. Therefore, they chose to support themselves in certain places so as not to hinder their core objective of planting a church. In the main, there are often two types of labourers in the vineyard, or officers of the temple of God: those who ministered in holy things and those who waited on the altar (v 13). This was ordained of God, that Gospel ministers should be supported by those who receive the good news for modern man—the Gospel of peace (v 11-15; Galatians 6:6; Hebrews 7:1-11; Luke 10:7; Matthew 10:10). Beloved, the Bible says in no uncertain terms, that it is more honourable to give than to receive. Even so the Apostle of Jesus Christ, Paul, claims he has greater cause for glorifying by preaching the Gospel without charge.

> *"For though I preach the gospel, I have nothing to glory of: for necessitiy is laid upon me; yea, woe is unto me, if I preach not the gospel! For if I do this willingly, I have a reward: but if against my will, a dispensation of the gospel is committed unto me. What is my reward then? Verily that, when I preach the gospel, I may make the gospel of Christ without charge, that I abuse not*

Chapter 2: Attaining the Secret Place of Divine Love

my power in the gospel. For though I be free from all men, yet have I made myself servant unto all, that I might gain the more. And unto the Jews I became as a Jew, that I might gain the Jews; to them that are under the law, as under the law, that I might gain them that are under the law; To them that are without law, as without law, (being not without law, as without law to God, but under the law to Christ,) that I might gain them that are without law; To the weak became I as weak, that I might gain the weak: I am made all things to all men, that I might by all means save some. And this I do for the gospel's sake, that I might be partaker thereof with you. Know ye not that they which run in a race run all, but one receiveth the prize? So run, that ye may obtain. And every man that striveth for the mastery is temperate in all things. Now they do it to obtain a corruptible crown; but we an incorruptible. I therefore so run, not as uncertainly; so fight I, not as one that beateth the air: But I keep under my body, and bring it into subjection: lest that by any means, when I have preached to others, I myself should be a castaway" (I Corinthians 9:16-27).

Paul went ahead to preach his doctrine of selflessness in the service of God's people as a way of echoing God's benevolence in the atonement of our sins through the sacrifice of His only begotten Son. Paul's actions therefore mirror the goodwill gesture of all three persons in the Godhead who have had to make tangible sacrifices to justify to themselves, their love for us, while we were all sinners! The apostle's actions there succinctly reconcile (John 3:16 to I John 3:16), as he went out to spiritually empower his brethren without relying on any formal collections in church. To paraphrase him: If I willingly co-operate with God I have a reward (v 25). If I fulfil my office by simply doing what I am supposed to do, I have nothing extra to buttress my claim to any sort of glorification, for I have nothing practically to show. However, if I fulfil the office beyond the requirement of duty, I more than stand a chance to claim special reward (v 17). Accordingly, in his stewardship Paul claims to live free from all obligations to men, yet he serves every man as if he was their personal slave (v 19). He does all this to gain an insight of the person in order to be able to influence him in the direction of the Gospel, and ultimately win his soul over to Christ. Paul made sure to empathise, and not distance himself mentally or emotionally from the plight of his flock. Rather, he resolved to live like them in order to gain them. The easiest way to gain the hearts and soul of any human being is through empathy. Cognitive empathy ensures that you are able to share their world-view or reason with him or her on common grounds. Furthermore, emotionally empathising with someone would entail an immidiate-felt sympathy for their welfare, well-being, and basic needs. Reasoning with anybody without showing emotions is hopeless. Finally, having reasoned with them mentally to obtain their world-view, as well as keying into their basic needs, interests and welfare; sharing in their displeasure by showing compassion, it would be conducive to common sense, that such a conscientious partner would seek to follow all this up by engaging in some sort of action or decision geared towards serving or providing something in the interest of the aggrieved party. This latter stage of empathy is generally referred to as empathetic concern.

The versatile application of our emotional intelligence or quotient, it is what differentiates us from other either wholly spiritual creatures like angels, wanting a soul; or wholly natural persons like natural people who have opted to stay aloof of their spiritual essence. Emotional intelligence that is subject to the promptings of the Holy Spirit, through our own spirits with a view to birthing Jesus Christ in us, on us, for us, with us, and as us is the spiritual aspect to our being. In this state we will have the potential to intervene in critical moments; in strained social contexts, we will have the capacity to magnify the Lord. And like the song-writer rightly says:

> *"Where there is hatred, we will show His love*
> *Where there is injury, we will never judge*
> *Where there is striving, we will speak His peace*
> *Where there is blindness, we will pray for sight*
> *Where there is darkness, we will shine His light*
> *Where there is sadness, we will bear their grief"*

Now, chosen one of God, if you are like Paul who is capable of the following: knowing how to be content under all circumstances; how to abase as well as how to abound in all places, in all things; how to be full; how to be hungry; how to suffer need, and above all to be of the awareness that nothing is impossible through Christ, you will be able to deliver under the most impossible circumstances in life (Philippians 4:11-13; Matthew 17:20; Mark 9:23; 11:22-24; John 14:12-15; 15:7,16).

This is the power that is capable of uniting the church that has been split along class, intellectual, cultural, economic, political and even racial lines today for the betterment of all mankind. It is the singular reason Paul was determined not to see his congregation as anything else other than our Saviour Jesus Christ crucified:

> *"And I, brethren, when I came to you, came not with excellency of speech or of wisdom, declaring unto you the testimony of God. For I determined not to know any thing among you, save Jesus Christ, and him crucified. And I was with you in weakness, and in fear, and in much trembling. And my speech and my preaching was not with enticing words of man's wisdom, but in demonstration of the Spirit and the power: That your faith should not stand in the wisdom of men, but in the power of God"* (I Corinthians 2:1-5).

Paul also touched on one of the main causes of dementia among Christians is particular, and human beings as a whole. He teaches that Christians should focus on the bright future that lies ahead in the glorious calling of Christ, instead of getting themselves stuck in their unattractive past. Brethren, the dilemma of seeing the glass as either half-full or half-empty; of perceiving opportunity where others see dispair; of sowing while others still procrastinate in a drought-stricken country signposts the demesne of devout Christian living (Hebrews 11:6; 8-10; II Corinthians 10:3-6). The man of God calls for unity in diversity amongs believers. In other words, while we may have come from different cultural backgrounds, still we should not lose sight of the fact we are after a common goal and that our future is harmonised and stays hinged upon the solid virtues and commandments of the powerful kingdom culture of our Saviour Jesus Christ. It is only Christ who can render us the perfection we all so dearly crave:

> *"Brethren, I count not myself to have apprehended: but this one thing I do, forgetting those things which are behind, and reaching forth unto those things which are before, I press toward the mark for the prize of the high calling of*

> *God in Christ Jesus. Let us therefore, as many as be perfect, be thus minded: and if in any thing ye be otherwise minded, God shall reveal this unto you. Nevertheless, whereto we have already attained, let us walk by the same rule, let us mind the same thing. Brethren, be followers together of me, and mark them which walk so as ye have us for an ensample. (For my many walk, of whom I have told you often, and now tell you even weeping, that they are the enemies of the cross of Christ: Whose end is destruction, whose God is their belly, and whose glory is in their shame, who mind earthly things). For our conversation is in heaven; from whence also we look for the Saviour, the Lord Jesus Christ: Who shall change our vile body, that it may be fashioned like unto his glorious body, according to the working whereby he is able even to subdue all things unto himself"* (Philippians 3:13-21).

Hence, the ideal, complete and glorified state of human perfection is only achieveable through Christ. The Word affords us a full end, even a purely consummate state of existence, like Christ after the resurrection (Luke 13:32; John 17:23; II Corinthians 12:9; Hebrews 2:10; 5:9; 7:19; 9:9; 10:1, 14; 11:40; 12:23; James 2:22; I John 2:5; 4:12, 17-18). It is only through Jesus that Christian believers attain fulfilment (Luke 2:43; John 19:28); and can therefore triumph, even as we aspire to accomplish all our main objectives in life (John 4:34; 5:36; 17:4; Acts 20:24). Thus, like Paul we are all in a constant search self-assertion and perfection; we are here to achieve the highest, purest expression of our purpose in life. Hence life itself seems to be a kind of metaphorical bootcamp where desperately devoted knights of the round table, all in quest of the holy grail of self-perfection and glorification seem to be caught in a fierce tussle for greater glory (Matthew 11:12-13). Paul says he had not yet laid hold upon the prize of resurrection, perfection, and glorification (v. 12-14, 20-21). In his life-long quest for the grail, he resolved to forget the ground he had covered in the race (I Corinthians 9:24-27). He never rests on his laurels. He refuses to waste precious time ruminating and rummaging hopelessly over the past (v 13). Rather, he reaches forth to that which is affordable—that which lies before him in the race for glory. He strains every nerve and flexes every muscle fibre, while exhausts every modicum of his strength to conquer. He makes it clear that his future depends on it. It is the race of his life (v 13). Therefore he must press toward the mark (v14), that is to

Chapter 2: Attaining the Secret Place of Divine Love

say, the man of God goes all out for gold. He surges forth, after the white line in hot pursuit, just in case he might get beaten to the contest or even run the risk of being disqualified, knowing full well all other contenders in the stadium have their eyes fixed at the ultimimate prize (v 14; I Corinthians 9:24).

According to Paul what all believers should be looking forward to is the rapture which could take place any time (v 20; Titus 2:13). The rapture is supposed to take place before the second advent. The former marks the time the saints are expected to be caught up in the air with the Messiah, whereas the latter event should happen only when Christ returns with His saints to rule and rid the earth of every evil, after the tribulation; after destroying the anti-Christ, within the period of a thousand years, and after which He will hand the kingdom back to His Father as it was before Adam and Eve undertook their sinful career (II Thess. 2:7; Revelation 1:19; 4:1).

"Who shall change our vile body", Here, the Apostle Paul is prophesying the eventual transformation of our sinful bodies from the current state of humiliation. He alludes to the low state of sin and shame which the human body has been so ludicrously reduced to. Instead of it being deathless, immortal, glorious, and powerful as the paramount head of all God's creation, as it was originally meant to be, it has now turned vile, depraved, sinful, and sickly, even mortal or fragile and subject to the lowest humiliation and eternal ruin (II Corinthians 4:16; Romans 1:18-32; 6:19; Genesis 3:19). Fortunately, nonetheless, through submission to Christ, our body will be changed from mortality to immortality; from a natural body to a spiritual body; from corruption to incorruption; and from weakness and humiliation to glory and power (v 21; I Corinthians 15:35-38). It will be flesh and bone like Christ's body of glory (v 21; Luke 24:39; Zechariah 13:6).

Brethren, we can keep waxing poetic on scientific research and technological advancement as an index to human transformation; we can even proceed to carry out all kinds of scientifice experimentation regarding cognitive control; undertake an indepth, piece-meal neurological analysis of the human brain with a view to impacting human psychological and mental self-control (to boost our IQ and EQ)as much as we possibly can afford. Nevertheless, we should always bear in mind that the power that made the body (Son of man), and all things originally, will be the power that makes the resurrection bodies in a moment (I Corinthians 15:51) and subdue all things to God again, in a perfect state (I Corinthians 15:24-28; Hebrews 2:9-18).

In his seminal works, William Shakespeare, the eminent British playwright and poet hinted at this human dilemma over four hundred years ago. Hence a critical appraisal of the existentialist purview of these so-called great tragedies—whether in King Leah, where he dramatizes the dementia of a crazy king over the inheritance of his daughters; or in Othello, the Moor of Venice, in which the central theme is on the misunderstandings that resulted from a clash of cultures—between that of the central personage, Othello, and characters of his adopted land, Venice. Consequently, the obscurity of his complex ecology is grossly exploited by his fiendish subordinate, Iago, who was a perfect villain. In Macbeth, however, Shakespeare exposes the impetuosity of human action with regards to our drive for power, fortune and fame. Lastly, in Hamlet, Prince of Denmark, we are presented with the ludicrous tendency of aristocratic inaction—a world at the threshold of ruin and disaster: led by privileged fools, and absentee landlords. In all four plays, the characters are presented as helpless pawns on a chessboard which are being manipulated by heathen forces, suggestive of spiritual forces haunting the human tragic universe of Shakespearean plays to frustrate our best intentions. Hence, there is no neutrality with regards to this inter-galactic warfare between good and evil on earth. Shakespeare described this as the power of the tragic universe which exploits loopholes in our character traits to bring about our downfall. Brethren, from what ever perspective you strive to dissect these theatrical pieces, Shakespeare's statement of intent on all four plays is usually summed up to read as follows: *In the end humankind is called upon to make a choice, and the tragedy is that the choice is impossible!* Thus, a survey of Shakespeare's progenitors, which comprises a critique of most of the works of renown Theban play-writes of Greek tragedy such as Sophocles, Aeschylus, and Euripides, postulates the irrefutable verdict that human wisdom without the guidance of the Holy Spirit is nothing but a recipe for life-long suffering, mixed with tragedy and deep sorrow. All in all, the Greek concept of catharsis, aimed at pent-up emotional discharge as a psychological therapy to alleviate tensions, or even the permanent relief of the condition, is the Pagan variant of the supernatural born-again experience of Christian believers to achieve the cleansing or circumcision of hearts and minds to serve God in righteousness, through the Spirit baptism.

Hence our limitation in terms of self-management of emotional intelligence or cognitive self-control are self-imposed. We rebel against our Maker who is Omnipotent, (Psalm 139:19-20), Omniscient (Psalm 139:1-5), and Omnipresent (Psalm 139:7-13), and expect to get a balance in our spiritual and natural life. The mental chaos or split personality of the ungodly often serves as a reminder of the existentialist kindergarten rhyme to this effect of:

> *"Oh The grand old Duke of York,*
> *He had ten thousand men;*
> *He marched them up to the top of the hill,*
> *And he marched them down again.*
>
> *And when they were up, they were up,*
> *And when they were down, they were down,*
> *And when they were only half-way up,*
> *They were neither up nor down."*

And in this fracas, permit me to say, intellectuals rank paramount. Beloved in Christ, always bear in mind that most intellectuals are apostates, as they often seek to usurp divine power through half-baked philosophies, usually puffed up from their vain imagination. In fact, intellectuals are end time giants. They are the Goliaths of our generation. They build a reputation for themselves as self-made men, who are always keen to battle to the last calory of their strength, just to defend their egos, while arrogating God's glory wholly onto themselves, committing all sorts of moral and ethical transgressions in their sinful career. Intellectual knowledge: be it high art, philosophical, scientific, legal or technological without acknowledging God as the Source of all human understanding and enlightenment is tantamount to wizardry. The Apostle Paul pitched it as follows:

> *"For men shall be lovers of their own selves, covetous, boasters, proud, blasphemers, disobedient to parents, unthankful, unholy, Without natural*

affection, trucebreakers, false accusers, incontinent, fierce, despisers of those that are good, Traitors, heady, highminded, lovers of pleasures more than lovers of God; Having a form of godliness, but denying the power thereof: from such turn away. For of this sort are they which creep into houses, and lead captive silly women laden with sins, led away with divers lusts, Ever learning, and never able to come to the knowledge of the truth. Now as Jannes and Jambres withstood Moses, so do these also resist the truth: men of corrupt minds, reprobate concerning the faith. But they shall proceed no further: for their folly shall be manifest unto all men, as theirs also was"
(II Timothy 3:2-9).

Useful scriptural references to portray the limitations of mortal flesh before the preeminence of God: human mental, intellectual and psychological weakness in the absence of God here include the following:

"O Lord, I know that the way of man is not in himself: it is not in man that walketh to direct his steps" (Jeremiah 10:23).

"Wherefore, I also, after I heard of your faith in the Lord Jesus, and love unto all the saints, Cease not to give thanks for you, making mention of you in my prayers; That the God of our Lord Jesus Christ, the Father of glory, may give unto you the spirit of wisdom and revelation in the knowledge of him: THE EYES OF YOUR UNDERSTANDING BEING ENLIGHTENED; that ye may know what is the hope of his calling, and what the riches of the glory of his inheritance in the saints, And what is the exceeding greatness of his power to us-ward who believe, according to the working of his mighty power" (Ephesians 1:15-19).

"The Voice said, Cry. And he said, What shall I cry? All flesh is grass, and all the goodness thereof is as the flower of the field: The grass withereth, the flower fadeth: because the Spirit of the Lord bloweth upon it: surely the people is grass. The grass withereth, the flower fadeth: but the word of our God shall stand for ever" (Isaiah 40:6-8).

Chapter 2: Attaining the Secret Place of Divine Love 63

> *"The steps of a good man are ordered by the Lord: and he delighteth in his way. Though he fall, he shall not be utterly cast down: for the Lord upholdeth him with his hand"* (Psalm 37:24).

As for our perception, God made sure that we are equipped with supernatural levels that cannot be readily determined by the carnal mind. As a matter of fact, to every sense, there is a superior layer to support it in times of need. Therefore, just as we can see, we can also perceive; if we smell, we can also discern; if we touch, we can also feel; if we hear, we can understand; if we taste, we can also assimilate. Deeply spiritual people have each of the above ten senses perfectly developed by the Holy Ghost who is our Comforter. The Spirit of the fear of the Lord is full of wisdom from above that possesses the following characteristics: pure—chaste, holy and clean; peaceable, (also in Hebrews 12:14); gentle—meek, modest, and kind; easily entreated—not stubborn or obstinate, but yielding to others; full of mercy—always forgiving and performing acts of kindness; full of good fruit (also Galatians 5:22-23); without partiality—having no respect of persons (also James 2:1-10); and finally without hypocrisy—open, honest, genuine, and true (James 3:17-18). All in all, brethren, our hope is derived from the full expanse of our faith. In other words, it is our hope that gives shape to our faith. Faith itself is a gift from God. It is the revelation of our glorious ministration in Christ Jesus which surpasses all human understanding. In short, the Bible says, *"For since the beginning of the world men have not heard, nor perceived by the ear, neither hath the eye seen, O God, beside thee, what he hath prepared for him that waiteth for him."* (Isaiah 64:4). The hope of the unbeliever is pathetic: for theirs is limited to what they have already seen—that which is limited in time and space: earthly, sensual and demonic. We sell ourselves cheap to the world because we are hard put to reckon the difference between ourselves and things or inventions made to facilitate work; objects and gadgets meant to serve us; we easily yield to social profiling and/or stereotypes, political gerrymandering, economic subterfuge and cultural sabotage as well as other forms of worldly contraptions and conceits aimed at exploiting the simple piety of the masses so as to hoodwink them and ultimately hijack their divine inheritance. What's more, since most of us scarcely make any distinction whatsoever between what we chose to listen to or read, with the same attention to detail as we do when we carefully separate what is edible or consumable from what is not, even so, Apostle Paul cautions that we should control what things to ponder, as well as carefully sieving what material goes into our minds by way of reading or paying active or passive cognitive attention:

> *"Finally, brethren, whatsoever things are true, whatsoever things are honest, whatsoever things are just, whatsoever things are pure, whatsoever things are lovely, whatsoever things are of good report; if there be any virtue, and if there be any praise, think on these things"* (Philippians 4:8).

Under the circumstances it is therefore illusory for us to consider, even for once, leading our lives without the attention of our God. It is rather foolhardy, even an impossible task to ever imagine ourselves up against these forces of destruction, knowing that we fight not against flesh and blood, but against principalities and powers; against the forces of the darkness of this world; against spiritual wickedness in high places. If we have been barely able to make the right choices as individuals, it is therefore unlikely that we will succeed as a family; and if we are not a family, then we are not good enough to constitute a nation; and if a nation is divided within itself, then how can it even consider contributing to world peace? As all true Christians know, our success on this planet resides in our purpose in Christ which is about working together as one family (Romans 8:14-16). Christ institutionalised servant leadership in order to drive home the plain, and indelible truth that a successful life is when you have risen to the awareness that you are on earth, having been assigned by a good and great God for a fabulous purpose: namely, to contribute to the welfare and well being of your neighbour: for the Son of man came to the world not to be served, but to serve. Brethren, the best of us are here to serve. Hence the need for us to put up Jesus.

> *"Howbeit we speak wisdom among them that are perfect: yet not the wisdom of this world, nor of the princes of this world, that come to nought: But we speak the wisdom of God in a mystery, even the hidden wisdom, which God ordained before the world unto our glory: Which none of the princes of this world knew: for had they known it, they would not have crucified the Lord of glory"* (I Corinthians 2:6-8).

Brethren, we may not have been one of those forlorn princes who erred in persecuting the Prince of peace, but our downright negligence or passive obeisance in this regard does not portray us in any better light. The Word of God is the wisdom of God. Jesus is the Word, and therefore, the wisdom of God. All God's glory manifested on earth comes only by way of Jesus Christ. Therefore we also submit that Jesus is the glory of God. The abundance of life is made possible to us through Jesus (John 1:4; 3:16; 10:10; Philippians 1:21). That is why the Apostle Paul had to warn the Corinthians in his second letter addressed to them. The man of God preached about the purpose of the Gospel to the saints—edification. The Apostle of Jesus went on to point out what the saints are commanded to put off: debates: wranglings; envying: jealousies; wrath: indignation; backbiting: slanders; swellings: puffed up feelings; strife: contentions and whispering: murmurs. He also upbraided them against three kinds of mortal sins. Namely, homosexuality, popularly known as uncleanness; fornication, which is unauthorised sexual intercourse by two consenting parties, and finally lasciviousness—the act of demonstrating an offensive or uncouth sexual desire. Such members would have to be brought to judgment, otherwise my God will humble me before you, says Paul.

> *"Again, think ye that we excuse ourselves unto you? we speak before you in Christ: but we do all things, clearly beloved, for your edifying. For I fear, lest, when I come, I shall not find you such as I would, and that I shall be found unto you such as ye would not: lest there be debates, envyings, wraths, strifes, backbiting, whisperings, swellings, tumults: And lest, when I come again, my God will humble me among you, and that I shall bewail many which have sinned already, and have not repented of the uncleanness and fornication and lasciviousness which they have committed"*
> (II Corinthians 12:19-21).

Now, brethren, having been cleansed by the infallible Word of God we can now proceed to unveil the essential mystery of the Bible—Christ in you, and as you! A mystery which itself has got more layers than an onion. Remember: *"For ye are dead, and your life is hid with Christ in God"* (Colossians 3:3).

Chapter 3

THE FUNDAMENTAL MYSTERIES OF THE SECRET PLACE

"Then was the secret revealed unto Daniel in a night vision. Then Daniel blessed the God of heaven. Daniel answered and said, Blessed be the name of God for ever and ever: for wisdom and might are his: And he changeth the times and the seasons: he removeth kings, and setteth up kings: he giveth wisdom unto the wise, and knowledge to them that know understanding: He revealeth the deep and secret things: he knoweth what is in the darkness, and the light dwelleth with him. I thank thee, and praise thee, O thou God of my fathers, who hast given me wisdom and might, and hast made known unto me now what we desired of thee: for thou hast now made known unto us the king's matter" (Daniel 2:19-23).

We Are Born of God

This God is a Spirit and we are born of that Spirit. We have agreed early on that the things of the spirit are only communicated by the Spirit of God onto His anointed. That is why the Pharisees of the Old Testament Jews thought they knew God inside out, and were His, but Jesus confounded their thinking. The Messiah made them to understand that they were not born of God but they were born of their father, the devil:

> *"They answered and said unto him, Abraham is our Father. Jesus saith unto them, If ye were Abraham's children, ye would do the works of Abraham. But now ye seek to kill me, a man that hath told you the truth, which I have heard of God: this did not Abraham. You do the deeds of your father. Then said they to him, We be not born of fornication; we have one Father, even God. Jesus said unto them, If God were your Father, ye would love me: for I proceeded forth and came from God; neither came I of myself, but he sent me. Why do ye not understand my speech? even because ye cannot hear my word. Ye are of your father the devil, and the lusts of your father ye will do. He was a murderer from the beginning, and abode not in the truth, because there is no truth in him. when he speaketh a lie, he speaketh of his own: for he is a liar, and the father of it"* (John 8:39-44).

Accordingly, Jesus told them that if they were really the spiritual seed of Abraham they would have taken after him in faith. Abraham was a champion of faith. And also of obedience, and hence, righteousness; they only focused on killing. Killing a man (Jesus spoke as man), who told them the truth out of sheer love, which is not anything Abraham would have done. The Lord Jesus was speaking mysteries hidden over the ages from these Pharasees, by the deep veil—the Mosaic veil (II Corinthians 3:12-17). Logically, they could not understand His speech. They thought the deeds of the law would lead them to the righteousness of God. They just could not get themselves to understsand the Gospel truth which says that Jesus is the end of the law for righteousness to everyone that believes (Romans 10:4). They claimed to be God's children on the premise that they did not flirt with other gods—idolatry is spiritual fornication (we are not born of fornication), but Christ countered this by exposing their intentions and deeds: The fact that you do the works of the devil proves you are of the devil (I John 3:8). Since you seek to kill the Son of man you must be the offspring of him who murdered from the very beginning (v41-44)—like father, like son. Jesus emphasised that if God were their Father they would have loved Him, and would not seek to persecute Him instead, because they would have recognisd spiritually that they were of the same Father. Thus, like Nicodemus, they could not get the revelation to enable them crack that mystery.

Jesus Proves our Divinity

However, the regenerated, born again child of God is not like onto the ancient Jews. Brethren, we are well and truly born of God, especially because we believe that Jesus is the Christ, according to the Scriptures. In fact, Jesus testifies to our divinity:

> *"Jesus answered, Verily, verily, I say unto thee, Except a man be born of water and of Spirit, he cannot enter into the kingdom of God. That which is born of the flesh is flesh; and that which is born of the Spirit is spirit. Marvel not that I said unto thee, Ye must be born again. The wind bloweth where it listeth, and thou hearest the sound thereof, but canst not tell whence it cometh, and wither it goeth: so is every one that is born of the Spirit. Nicodemus answered and said unto him, How can these things be? Jesus answered and said unto him, Art thou a master of Israel, and knowest not these things? Verily, verily, I say unto thee, We speak that we do know, and we testify that we have seen; and ye receive not our witness. If I have told you earthly things, and ye believe not, how shall ye believe, if I tell you of heavenly things"* (John 3:5-12)?

Our Invincibility Derives from Jehovah's Seed

Hence, like the other Pharisees, Nicodemus could not believe our Lord Jesus because of the veil. To gain the gift of salvation which is the commodity Jesus came to sell to the world, you need to first of all, hear the Gospel; and then believe it. The final step is to keep and nurture the Seed to grow and bear fruit. The Seed itself, which is in us, buttresses our invincibility, since it is from the Lord:

> *"Whosoever is born of God doth not commit sin; for his seed remaineth in him: and he cannot sin, because he is born of God. In this the children of God are manifest, and the children of the devil: whosoever doeth not righteousness is not of God, neither he that loveth not his brother"* (I John 3:9-10).

Brethren, the Seed is planted by God Himself to confound the devil as we saw Jesus doing against the Pharisees who are the thief's agents and advocates: *"And I will put enmity between thee and the woman, and between thy seed and her seed; it shall bruise thy head, and thou shalt bruise his heel."* (Genesis 3:15). But is also worthwhile pointing out that the devil doesn't take that kindly and goes about planting his own seeds by night (Psalm 30:5). Jesus illustrates this evil phenomenon in the book of Matthew, through the Parable of the Tares:

> *"... The kingdom of heaven is likened to a man which sowed good seed in his field: But while men slept, his enemy came and sowed tares among the wheat, and went his way. But when the blade was sprung up, and brought forth fruit, then appears the tares also. So the servants of the householder came and said unto him, Sir, didst not thou sow good seed in the field? from whence then hath it tares? He said unto them, An enemy hath done this. The servants said unto him, Wilt thou then that we go and gather them up? But he said, Nay; lest while ye gather up the tares, ye root up also the wheat with with them. Let both grow together until the harvest: and in the time of harvest I will say to the reapers, Gather ye together first the tares, and bind them in bundles to burn them: but gather the wheat into my barn"* (Matthew 13:24-30).

Friend, as the parable demonstrates, the good seed is Jesus and the bad seed is Lucifer. The good Seed births those who walk after and/or are led by the Spirit which is what we are. Meanwhile the bad seed brings forth fruits of the flesh which are subject to condemnation and who include the devil himself and his fallen angels or demons, unbelievers, apostates and all sinners and transgressors. The good seed produces the fruit of the Spirit, earthly manifestation of spiritual life (Galatians 5:22-23; I Corinthians 13; Ephesians 5:9; Philippians 4:8). Whereas the evil seed becomes the genesis of all fleshly life and rotten fruits (Galatians 5:19-21; Mark 7:21-23; Romans 1:29; I Corinthians 6:9).

Chapter 3: The Fundamental Mysteries of the Secret Place   71

Our Divine Origin is Seen by the Love we Bear One Another

Therefore, the fruit of the Spirit is the love we bear one another in Christ:

> *"Beloved, let us love one another: for love is of God; and every one that loveth is born of God, and knoweth God"* (I John 4:7).

> *"Hereby perceive we the love of God, because he laid down his life for us: and we ought to lay down our lives for the brethren"* (I John 3:16).

> *"A new commandment I give unto you , That ye love one another, as I have loved you, that ye also love one another. By this shall all men know that ye are my disciples, if ye have love one to another"* (John 13:34-35).

Friend, like I mentioned earlier, love is the standard of godliness. There is no higher order than love: it is greater than faith, and even greater than hope! Agape love is God's glory in the highest, forever! Jesus described it ot His disciples in such terms as:

> *"As the Father hath loved me, so have I loved you: continue ye in my love. If ye keep my commandments, ye shall abide in my love; even as I have kept my Father's commandments, and abide in his love. These things have I spoken unto you, that my joy might remain in you, and that your joy might be full. This is my commandment, That ye love one another, as I have loved you. Greater love hath no man than this, that a man lay down his life for his friends. Ye are my friends, if ye do whatsoever I command you"*
> (John 15:9-14).

Thus Agape love is therefore love that flows from faith in God, *"And hope maketh not ashamed; because the love of God is shed abroad in our hearts by the Holy Ghost which is given unto us."* (Romans 5:5). And He, it is the One who pushes you to act carry on in fulfilment of the purpose of God in your life. The Spirit of God operates solely in truth and righteousness. It therefore follows that this calibre of love is for the general good—a blessing to those who obey and willingly pursue the righteous path of God:

> *"For God so loved the world, that he gave his only begotten Son, that whosoever believeth in him should not perish, but have everlasting life"* (John 3:16).

Indeed, the first part of that verse depicts the robustness in terms of length, breadth, and depth of God's love, as stated by Paul in his famous letter to the Romans:

> *"For when we were yet without strength, in due time Christ died for the ungodly. For scarcely for a righteous man will one die: yet peradventure for a good man some would even dare to die. But God commendeth his love towards us, in that, while we were yet sinners, Christ died for us. Much more then, being now justified by his blood, we shall be saved from wrath through him. For if, when we were enemies, we were reconciled to God by the death of his Son, much more, being reconciled, we shall be saved by his life. And not only so, but we also joy in God through our Lord Jesus Christ, by whom we have now received the atonement"* (Romans 5:6-11).

Hence, from the above verses we can now fathom how profound and grave our former state was when the Lord decided to come to our rescue at the cost of His life. First off, we were without strength—weak, dying, helpless to resist sin and act correctly in the sight of God, and helpless and hopeless to deliver ourselves from misery. Secondly, we were ungodly, that is to say sinful, morally depraved, Satan-driven and enslaved. Thirdly, we were sinners adept at missing the bull's eye of success in spiritual battles against the devil and his fallen angels and demons; we were also powerless when it comes to seeking our salvation. And finally, we were sworn enemies of God. We hated our God and His righteousness and were therefore at war with His values and agents.

Brethren, this was the state of the Gentiles when Christ died for us. Now Apostle Paul submits that life is full of examples of men dying for friends, loved ones, and great men, but it is utterly counter-intuitive for one to die for enemies! Friend, that is what Christ did for us. He further argues that, and this is the denouement of his thesis: if Christ died for us while we were yet ungodly, sinners, and enemies, how much more will he do for us now that we have become reconciled, godly, and friends? If He saved us by His vicarious death, shedding His unblemished blood on our behalf, how much more can he save us by His holy and powerful life (also see Romans 8:31-34; Hebrews 7:25).

It is in this light that Apostle Paul was exhorting the Ephisians to seek the face of God in order to come to the full knowledge of God's love which surpasses human knowledge and dwarfs human understanding:

> *"That Christ may dwell in your hearts by faith; that ye, being rooted and grounded in love, May be able to comprehend with all saints what is the breadth, and length, and depth, and height; And to know the love of Christ, which passeth knowledge, that ye might be filled with all the fulness of God"* (Ephesians 3:17-19).

We therefore conclude the matter by upholding the truth that, God's love is infinite and mega-abundant—beyond the greatest abundance we may request or ever command from even the wildest stretch of our imagination, according to His riches and glory by Christ Jesus our Lord. His ability is fused up with His enthusiasm to commit meticulously to His people. There are no limitations in requesting supplies from God in accordance with the promise (II Peter 1:4).

We Are of God Because we Do Believe in Christ

Moreover, it is our belief in Christ which is emblematic of our godliness:

> *"Whosoever believeth that Jesus is Christ is born of God: and every one that loveth him that begat loveth him also that is begotten of him"* (I John 5:1).

Paul says Christ is our righteousness:

> *"For Christ is the end of the law for righteousness to every one that believeth… That if thou shalt confess with thy mouth the Lord Jesus, and shall believe in thine heart that God hath raised him from the dead, thou shalt*

> be saved. For with the heart man believeth unto righteousness; and with the mouth confession is made unto salvation. For the scripture saith, Whosoever believeth on him shall not be ashamed. For there is no difference between the Jew and the Greek: for the same Lord over all is rich unto all that call upon him. for whosoever shall call upon the name of the Lord shall be saved (i.e. Jesus Christ)" (Romans 10:4, 9-13).

> "As ye have therefore received Christ Jesus the Lord, so walk ye in him: Rooted and built up in him, and stablished in the faith, as ye have been taught, abounding therein with thanksgiving. Beware lest any man spoil you through philosophy and vain deceit, after the tradition of men, after the rudiments of the world, and not after Christ. For in him dwelleth all the fulness of Godhead bodily. And ye are complete in him, which is the head of all principality and power" (Colossians 2:6-10).

Our faith in Christ as Son of God testifies, we have overcome the world:

> "For whatsoever is born of God overcometh the world: and this is the victory that overcometh the world, even our faith" (I John 5:4).

Brethren, to start with, let us take a survey on some of the key Biblical references showing how we have overcome the world through faith:

First of all, through faith we are blessed with bodily healing which is a token of our eventual salvation. Hence, Jesus delivered healing to the the centurion through faith (Matthew 8:10). Also, through faith, Peter used the healing of the lame man in the book of Acts to confirm the deity of Jesus (Acts 3:16).

Secondly, through faith our protection from natural disasters and spiritual hazards is guaranteed, as explained by Jesus when He rebuked the wind in the book of Matthew (Matthew 8:26). This was also evident when the Lord rescued Peter from sinking into the sea as the latter had suddenly lost sight of Jesus having been overwhelmed by the circumstances around the raging sea (Matthew 14:31). In fact, we have overcome the world through faith because we rely on God for our daily supply of food, which means we are exempt from all natural catastrophes or economic crisis regarding food shortages (Matthew 16:8-10). Moreover, through faith, we have obtained divine forgiveness like the lady in the book of Luke (Luke 7:50). David also covered this blessing in the Psalms: *"Blessed is he whose transgression is forgiven, whose sin is covered. Blessed is the man unto whom the Lord imputeth not iniquity, and in whose spirit there is no guile"* (Psalm 32:1-2). This is because God has appointed His Son, Jesus Christ to be propitiation or covering for our sins (Romans 3:25).

Additionally through faith, we can perform miracles: *"And Stephen, full of faith and power did great wonders and miracles among the people"* (Acts 6:8). The Apostle Paul was also able to minister the Spirit to the Galatians, and performed miraculous feats of valour through faith in Christ (Galatians 3:5). Brethren, we also obtain heart purity through faith. Purification of the heart is an absolute prerequisite for the transformation of souls prior to the new birth (Acts 15:9; 10:44-48). It therefore follows that you cannot become a new creature without purity of heart as prescribed by the Gospel (II Corinthians 5:17-18; II Th. 2:13; I John 1:9; 2:29; 3:5-10; 5:1-4, 18). Furthermore, by faith we become sanctified, set aside for divine purposes as proclaimed by our Lord in the book of Acts (Acts 26:18). Also, the Bible says all human beings have fallen short of the glory of God; that our righteousness in the flesh is nothing worthier than a dirty rag in the sight of the Most High. However, by faith in Christ, we have been granted the said righteousness through grace (Romans 3:22; 9:30). Therefore, beloved, justification is another blessing we have obtained by the grace of God as a reward of our faith in Christ (Romans 3:28-31; 4:1-25; 5:1; Galatians 2:16; 3:8, 24).

Consequently, being justified by faith in Christ we have gained access to His grace and like the patriarch Abraham, our youth is renewed like the eagle's (Romans 4:17-20; Psalm 103:5); we are spiritually, mentally and physically stable by keeping the faith we have in Christ (I Corinthians 16:13; II Corinthians I:24); our Christian life style has catapulted us into the newness of life in Christ (II Corinthians 5:7; Hebrews 10). Beloved, life in Christ through faith is a marvellous experiences with multiple advantages which I am going to enlist now to be developed in the subsequent passages and chapters of this book—Holy Spirit guidance (Galatians 3:2,14); sons of God (Galatians

3:26); salvation (Acts 4:12; Ephesians 2:8-9); Christ Indwelling (Ephesians 3:17); baptism into Christ (Colossians 2:12); works of power (I Thessalonians 1:3; II Thessalonians 1:11); Godly edifying (I Timothy 1:4); boldness (I Timothy 3:13); Assurance (Hebrews 10:22); good profession (Hebrews 10:23); patience (James 1:3; I Peter 1:7); inheritance (James 2:5); power to resist the devil (I Peter 5:9); edification (Jude 20) and many faith exploits as reported in the book that celebrates the heroes of faith, (Hebrews 11).

Baptism in Christ, not into water: the secret of redemption (I Corinthians 12:13; Galatians 3:27),

> *"In whom also ye are circumcised with the circumcision made without hands, in putting off the body of the sins of the flesh by the circumcision of Christ: Buried with him in baptism, wherein also ye are risen with him through the faith of the operation of God, who hath raised him from the dead. And you, being dead in your sins and the uncircumcision of your flesh, hath he quickened together with him, having forgiven you all trespasses"*
> (Colossians 2:11-13).

Hence, we have been circumcised, not by incising the foreskin of any of our members, but by spiritual circumcision of Christ in putting off the body of sins of the flesh. Christ consented to become circumcised in order to fulfil all the law that he may become a true mediator between God and man. Therefore, through Him we are spared all the fetters and shackles that come with the burden of the Mosaic law, and have effectively been redeemed through the nailing of all our sins on the cross (I Peter 2:24).

Thus, here we are not talking about water baptism, but spiritual baptism. In fact, baptism here implies the baptism into Christ and into His body through the Holy Spirit (Romans 6:1-10; I Corinthians 12:13; Galatians 3:27). Ultimately, water baptism is only a token of spiritual baptism (I Peter 3:21). Brethren, we are talking about the baptism which symbolises spiritual resurrection from death in sins, trespasses, iniquities, and transgressions (Ephesians 2:1-9). Such a baptism is nothing else but the supernatural operation of God. It is beyond the reach or comprehension of the human preacher. The circumcision is rendered perfect through faith in Christ, not through the operation of the minister. Only God can resurrect or quicken from death in sins and trespasses. It is His sole prerogative.

The physical manifestation of our spiritual blessings in Christ (Ephesians 1:3; 2:4-7), walking in the newness of life, free from all earthly encumbrances and demonic shackles

> *"Therefore if any man be in Christ, he is a new creature: old things are passed away; behold, all things are become new. And all things are of God, who hath reconciled us to himself by Jesus Christ, and hath given us the ministry of reconciliation; To wit, that God was in Christ, reconciling the world unto himself, not imputing their trespasses unto them; and hath committed unto us the word of reconciliation"* (II Corinthians 5:17-19).

The *old things* we have put off through faith in Christ are all the works of the flesh as recorded in Galatians 5:19-22. Nevertheless, the love of God which is in Christ has afforded us the following benefits:

1. God has reconciled Himself through Christ to all men
2. God has forgiven the sins of all those who have confessed and are reconciled to Him
3. God has imparted to those reconciled to Him, the Word of reconciliation
4. God has appointed the reconciled ambassadors for Christ to win souls for the kingdom
5. Through the exchange on the cross, God made Chrsit an offering for sin, that man might become righteous before God.

God has abolished all law observances for those who seek abode in Christ and has granted us a superior dispensation by grace:

> *"For Christ is the end of the law for righteousness to everyone that believeth. For Moses describeth the righteousness which is of the law, That the man which doeth those things shall live by them. But the righteousness which is*

of faith speaketh on this wise, Say not in thine heart, Who shall ascend into heaven? (that is, to bring Christ down from above:) Or, Who shall descend into the deep? (that is, to bring up Christ again from the dead). But what saith it? The word is nigh thee, even in thy mouth, and in thy heart: that is, the word of faith, which we preach" (Romans 10:4-8).

Brethren, as you would appreciate from the above verses, our deliverance from the curse of the law was long overdue! Perfect compliance was required by the law of Moses. Since nobody was able to accomplish this, all men were condemned by the law and cursed by it (Galatians 3:19-25; Romans 5:20; Hebrews 9:10). Beloved, while Jesus came to love, heal and to forgive, the law, on its part, not only mandated to condemn us, but it was officially enforced to expose our short-comings in terms of achieving salvation. Christ is the end of the law of sacrifices, types, rituals, and outward religion which foreshadowed Him and the spiritual realities of of the New Testament.

Also, while law righteousness demanded perfect submission to the precepts or ordinances of the law, faith righteousness beckons only for confession of sins and total surrender to God who, by the Holy Spirit, grants freedom from the law of sin and death, transforming the mind and heart (II Corinthians 5:17-18; I Corinthians 6:11), and while fulfilling in mankind the righteousness of the law (Romans 8:3). The law of faith also renders us righteous in Christ (I Corinthians 1:30; II Corinthians 5:21; Romans 4:1-25; 10:6-13). The Apostle Paul went on to draws a parallel with the Old Testament law, in terms of availability: Hence, men do not have to search for Christ or the Word of the gospel, for it is nigh them, and only needs to be acted upon. Like the law in Deuteronomy 30:12-14: we do not have to search for it; it is already available if only we would recognise or acknowledge it. Thus, we do have the gospel remedy, if only we will give our consent to its soul-saving application. Finally, just like the Bible says it clean and clear, Christ descended into the lower parts of the earth to liberate the righteous who had been languishing under the shackles of captivity by the devil (Matthew 12:40; Ephesians 4:8-10; Hebrews 2:14-15), so is that self-same Gospel of Jesus Christ lying before us today: plain and easy to obey. The doctrine of the death and resurrection of Christ is fully effective to save and deliver. It is near us. It is easy to be confessed with our mouths and be believed in our hearts, should we elect to be saved and be delivered by it. It is nothing but the Word of faith, and if acted upon diligently as prescribed in the Bible, we shall obtain our salvation forthwith.

> *"Blotting out the handwriting of ordinances that was against us, which was contrary to us, and took it out of the way nailing it to the cross; And having spoilt principalities and powers, he made a show of them openly, triumphing over them in it"* (Colossians 2:14-15).

Dear reader, that is why we are more than conquerors through Christ that loved us, and gave His life for us. It is the greatest show of love ever! We are truly born of God. No trace or detail of the ancient writing can be seen afterward. Beloved, the Mosaic law which was entirely against our very being and nature had had to be discarded once and for all, otherwise redemption would have only been a far cry. This is because the law made no provision for redemption. It only slaughtered and slew all men because they all fell short of its gruesome demands, for the law always esteemed their sins beyond pardon. Jesus took this implacable enemy contraption away from our midst; out of our path, so as to liberate us permanently from its perpetual curse that loomed over us like an eternal death penalty. Brethren, since it is out of our way, let us make sure we do not stumble over it any longer. We should keep it in check, absolutely out of the way. Amen.

We Are The Sons of God: Present Reality

Beloved in Christ here is another crystal clear evidence of our divinity: We ARE the sons of God. Please pay keen attention to the grammatical aspect in place here. The form is the Simple Present which designates whole, complete states, and in this particular case, PRESENT TENSE. The great book does not say WE WILL BECOME or any other alternative linguistic nuance to suggest a continuous, tentative or conditional aspect which might have designated a kind of incomplete, hypothetical or somewhat mysterious project of divine contrivance. It is not in the making. It is done. Accomplished. Thus our faith in Christ has procured the Holy Spirit cleansing once and for all! This our reality:

> "Beloved, what manner of love the Father hath bestowed upon us, that we should be called the sons of God: therefore the world knoweth us not, because it knew him not. Beloved, now we are the sons of God, and it doth not yet appear what we shall be: but we know that, when he shall appear, we shall be like him; for we shall see him as he is" (I John 3:1-2).

Friend, just imagine the measure of love the Father has bestowed upon us! And all this without merit onto us, like spoils of war (Ephesians 3:17-19; Romans 8:35-39). Henceforth, we are sons, albeit, not in the sense of being begotten, as in the case of Christ, who is the only begotten Son of God (John 1:14, 18; 3:16, 18). Because of our complete transformation: both on the inside and on the outside—in terms of change of lifestyle, the world will reject us, just as it did to our Lord and Saviour, Jesus Christ. If we continue working righteousness, then, at the rapture, we will inherit His glorified human body (Philippians 3:20-21; I Corinthians 15:51-54; Colossians 3:4). We will definitely maintain our different bodies, in terms of colour, shape, features and characteristics, as we had on earth. Thus, the hope of the rapture should serve as an incentive to encourage us to purify ourselves in the manner of Christ (I John 1:7, 9; 2:6; 3:5-10; 5:1-4, 18).

> "That was the true Light, which lighteth every man that cometh into the world. He was in the world, and the world was made by him, and the world knew him not. He came unto his own, and his own received him not" (John 1:9-11).

The world will not approve of, or acknowledge the doctrine and way of life of the adopted sons and daughters in Jesus, because it did not accept Christ, who is the Author and Perfecter of our faith:

> "But as many as received him, to them gave he power to become the sons of God, even to them that believe on his name: Which were born, not of blood, nor of the will of the flesh, nor of the will of man, but of God" (John 1:12-13).

Chapter 3: The Fundamental Mysteries of the Secret Place

To be precise, we have been granted access into the First Family; freely given the power of attorney; given the liberty and right for each and everyone of us to be saved if we will, not by might or merit; not by any good work of ours or accomplishments, such as showing perfect loyalty to the Mosaic law, but by grace through faith; we have been adopted, as joint-heirs with Christ, glorified. According to the Bible:

> *"For as many as are led by the Spirit of God, they are the sons of God. For ye have not received the Spirit of bondage again to fear; but ye have received the Spirit of adoption, whereby we cry, Abba, Father. The Spirit itself beareth witness with our spirit, that we are the children of God: And if children, then heirs; heirs of God, and joint-heirs with Christ; if so be that we suffer with him, that we may be also glorified together"* (Romans 8:14-17).

> *"But God who is rich in mercy, for his great love wherewith he loved us, Even when we were dead in sins, hath quickened us together in heavenly places in Christ Jesus: That in the ages to come he might shew the exceeding riches of his grace in his kindness toward us through Christ Jesus. For by grace are ye saved through faith; and that not of yourselves: it is the gift of God: Not of works, lest any man should boast"* (Ephesians 2:4-9).

Thus, having been spiritually resurrected from our sinful past, we have been adopted as sons because we have received the Spirit and nature of God—which is of strength and of a sound mind (II Timothy 1:7). The so-called old man, which is the spirit of bondage—the spirit and nature of Satan is that of servitude and has been cleansed by the blood of Jesus, and nailed upon the cross of Calvary.

God Has Re-christened Us

Jesus is all and all: *"And that he died for all, that they which live should not henceforth live unto themselves, but unto him which died for them, and rose again."* (II Corinthians 5:16). Thus in Christ there is no other nationality like American, Chinese, Cameroonian, Greek or Jew. The love of God knows no bounds—it literally permeates all humanity in time and space, just like the sun shining, shines to give warmth to every creature or human being, and the rain falling, falls to water the whole earth for the good of every individual or nation, without discrimination; so is the anointed name of Jesus which is given onto us in love:

> *"Even unto them will I give in mine house and within my walls a place and a name better than of sons and of daughters: I will give them an everlasting name, that shall not be cut off"* (Isaiah 56:5).

> *"And the Gentiles shall see thy righteousness, and all kings thy glory: and thou shalt be called by a new name, which the mouth of the Lord shall name"* (Isaiah 62:2).

> *"And ye shall leave your name for a curse unto my chosen: for the Lord God shall slay thee, and call his servants by another name"* (Isaiah 65:15).

> *"He that hath an ear, let him hear what the Spirit saith unto the churches; To him that overcometh will I give to eat of the hidden manna, and will give him a white stone, and in the stone a new name written, which no man knoweth saving he that receiveth it"* (Revelation 2:17).

> *"Him that overcometh will I make a pillar in the temple of my God, and he shall go no more out: and I will write upon him the name of my God, and the name of the city of my God, which is new Jerusalem, which cometh down out of heaven from my God: and I will write upon him my new name"* (Revelation 3:12).

Brethren, the importance of names need not be overemphasised. God takes names very seriously. Naming is power. In fact, one of the first delegation of duty and power onto man was when the Lord, having created all the things of the world, putting man in charge, came to see how Adam would call them. Hence, the Bible says whatever Adam called those things that was their names thereof (Genesis 2:19). The naming of God's creations lends man great authority, and places him in the diver's seat of things, even as custodian of the property of God on earth.

Similarly, when Abram came under God's full command through faith, and was given the title, *father of all nations,* the Lord changed his name into Abraham—meaning, *father of all nations.* In the same token, when Jacob received the blessings of Jehovah, the Almighty changed his name from Jacob (meaning a confidence trickster), into Israel (prince of God). Consequently, Jesus Christ, as the only begotten Son of the Father, inherited His Father's name in all glory:

> *"Let this mind be in you, which was also in Christ Jesus: Who, being in the form of God, thought it not robbery to be equal with God: But made himself of no reputation, and took upon him the form of a servant, and was made in the likeness of men: And being found in fashion as a man, he humbled himself, and became obedient unto death, even the death of the cross. Wherefore God also hath highly exalted him, and given him a name which is above every name: That at the name of Jesus every knee should bow, of things in heaven, and things in earth, and things under the earth; And that every tongue should confess that Jesus Christ is Lord, to the Glory of God the Father"* (Philippians 2:5-11).

Brethren, it cost Christ more than a fortune in self-humiliation in order to earn the name that has procured our exaltation, through the power of attorney granted us, by His grace through faith. Jesus consecrated to emptying Himself of all His unquestionable divinity: laid aside His divine form; arrogated onto Himself no reputation; assumed the form of a servant; was made in the likeness of men; humbled Himself, and became obedient onto death. Those are the seven levels of the so-called *"Kenosis"*—emptying of Christ from His divine form to human form.

This was all done out of love (I Corinthians 13). The name is the strong tower to which all believers seek refuge in times of trouble (Joel 2:32; Romans 10:13). It therefore nullifies all other names as far as our race for salvation is concerned, at least from the perspective of His disciple, Peter:

> *"Then Peter filled with the Holy Ghost, said unto them, Ye rulers of the people, and elders of Israel, If we this day be examined of the good deed done*

> *to the impotent man, by what means he is made whole; Be it known unto you all, and to all the people of Israel, that by the name of Jesus Christ of Nazareth, whom ye crucified, whom God raised from the dead, even by him doth this man stand here before you whole. This is the stone which was set at nought of you builders, which is become the head of the corner. Neither is there salvation in any other: for there is none other name under the heaven given among men, whereby we must be saved"* (Acts 4:8-12).

Brethren, we have become partakers of the name by grace through faith in Christ Jesus. If we are joint-heirs with Him to the throne of God, then we should also share His glorious name—Jesus Christ of Nazareth, the resurrected Son of the living God. The Bible says that He passed unto those who received Him, unlimited anointed powers to become sons of God:

> *"Even unto them will I give in mine house and within my walls a place and a name better than of sons and of daughters: I will give them an everlasting name, that shall not be cut off"* (Isaiah 56:5).

This was Jesus speaking through the prophet Isaiah. For the Gospel also teaches that whosoever receiveth a prophet in the name of a prophet, gets a prophet's reward. And whosoever welcomes a righteous man in the name of a righteous man gets the reward of a righteous man. Friend, have you received Jesus as your Saviour?

1. We Are Gods—Sons of The Most High

Friend, it is high time we started getting used to this powerful revelation—we are gods! Yes, brethren. God, who cannot lie, declared it in the Spirit through His prophet David:

> *"God standeth in the congregation of the mighty; he judgeth among the gods… I have said, Ye are gods; and all of you are children of the most High"*
> (Psalm 82: 1, 6).

And Jesus Christ—the One who is holy; the One who is harmless; the One who is undefiled; the One who is separate from sinners; and finally, the One who is set above the heavens—confirmed His Father's proclamation, testifying to our divine heritage:

> *"Jesus answered them, Is it not written in your law, I said, Ye are gods? If he called them gods, unto whom the word of God came, and the scripture cannot be broken; Say ye of him, whom the Father hath sanctified, and sent into the world, Thou blasphemest; because I said, I am the Son of God? If I do not the works of my Father, believe me not. But if I do, though ye believe not me, believe the works: that ye may know, and believe, that the Father is in me, and I in him"* (John 10:34-38).

Jesus argues that if the Scriptures which is the infallible Word of God declares that all believers are children of God, why should it be blasphemy of Me to claim deity who am the Son of the Most High, and one with Him? If you believe the Scripture as truth, then you will believe My works as the works of God.

Brethren, the point the Messiah was trying to make here is one which is essential to Christianity as a whole: there is no miracle for unbelievers. That is to say, if you cannot believe the Gospel of Jesus as being the Word of God, you cannot also believe the evidence that is addressed to the senses, and may then proceed to ascribe the works of God to Satan, which is tantamount to downright blasphemy! Anybody born of God must proceed to do great works (Daniel 11:32; John 14:12; Ephesians 2:10). That is why it is said that faith without works is dead (Jas.1:22-25; 2:20-26). All God's children are led by the Spirit to do great works (Ephesians 2:10). Any work outside the Spirit, regardless of its intents, quantity or quality, is considered anathema, or better still, dirty rags, in the sight of God.

Back to our deity, friend. Yes, we are gods because God Himself has said so, and His only begotten Son whom He sanctified and sent into the world for our salvation, has confirmed it. Now, consider this, beloved: man is a spirit. He lives in a body and has a soul. This is very important because angels, for example, don't have souls. They are ministering spirits at the service of God and man (Hebrews 1:4-7). They are therefore bereft of any intellect or I.Q., and do not command any measure of emotional intelligence or E.Q, either. Come to think of it, friend: lizards only give birth to lizards, cats to cats—thus a God can only engender gods—people in His image. That is to say, living souls and/or quickening spirits who look like Him in terms of character, traits or behavioural patterns:

> *"And God said, Let us make man in our image, after our likeness: and let them have dominion over the fish of the sea, and over the fowl of the air, and over the cattle, and over all the earth, and over every creeping thing that creepeth upon the earth. So God created man in his own image, in the image of God created he him; male and female created he them"*
> (Genesis 1:26-27).

The deity of mankind is in place, within the framework of God's creative genius, and operational paradigm. Having made everything afther their kind, it is axiomatic that man is created to be god. And the outcome was quite satisfactory to Him, which means that we are made perfect—we are gods!

> *"And God saw every thing that he had made, and, behold, it was very good…"*
> (Genesis 1:31).

Therefore, we conclude: man is a spirit because he was created by a Spirit. Man is god because He was engendered by God Himself. Amen.

2. We Are Born Of The Incorruptible Sperm (Seed) Of God

Consequently, we are the bona fide, regenerated born again, quickened, empowered children of God destined to overcome all the wiles and intricacies of the devil's wicked plan:

> *"Finally, my brethren, be strong in the Lord, and in the power of his might. Put on the whole armour of God, that ye may be able to stand against the wiles of the devil. For we wrestle not against flesh and blood, but against principalities, against power, against the rulers of the darkness of this world,*

against spiritual wickedness in high places. Wherefore take unto you the whole armour of God, that ye may be able to withstand in the evil day, and having done all, to stand. Stand therefore, having your loins girt about with truth, and having on the breastplate of righteousness; And your feet shod with the preparation of the gospel of peace; Above all, taking the shield of faith, wherewith ye shall be able to quench all fiery darts of the wicked. And take the helmet of salvation, and the sword of the Spirit, which is the word of God: Praying always with all prayer and supplication in the Spirit, and watching thereunto with all perseverance and supplication for all saints"
(Ephesians 6:10-17).

In this regard, therefore, and according to the above Scripture, we are blessed with the ability to stand against all enemy threats; the ability to weather every demonic storm or attack; and finally, we are anointed with the Holy Ghost and with power in Christ Jesus to quench each and every one of Satan's fiery darts. To accomplish this we must be strong in the Lord, be strong in His power, put on the whole armour of God, stand, have our loins girt with truth, put on the breastplate of righteousness, have our feet shod with the preparation of the Gospel of peace, take up the shield of faith, put on the helmet of salvation, take the sword of the Spirit—which is the *rhema* Word—of God, and keep watching in prayer and supplication.

Having said that, suffices to submit right here that the Lord Jesus was thus the incarnated Word of God. Therefore, as He is, so are we in this world: *"Beloved, now are we the sons of God, and it doth not yet appear what what we shall be: but we know that, when he shall apear, we shall be like him; for we shall see him as he is"* (I John 3:2). *"Herein is our love made perfect, that we may have boldness in the day of judgment: because as he is, so are we in this world"* (I John 4:17). This is so because we are incarnated, regenerated, born again by the SEED or sperm of God; as Peter concludes:

"Being born again, not of corruptible seed, but of incorruptible, by the word of God, which liveth and abideth for ever. For all flesh is as grass, and all the glory of man as the flower of grass. The grass withereth, and the flower

thereof falleth away: But the word of the Lord endureth for ever. And this is the word which by the gospel is preached unto you" (I Peter 1:23-25).

To crown it all, brethren, since the Bible holds that corruption will not inherit incorruption, therefore we can safely state here that the born again mystery that takes place in the Holy Spirit enables us to become the incorruptible seed to inherit the kingdom of God. Through the Word of God we shall live forever.

Book The Second

THE FOUR PILLAR OF SALVATION

INTRODUCTION

Salvation is God's greatest gift to mankind. It is the gift of eternal life which takes the form of His only begotten Son, Jesus Christ of Nazareth who is the blessed and only Potentate, the King of kings, and Lord of lords. Therefore there is no salvation without Christ: all the other religions whose doctrines either directly or implicitly ignore the appellation of His name which God the Father has raised above every other name (Philippians 2:9-11), may just as well be likened to the old adage of pouring water on a duck's back, which comes to nought. Beloved in Christ, the word of God, the Rhema Word makes it abundantly clear in both the Old and the New Testament that deliverance is granted only by calling the name of the Lord:

> *"And it shall come to pass, that whosoever shall call on the name of the Lord shall be delivered: for in mount Zion and in Jerusalem shall be deliverance, as the Lord hath said, and in the remnant whom the Lord shall call"*
> (Joel 2:32).

The name that is given to us on earth as synonymous with deliverance is no other than that of Jesus. Some false prophets and many other religious dogmas contrive to undermine this gospel truth by referring to Him only as the Son of God while chanting His Father's other names in churus. Brethren, it is absolutely immaterial how many times you call on the other names of the

Father, unless you call the name Jesus, you can as well kiss salvation goodbye! First of all, it is important to be aware of the fact that the Gospel spells it out in concrete terms that salvation comes through the Son, not the Father:

> *"For God so loved the world, that he gave his only begotten Son, that whosoever believeth in him should not perish, but have everlasting life"* (John 3:16).

Brethren, judging from the premise that the Word of God is the only entity, given that it was that which created heaven and earth, and also created us, as clearly stipulated at the opening chapters in the book of Saint John, we can safely conclude that Jesus is that Word: for He truly is the incarnation of the Word. Now, according to the Psalmist, God has magnified His Word above all His names:

> *"I will worship toward the holy temple, and praise thy name for thy lovingkindness and for thy truth: for thow hast magnified thy word above all thy name"* (Psalm 138:2).

Consequently, the Word is the Gospel of Jesus Christ which is essential to salvation. Throughout Scripture, there has not been any salvaging prophecy without a release of the Gospel. From Abraham through Moses to John the Baptist, God's message was one and the same: the coming of the Messiah, Immanuel (Isaiah 7:13-18; Matthew 1:18) who heals, delivers, baptizes in the Holy Spirit, and is coming again! In fact, the emblematic phrase of the Gospel was captured in the book of Acts by Peter:

> *"The word which God sent unto the children of Israel, preaching peace by Jesus Christ; (he is Lord of all) That word, I say, ye know, which was preached throughout all Judaea, and began from Galilee, after the baptism which John preached; How God anointed Jesus of Nazareth with the Holy Ghost and with power: who went about doing good; and healing all that were oppressed of the devil; for God was with him"* (Acts 10:36-38).

Introduction

Peter's gospel was the first of its kind to a Gentile: a man called Cornelius of Caesarea. Although the Bible presents him as *"A devout man, and one that feared God with all his house, which gave much alms to the people, and prayed to God."* Yet, Jehovah had to initiate him into the kingdom path of righteousness by insisting he go and look for Peter: *"He lodgeth with one Simon a tanner, whose house is by the sea side: he shall tell thee what thou oughtest to do."*—hear the Word of God, which is the Gospel of Jesus Christ, as quoted above.

Ultimately, the Word of God, the Perfect Law or the Gospel of Jesus Christ is exactly what Paul the Apostle describes in his seminal work—the epistle to the Romans Chapter 1: *"For I am not ashamed of the gospel of Christ: for it is the power of God unto salvation to every one that believeth; to the Jews first, and also to the Greek."* (v 16).

The Word and the Name are intertwined. The Name Jesus itself is divine: begotten of the Father, and glorified: *"I am come in my Father's name,…"* (John 5:43):

> *"Wherefore God also hath highly exalted him, and given him a name which is above every name. That at the name of Jesus every knee should bow, of things in heaven, and things in earth, and things under the earth; And that every tongue should confess that Jesus Christ is Lord, to the glory of God the Father"* (Philippians 2:9-11).

That is why Jesus had the boldness to declare as He did in the book of John:

> *"…I am the way, the truth, and the life: no man cometh unto the father but by me"* (John 14:6).

And the Apostles were all strongly schooled in this apostolic doctrine such that wherever they found themselves preaching, teaching or healing, the name of Jesus was always key:

> *"Then Peter filled with the Holy Ghost, said unto them, Ye rulers of the people, and elders of Israel, If we this day be examined of the good deed done*

to the impotent man, by what means he is made whole; Be it known unto you all, and to all the people of Israel, that by the name of Jesus Christ of Nazareth, whom ye crucified, whom God raised from the dead, even by him doth this man stand here before you whole. This is the stone which was set at nought of you builders, which is become the head of the corner. Neither is there salvation in any other: for there is none other name under heaven given among men, whereby we must be saved" (Acts 4:8-12).

Chapter 1

YOU NEED DELIVERANCE

Two categories of Christians are easily discernible today. The first category is largely made up of those who know so much that they esteem themselves versed in the Word to the extent of being infallible. The problem here is therefore not that they are ignorant of the truth, but that they have virtually stopped listening. They have become so stiff-necked, and rather hardhearted that they cannot readily lend themselves to, or make themselves amenable to the ways of God, and have, therefore, become way too insensitive to the plight of others around them, which in turn undermines any prospects of God ever considering the option of using them for His sublime purpose: namely, as the supreme vessels of blessings they were meant to be. Many in this class include church dignitaries whose ministries have become barren and bereft of any great testimonies, or prophecies, signs, wonders and miracles which constitute the blessed emblem ordained to accompany the Gospel of Jesus Christ. Hence, they can simply be likened to the Scribes, Pharisees or Sanhedrins of the first century synagogues who were so set in their ways and stuck in their minds that the Lord described them as *old wine skins*, incapable of taking the pressure of *new wine* without giving way.

On the other hand, there are those who are resigned to their fates; those who, to all intents and purposes, seem to have given up on all matters divine. They have grown so bitter, having taken punches upon punches over the years from numerous incessant life battles that have put their morale on the wane. Like the man in agony, who accosted the nine normal disciples of Jesus left behind (for his terminally afflicted son) after the Lord had gone to the mount of transfiguration with Peter, James and John, this melancholy tribe have invested all their life fortune in a man-made religion—church, and have now turned around to blame their calamity on the Spirit of Jesus Christ (Matthew 17:14-21). Beloved in Christ, not all churches are of Christ. The true church of Christ is Spirit-filled and Spirit-led. The Holy Spirit is head of all future prophecies:

> *"I have yet many things to say unto you, but ye cannot bear them now. Howbeit when he, the Spirit of truth, is come, he will guide you into all truth: for he shall not speak of himself; but whatsoever he shall hear, that shall he speak: and he will shew you things to come. He shall glorify me: for he shall receive of mine, and shall shew it unto you. All things that the Father hath are mine: therefore said I, that he shall take of mine, and shall shew unto you"* (John 16:12-15).

> *"He that hath ear, let him hear what the Spirit saith unto the churches"* (Revelation 2:7).

> *"Until the day in which he was taken up, after that he through the Holy Ghost had given commandments unto the apostles whom he had chosen"* (Acts 1:2).

Friend, it took the woman with the issue of blood twelve years to finally catch up with the true church of Christ! (Matthew 9:19-22)

Anyway, brethren, many backsliders and several other itinerant church goers, who often esteem themselves victims of the much institutionalised religious conservatism, would naturally fill the ranks of this spiritually destitute class; they have managed to amass and nurture tons and tons of grievances against unscrupulous church leadership ever accused of financial impropriety, salacious malpractices as well as other universally acknowledged acts of religious delinquency relating to gross miscarriage or abuse of moral congruence in human communities. Apostates, unbelievers and others of that ilk, tend to blame God for actions undertaken by worldly free agents. Accordingly, when these masses

Chapter 1: You Need Deliverance 97

are victorious and jubilant, it is as a result of their personal competence. They arrogate all the praises onto themselves and take all the accolades ,and wallow in self-deceit or vainglory. When things go awry, alas, they quickly recoil in utter desperation, heaping every blame on God whom they have barely acknowledged as their eternal Father. The Apostle Paul took a swipe at such in one of his letters to Timothy (I Timothy 5:8): *"But if any provide not for his own, and specially for those of his own house, he hath denied the faith, and is worse than an infidel."* The setback suffered here might be twofold: natural negligence or spiritual blindfold. The former because God Himself cried out loud in the Old Testament book of the prophet, Hosea, saying that His people are ignorant to a fault, even to their own detriment:

> *"My people are destroyed for lack of knowledge: because thou hast rejected knowledge, I will also reject thee, that thou shalt be no priest to me: seeing thou hast forgotten the law of thy God, I will also forget thy children"* (Hosea 4:6).

> *"But be ye doers of the word, and not hearers only, deceiving your own selves. For if any man be a hearer of the word, and not a doer, he is like unto a man beholding his natural face in a glass: For he beholdeth himself, and goeth his way, and straightway forgetteth what manner of man he was. But whoso looketh into the perfect law of liberty, and conitnueth therein, he being not a forgetful hearer, but a doer of the work, this man shall be blessed in his deed"* (James 1:22-25).

Brethren, the law here refers to the new covenant with our Lord Jesus Christ that has made us joint-heirs with Christ to the throne of the Most High God. That is what has the power and Spirit to transform lives, should you diligently pursue all the ordinances, according to the commandments of our Lord Jesus.

However it is also important to bear in mind that we inherited a cursed earth from Adam and Eve as revealed in the book of Genesis 3:17-19. As descendants of Adam and Eve, we are born into sin even though we may not have committed any sins in the similitude of those of Adam and Eve. Hence, in the psalms, David prayed:

> "Behold, I was shappen in iniquity; and in sin did my mother conceive me" (Psalm 51:5).

Dear reader, we need deliverance due to our unrighteous past of which there is no exception, and this regardless of how righteous or holy we pretend to be today. We are either subsumed under the Adamic stock, who are formed after the first Adam, made a natural man; a living soul and destined or cursed to end up as mere dust (Genesis 3:14-19). Otherwise, upon repentance and yielding to God's purpose, we are transformed in faith by God's grace in the supernatural process of the born-again miracle into the kingdom of God.

The intergalactic warfare between good and evil means that we are ultimately called to make a choice on which side of the dial we intend to pursue our spiritual career: blessings with God or curses with Lucifer. The Psamists launched their recital by putting into perspective some of the benefits, should one choose wisely. Conversely, the inexorable fallout for erring in this endeavour are dire and multifarious:

> "Blessed is the man that walketh not in the counsel of the ungodly, nor standeth in the way of sinners, nor sitteth in the seat of the scornful. But his delight is in the law of the Lord; and in his law doth he meditate day and night. And he shall be like a tree planted by the rivers of water, that bringeth forth his fruit in his season; his leaf also shall not wither; and whatsoever he doeth shall prosper.
> The ungodly are not so: but are like the chaff which the wind driveth away. Therefore the ungodly shall not stand in the judgment, nor sinners in the congregation of the righteous. For the Lord knoweth the way of the righteous: but the way of the ungodly shall perish" (Psalm 1:1-6).

Moses, the law-giver made a life-saving appeal, even a spirit-filled proposition to the children of Israel in the wilderness. The divine ultimatum involved the contending forces of blessings or curses being up for grabs, as the children of Israel laboured to overcome their evil past and embrace the new dispensation that was being rolled out to them by Jehovah through His servant Moses:

> "Behold, I set before you this day a blessing and a curse; A blessing, if ye obey the commandments of the Lord your God, which I command you this day:

> *And a curse, if ye will not obey the commandments of the Lord your God, but turn aside out of the way which I command you this day, to go after other gods, which ye have not known"* (Deuteronomy 11:26-28).

Even the prophet Jeremiah caught the ill-fated vision concerning half-baked allegiance to God by some Christian fence-sitters:

> *"Thus saith the Lord: Cursed be the man that trusteth in man, and maketh flesh his arm, and whose heart departeth from the Lord. For he shall be like the heath in the desert, and shall not see when good cometh; but shall inhabit the parched places in the wilderness, in a salt land and not inhabited. Blessed is the man that trusteth in the Lord, and whose hope the Lord is. For he shall be as a tree planted by the waters, and that spreadeth out her roots by the river, and shall not see when heat cometh, but her leaf shall be green; and shall not be careful in the year of drought, neither shall cease from yielding fruit"* (Jeremiah 17:5-8).

Furthermore, the Apostle Paul dissects the spiritual cause of those who misfire in this regard, as coming under the spell of demonic power which schemes to blur their vision for a better tomorrow and eventually seals their fates from obtaining a redeemed future in Christ:

> *"But if the gospel be hid, it is hid to them that are lost: In whom the god of this world hath blinded the minds of them which believe not, lest the light of the glorious gospel of Christ, who is the image of God, should shine unto them. For we preach not ourselves, but Christ Jesus our Lord; and ourselves your servants for Jesus' sake. For God, who commanded the light to shine out of darkness, hath shined in our hearts, to give the light of the knowledge of the glory of God in the face of Jesus Christ"* (II Corinthians 4:3-6).

That is why we all need deliverance. Deliverance is not limited to any select or damned group: it is for all mankind without exception. Clearly, deliverance cannot be imposed on anyone, but we all are in dire need of it; for we all are in the transgression having been born into an inheritance that has put on the wrong helmet: that which is righteously unbecoming. We do need coats of skin, as garment for all weather, and not tattered leaves from the volatile, disintegrating, natural environment—a cursed spectre had been levied on Adam and Eve, our forefather by Jehovah, and a terrible future awaits us should we fail to repent of our past sinful career (Genesis 3). Even so, the Messiah's statement of intent revealed in Luke 4:18-19 makes it clear that for us all, deliverance is a must-have:

> *"The Spirit of the Lord is upon me, because he hath anointed me to preach the gospel to the poor; he hath sent me to heal the brokenhearted, to preach deliverance to the captives, and recovering of sight to the blind, to set at liberty them that are bruised, to preach the acceptable year of the Lord"* (Luke 4:18-19).

Now, it would be downright falsehood for anyone to claim exclusion from all of the aforementioned classes of people. As a matter of fact, it is either you are poor, materially or spiritually; brokenhearted socially speaking, or are as such due to financial constraints. Being a captive does not necessarily mean that you are arrested physically by the forces of law and order held captive by thugs. In spiritual terms, however, it may mean you have become a slave to some delinquent act or deed, even an obsession or an addiction to something dishonourable. Nor does blindness exclusively refers to loss of sight, no! The *blind* here essentially imply the lost to the Gospel of peace, such as have been excluded from experiencing the mysterious truths embedded in the miracles which are meant to be signs or proofs addressed to consolidate the gains of their belief by addressing their senses to give them hope in a resplendent future—to those who have fallen prey to the devil's malignant sleight-of-hand. Brethren, the *bruised* ones are definitely those that are being possessed and tossed around in scorn, at Lucifer's whim.

Beloved in Christ, even if you look at the Grand Commission given to us all in the book of Saint Matthew 28:18-20, it is quite obvious that all God's creatures on the face of this earth badly need deliverance in Christ:

> *"…All power is given unto me in heaven and in earth. Go ye therefore, and teach all nations, baptizing them in the name of the Father, and the Son,*

and the Holy Ghost: Teaching them to observe all things whatsoever I have commanded you: and, lo, I am with you alway, even unto the end of the world. Amen" (Matthew 28:18-20).

To all intents and purposes, the emphasis on the phrase: *and teach all nations,* speaks volumes of the generalised nature of this divine plea, with reference to our basic need, right and welfare. Time and time again, we are reminded of the fact that we all have failed to live up to the glorious expectations and precepts of the Most High, and therefore have fallen short of being heirs to His glorious heritage in heaven and on earth:

"...for there is no difference: For all have sinned, and come short of the glory of God" (Romans 3:21-24).

By and large, sinning here is twofold: it refers to either our iniquities, or simply falling foul of the commandments or statutes of God. Nevertheless our iniquities abound and are otherwise known as *works of the flesh.* (Galatians 5:19-21). They include adultery or unlawful sexual relations between men and women, single or married; fornication, same as adultery above; uncleanness, whatever is the opposite of purity; including sodomy, homosexuality, lesbianism, pederasty, bestiality, and all other forms of sexual perversion. Also, lasciviousness, licentiousness, lustful tendencies, unchaste ways, and lewdness. In short, lasciviousness is about encouraging sexual arousal or partaking in activities, thoughts or actions tending to provoke or stir up sex sin and lust. Also, idolatry: any extravagant out-pouring of strong emotions on things on earth; witchcraft: sorcery, practising or dealing with evil spirits; magical incantations and casting spells and charms upon one by means of drugs and potions or enchantments of various kinds to either afflict pain or give blessing. Another is hatred, bitterness, abhorrence, malice and ill-will against anyone; the tendency to nurse grudges against or be passionately angry at someone; variance, which is tantamount to being at odds or in discord with: constantly debating, quarrelling and disputing with one another. Emulations, which amounts to seeking comparison with others: to compare yourself up or down against someone else out there. This births vaulting ambition, as you seek to climb to the top on the shoulders of others. Emulation usually causes envy, jealousy, indignation, arrogance or depression. There is also wrath, which is about moral indignation and pure fierceness. Turbulent passion or rampant rage , and determined and lasting anger. Strife is another one. With strife, we are constantly caught up in bitter contentions, disputations and jangling. We strife over minor issues and get angry. In short many a time it is only a contest for superiority and social status which may entail strenuous endeavours to equal or settle scores with rivals. Moreover, there is the sin of sedition which is characterised by actions or speeches aimed at stirring up social disorder or strife capable of undermining the peace in governments, religious denominations, communities or even among family members at homes. Furthermore, there is heresies: the tendency to reject sound Christian doctrine in favour of man-made rituals and dogmas, as well as philosophical hypothesis instead of the gospel truth. Then there is also envying: a purveyor of pain, ill-will, and jealousy at the good fortune or blessings of another. Envying is an absolute monster! A passion that degrades and dehumanises a person and ultimately ruins them in utter disgrace. Finally, we have murders: to slay someone. But it is also connected to character assassination; to steal the joy of another through heinous acts of sabotage or subterfuge which are all acts of betrayal for personal gain. Drunkenness is another sin that is frowned at both in heaven and on earth. Such a passion can render its victim a true slave to their addictive habit—given to drinking bouts. To revel here refers to social acts of entertainment that spin out of control, leading to lascivious and boisterous feasting, employing obscene music, and other sinful acts capable of birthing extreme sensual pleasures of salacious intent.

Early on, the psalmist had also sought to throw light on this basic fact that sinfulness, transgressions and other acts of malignant aspect in human character are nothing that could be twisted in order to stigmatise a certain group of people or nation, for it is global and has penetrated every strata of human civilisation as far back as Adam and Eve:

> *"The fool hath said in his heart, There is no God. They are corrupt, they have done abominable works, there is none that doeth good. The Lord looked down from heaven upon the children of men, to see if there were any that did understand, and seek God. They are all gone aside, they are all together become filthy: there is none that doeth good, no, not one"* (Psalm 14:1-3).

Chapter 1: You Need Deliverance

There seem to be a correlation between sinfulness and mental apathy. With clear emphasis on the phrases: *The fool hath said...*, *to see if there were any that did understand*, it is therefore no wonder we are constantly addressed with the same metaphor, over and over again: mankind is referred to as *a flock of sheep* with Christ as the Shepherd:

> "All we like sheep have gone astray; we have turned everyone to his own way; and the Lord hath laid on him the iniquity of us all" (Isaiah 53:6).

Such derogatory terms are in place here since the Bible says, "*The fear of the Lord is the beginning of knowledge: but fools despise wisdom and instruction*" (Proverbs 1:7). The preacher of the book of Ecclesiastes also went on to question our cognitive ability to make sound choices in sinfulness:

> "For there is not a just man upon earth, that doeth good, and sinneth not" (Ecclesiastes 7:20).

The prophet Jeremiah also caught the vision of humankind's inherent sinful nature in the following lines:

> "The heart is deceitful above all things, and desperately wicked: who can know it?" (Jeremiah 17:9)

Without controversy, our natural Adamic self lends itself to evil deeds. This is particularly due to the curse upon our nature by God, which is exploited by the devil to prey on us at his whim. Even God testified to this regarding the high rate of apostasy that had plagued the city of Sodom and Gomhorrah before He decided to destroy it in a flood:

> "And God saw that the wickedness of man was great in the earth, and that every imagination of the thoughts of his heart was only evil continually. And it repented the Lord that he had made man on the earth, and it grieved him at his heart. And the Lord said, I will destroy man whom I have created from the face of the earth; both man, and beast, and the creeping thing, and the fowls of the air; for it repenteth me that I have made them"

(Genesis 6:5-7).

Generations after the floods: more precisely during the time of King David, the situation had hardly improved in the sight of the Almighty, as the psalmist reports:

> "... there is none that doeth good. The Lord looked down from heaven upon the children of men, to see if there were any that did understand, and seek God. They are all gone aside, they are all together become filthy: there is none that doeth good, no, not one" (Psalm 14:1-3).

Friend, if there are any lessons to learn from the doomed fates of those unfortunate city dwellers of old, it would be nothing else but repentance to receive God's deliverance through faith in Christ. Our Lord and Saviour Jesus Christ revealed this truth to Nicodemus in the book of Saint John:

> "...Verily, verily, I say unto thee, Except a man be born again, he cannot see the kingdom of God... Verily verily, I say unto thee, Except a man be born of water and of the Spirit, he cannot enter into the kingdom of God. That which is born of flesh is flesh; and that which is born of Spirit is spirit. Marvel ye not that I said unto thee, Ye must be born again. The wind bloweth where it listeth, and thou hearest the sound thereof, but canst not tell whence it cometh, and wither it goeth: so is everone that is born of the Spirit" (John 3:3, 5-8).

> "There is therefore no condemnation to them which are in Christ Jesus, who walk not after the flesh, but after the Spirit. For the law of the Spirit of life in Christ Jesus hath made me free from the law of sin and death. For what the law could not do, in that it was weak through the flesh, God sending his own Son in the likeness of sinful flesh, and for sin, condemned sin in the flesh: That the righteousness of of the law might be fulfilled in us, who walk not after the flesh, but after the Spirit" (Romans 8:1-4).

Brethren, as Jesus proved to Nicodemus, differentiating between the supreme power of the Holy Spirit in comparison to the forces or laws of nature, by using the wind metaphor, so did Paul likewise demonstrate in his epistle to the Romans.

The man of God simply demonstrates how sin had reigned from Adam to Moses, but was not active before the law came into force because it did not have any reason to assert itself. However, once the commandment was introduced, sin came alive in full force, and by its lust compelled him to fall foul of its precepts and thus became condemned (Romans 7:7-25). Nevertheless, by putting up Jesus through faith, he became free from condemnation, was free from the law of sin, was free from eternal death, sin got condemned in his flesh, he fulfilled righteousness, he had life and peace, he became Spirit-filled, his body was dead to sin, his flesh was crucified with Jesus, and ultimately got him walking in the Spirit, and hence in the newness of life, and no longer after the sinful flesh (Romans 8:1-13). That is why we are exhorted to let ourselves be transformed by the cleansing power of the Word in faith. We are called upon to accept Jesus as our Lord, and let the Spirit communicate with our spirit to effect a divine fusion that births Jesus in us which is the deep secret or mystery of the Gospel of Jesus Christ. We need to declare the name of Jesus into salvation, having believed the Rhema Word for His righteousness in our hearts through the Holy Spirit of God.

Chapter 2

YOU CANNOT SAVE YOURSELF

"What shall we say then? Is the law sin? God forbid. Nay, I had not known sin, but by the law: for I had not known lust, except the law had said, Thou shalt not covet. But sin, taking occasion by the commandment, wrought in me all manner of concupiscence. For without the law sin was dead. For I was alive without the law once: but when commandment came, sin revived, and I died. And the commandment, which was ordained to life, I found to be unto death. For sin, taking occasion by the commandment, deceived me, and by it slew me. wherefore the law is holy, and the commandment holy, and just, and good. Was then that which is good made death unto me? God forbid. But sin, that it might appear sin, working death in me by that which is good; that sin by the commandment might become exceeding sinful. For we know that the law is spiritual: but I am carnal, sold under sin. For that which I do I allow not: for what I would, that do I not; but what I hate, that do I. If then I do that which I would not, I consent unto the law that it is good. Now then it is no more I that do it, but sin that dwelleth in me. For I know that in me (that is, in my flesh,) dwelleth no good thing: for to will is present with me; but how to perform that which is good I find not. For the good that I would I do not: but the evil which I would not, that I do. Now if I do that I would not, it is no more I that do it, but sin that dwelleth in me. I find then a law, that, when I would do good, evil is present with me. For I delight in the law of God after the inward man: But I see another law

in my members, warring against the law of my mind, and bringing me into captivity to the law of sin which is in my members. O wretched man that I am! who shall deliver me from the body of this death? I thank God through Jesus Christ our Lord. So then with the mind I myself serve the law of God; but with the flesh the law of sin" (Romans 7:7-25).

Friend, as we all seem desperate to make sense of our lives; better still, as we usually go all out to find meaning in our spiritual existence, in what often amounts to an existentialist struggle against our sinful nature, methinks the best way to exemplify the hopelessness of flesh and blood in this subtle confrontation for preeminence in mankind with sinful nature, would be to avail ourselves of the wisdom of this powerful passage, by scanning through the mysterious details contained in Saint Paul's letter to the Romans. Brethren, the above verses clearly depict the fierce struggle the Apostle Paul had had to put up in his desperate attempt to wriggle himself free from the firm grip of the shackles installed by sin and the powerlessness of the Mosaic law. The opening verse of his thesis simply serves to vindicate or exonerate the purpose and status of the law. In principle, therefore, the law was not enforced with an evil intent but was put in place for a good and sublime cause. Paul says that the law did not have any sinful aspect in itself, but he was sinful by nature. In fact, even before the advent of the commandment, he had come firmly under its vicious influences, albeit passively. Although he was alive in body, soul and spirit long before the law came into force, yet he was simply powerless in terms of conducting himself willingly according to its precepts because of the power of sin. Thus, although the law was just in its demands: exposing the evil of sin, still Paul had to suffer the consequences of disobedience to the law, not only due to the weakness of his flesh and blood, but also due to the powerlessness of the law in the wake of the resurgence of his sinful spirit. For example, at one point he acknowledges that he actually consented to the law but passive obeisance was not enough. He simply could not get himself to wholly act or lead his life according to the principle of those commandments because sin was in actual fact his slave-master. Even so, he let us know that he was not a total push-around to the spirit of sin. Somehow he did put up some resistance—he did not willingly acquiesced. He was not a willing slave. But was, nevertheless, a wretced slave to sin until he finally found a new slave-master which is Jesus Christ of Nazareth.

Chapter 2: You Cannot Save Yourself

> *"Therefore it is of faith, that it might be by grace; to the end the promise might be sure to all the seed; not to that ony which is of the law, but to that also which is of the faith of Abraham; who is the father of us all"* (Romans 4:16).

Friend, salvation comes from God. He is the Sole Proprietor of our deliverance. The invaluable gift can neither be earned by works nor achieved through man's wisdom. The Bible states it clearly and boldly that Christians can only obtain justification through faith in Christ Jesus who is the Author and Perfecter of our faith. In fact, throughout Scripture, we have seen many supreme vessels of God struggle with faith to keep their calling. This self-deceptive megalomaniac tendency is what the philosophical book of Proverbs warns against:

> *"Trust in the Lord with all thine heart; and lean not unto thine own understanding. In all thy ways acknowledge him, and he shall direct your paths"* (Proverbs 3:5-6).

Unfortunately, we usually esteem ourselves wise and often strive to take matters into our hands and flex our muscles, just to find out that we are not quite up to the task before we end up pleading to secure God's help. As far as deliverance is concerned, there is no neutrality. You are either gathering with Jesus, or you in league with the devil—busy scattering! Christ Himself said, if you are not with us, you are against us, period. The Bible says the path to damnation is usually wider than that which leads to salvation:

> *"There is a way which seemeth ight unto a man but the end thereof are the ways of death"* (Proverbs 14:12).

Brethren, we are always tempted to go for a quick fix. That is to say, succumbing to the allure of making some momentary home runs in stead of exercising patience and humility which will lead us to the ultimate promises of God through our Lord Jesus Christ in the end. According to the Bible, we are not justified by works of any kind, since salvation is never merited, but rather bestowed upon the faithful recipient by grace. Grace is God's undeserving mercy. In other words, we are saved thanks to the suffering, crucifixion and resurrection of our Lord and Saviour Jesus Christ.

All law keepers are being misled by the spirit of unbelief that reigns in darkness: choking the seed which the Lord has planted in them from taking root as well as blinding their eyes from apprehending, understanding and capturing the gospel truth by which they could obtain salvation:

> *"But if our gospel be hid, it is hid to them that are lost: In whom the god of this world hath blinded the minds of them which believe not, lest the light of the glorious gospel of Christ, who is the image of God, should shine unto them. For we preach not ourselves, but Christ Jesus the Lord; and ourselves your servants for Jesus' sake. For God, who commanded the light to shine out of darkness, hath shined in our hearts, to give the light of the knowledge of the glory of God in the face of Jesus Christ"* (II Corinthians 4:3-6).

Consequently, these law keepers reject "faith alone" (sola fide), misinterpreting James 2:20-26 in stressing that a person is not justified by faith alone. They argue that the Apostle Paul does not mean faith without works. Therefore these law keepers consider good works like charity, as prerequisites for our justification. They insist on procuring help where God does not need any. Even so, according to Scripture what James was saying, in effect, is quite contrary to their views. The Biblical truth is that if a man is saved by faith alone who has the seed in him, he will end up performing good deeds as a result of the change of nature (Romans 12:1-3), through the born again miracle. Any *good work* without Christ is the same as self-righteousness which is an emblem of demonic demolition. Beloved, self-righteousness is a mortal sin that has plagued mankind from inception, and the infamous, inglorious tower of Babel is an index to our self-aggrandisement:

> *"And the whole earth was of one language, and of one speech. And it came to pass, as they journeyed from the east, that they found a plain in the land of Shinar, and they dwelt there. And they said one to another, Got to, let us make brick, and burn them throughly. And they had brick for stone, and slime had they for morter. And they said, God to, let us build us a city and a tower, whose top may reach unto heaven; and let us make us a name, lest we be scattered abroad upon the face of the whole earth. And the Lord came down to see the city and the tower, which the children of men builded. And the Lord*

> *said, Behold, the people is one, and they have all one language; and this they begin to do: and now nothing will be restrained from them, which they have imagined to do. God to, let us go down, and there confound their language, that they may not understand one another's speech. So the Lord scattered them abroad from thence upon the face of all the earth: and they left off to build the city. Therefore is the name of it called Babel; because the Lord did there confound the language of all the earth: and from thence did the Lord scatter them abroad upon the face of all the earth"* (Genesis 11:1-9).

Thus, the new earth that had been replenished by the sons of Noah initially spoke one language, supposedly, Hebrew. Nevertheless, the propensity toward the pursuit of vainglory had resurfaced and mankind had totally lost the Spirit of the fear of God to the extent of craving self-importance, even self-indulgence. But their devilish blueprint would only lead to self-deceit and utter disaster as God is omnipotent, omniscient and omnipresent. The plural pronoun, *us*, here refers to the Holy Trinity. The same Godhead that convened to make us in His image (Genesis 1:26-29). The scattering of men abroad to occupy the different parts of the earth also meant that we would have to become separated from one another along racial, cultural and linguistic lines. The multiplicity of religions and ways of worship was also on the cards. All this, brethren, is the result of man's failure to live and work according to the will of God. Therefore we conclude:brethren, any work outside the realm of the Holy Spirit amounts to nothing but a piece of filthy rag in the sight of God.

Friend, work is ordained by God. Work is holy. It is an integral part of our divine heritage. Our God is a God of works: *"Many O Lord my God, are thy wonderous works which thou hast done, and thy thoughts which are to us-ward: they cannot be reckoned up in order unto thee: if I would declare and speak of them, they are more than can be numbered"* (Psalm 40:5). He made the heaven and the earth. In fact, the current world he made in six days (Genesis 1:1-31; Psalm 24:1). We are made in His image, and therefore we are blessed to carry out great works:

> *"Verily, verily, I say unto you, He that believeth on me, the works that I do shall he do also; and greater works that these shall he do; because I go unto my Father"* (John 14:12).

Unlike a lot of people out there, Jesus knew the source of all great works, which is from His Father! That is why Jesus was ordained with the Holy Spirit and power in order to equip Him for great works. Brethren, all great works are achieved through the Holy Spirit of God. Jesus whose quality and quantity of works remains unparalleled, made no secret as to the source of His achievements:

> "...Verily, verily, I say unto you, The Son can do nothing of himself, but what he seeth the Father do: for what things soever he doeth, these doeth the Son likewise. For the Father loveth the Son, and sheweth him all things that himself doeth: and he will shew him greater works than these, that ye may marvel" (John 5:19).

Brethren, the secret behind Jesus' miracles is that He never took a step without watching His Father. The sacred union with His heavenly Father made it impossible for Him to fail. Also, not only did He gleaned wisdom from the Father, but he was also humble and never sought to do His own will nor did he ever schemed to usurp the credits due to His God:

> "I can of mine own self do nothing: as I hear, I judge: and my judgement is just; because I seek not mine own will, but the will of my Father which hath sent me" (John 5:30).

> "Believe thou not that I am in the Father, and the Father in me? the words that I speak unto you I speak not of myself: but the Father that dwelleth in me, he doeth the works. Believe me that I am in the Father and the Father in me: or else believe me for the very works' sake" (John 14:10-11).

Beloved in Christ, the first Adam who was a living soul relied on God for great works. Adam could not have pulled that off without his God (Genesis 2:19-20). Adam manged to name all God's creatures because God was with Him. Similarly, Jesus Christ of Nazareth was able to go about doing good and healing all who were oppressed of the devil because He was One with His Father in the Spirit (Acts 10:38). And the Holy Spirit is in the Rhema Word that lives! Therefore, to do the works of God you have to believe in the

Gospel of Jesus Christ who is the incarnation of the Word in order to obtain the indwelling Spirit of God that will lead you to do the works of God:

> *"Then said they unto him, What shall we do, that we might work the works of God? Jesus answered and said unto them, This is the work of God, that ye believe on him whom he sent"* (John 6:28-29).

That said, all born again Christian believers who are one with Christ as prescribed in the book of Saint John chapter 15, are destined to do great feats of valour:

> *"Abide in me, and I in you. As the branch cannot bear fruit of itself, except it abide in the vine; no more can ye, except ye abide in me. I am the vine, ye are the branches: He that abideth in me, and I in him, the same bringeth forth much fruit: for without me ye can do nothing"* (John 15:4-5).

Jesus is therefore our sole Purvayor of works that is satisfactory to the Father. He alone can ordain the works to be made manifest by the Spirit of God. As we are grafted onto Him, therefore we cannot bypass Him to please the Father out of our own personal initiative:

> *"For we are his workmanship, created in Christ Jesus unto good works, which God hath before ordained that we should walk in them"* (Ephesians 2:10).

Beloved that is the only divinely sanctioned criteria for realisation of peak performance with regards to the ordinance of works in the Gospel of Jesus Christ. Anything outside the putative framework of Christ-like labour is therefore considered anathema. The Messiah is the standard:

> *"Now if any man build upon this foundation gold, silver, precious stones, wood, hay, stubble; Every man's work shall be made manifest: for the day shall declare it, because it shall be revealed by fire; and the fire shall try every man's work of what sort it is. If any man's work abide which he hath built thereupon, he shall receive a reward. If any man's work shall be burned, he shall suffer loss: but he himself shall be saved; yet so as by fire"* (I Corinthians 3:12-15).

Hence the Apostle Paul exhorts the church that you are not saved by works of any sort:

> *"For by grace are ye saved through faith; and that not of yourselves: it is the gift of God: Not of works, lest any man should boast"* (Ephesians 2:8-9).

So much about pretending to obtain salvation through self-righteousness in *good works*.

Moreover, keeping the law is like brandishing an evil camouflage:

> *"For whosoever shall keep the whole law, and yet offend in one point, he is guilty of all"* (James 2:10).

Hence the spiritual oxymoron of sinful men pretending to live up to the righteousness of God by themselves, inthe guise of upholding the decrepit laws of Moses. This way, needless to say they will never be able to attain God's sublime standards of perfection in Jesus Christ. For the Bible makes it crystal clear that God's foolishness is wiser than man, while His weakness is stronger than man. Moreover, His ways are not our ways, nor His thoughts our thoughts. For as the heavens are higher than the earth, so are His ways than our ways and His thoughts than our thoughts. In the Old Testament, it is our actions that counted. In the New Testament, it is our thoughts. For example, Jesus said just to think a bad thought is sin; to hate is synonymous with murder, while to lust is the equivalence of committing adultery: nurturing evil thoughts is as good as doing them in reality:

> *"Knowing that a man is not justified by the works of the law, but by the faith of Jesus Christ, even we have believed in Jesus Christ, that we might be justified by the faith of Christ, and not by the works of the law: for by the works of the law shall no flesh be justified"* (Galatians 2:16).

Friend, to make this more explicit it would be sensible to talk about the fundamental differences of the two testaments of the Bible. Accordingly, the Old Covenant is incomplete without the New Covenant. The essential promise

Chapter 2: You Cannot Save Yourself 115

of the Messiah's first advent is fulfilled only in the New Testament. All the prophecies and promises about God's plan for our salvation, His holy calling, the blessings granted to His elect through His purpose and grace were only fulfilled in the Messiah's first advent. Jesus manifested God's blessings by His personal appearance on earth; He abolished death that had reigned since Adam and Eve; brought life through His Gospel; brought immortality through His Gospel:

> *"Verily, verily, I say unto you. He that believeth on me hath everlasting life. I am the bread of life. Your fathers did eat manna in the wilderness, and are dead. This is the bread which cometh down from heaven, that a man may eat thereof, and not die. I am the living bread which caqme down from heaven: if any eat of this bread, he shall live for ever: and the bread that I will give is my flesh, which I will give for the life of the world"* (John 6:47-51).

The Bible says your salvation is in you. God has already given us the potential for the exercise of our faith (Romans 12:3). Thus, it is henceforth up to us to take up the gauntlet; go ahead and declare what we believe in. God's seed of salvation has already been inserted in us (Genesis 3:16), and He has clothed us with the garment of righteousness (Genesis 3:21; Isaiah 61:10). He has poured His Spirit on all flesh (Joel 2:28-29); and in our hearts (Jeremiah 31:31-34; I Corinthians 16-17). He has blessed us with all spiritual blessings in heavenly places in Christ Jesus (Ephesians 1:3), and made us sit in heavenly places (Ephesians 2:4-7). It is now our duty to believe in that righteousness within our heart, and speak out or declare our way onto salvation (Romans 10:10; II Corinthians 5:17):

> *"Whoever believeth that Jesus is the Christ is born of God: ...For what soever is born of God overcometh the world: and this is the victory that overcometh the world, even our faith. Who is he that overcometh the world, but he that believeth that Jesus is the Son of God?"* (I John 5:1,4-5).

Saving faith is about a change of heart and mind. The old mindset of the law keepers has to be destroyed to make way for a heart divine which is more natural to us and much more expedient for our eternal profit. We must not repeat the errors of the Jesheruns:

> "For they, being ignorant of God's righteousness, and going about to establish their own righteousness, have not submitted themselves unto the righteousness of God. For Christ is the end of the law for righteousness to everyone that believeth" (Romans 10:3-4).

In the New Testament, therefore, our bodies have become the temple of God (I Corinthians 3:16-17). On this score, our hearts are the holies of holies: the dwelling place of God. In fact, in the Old Testament, the priests were instructed in the book of Leviticus to always keep the flames in the altar, and never to put out the fire that glows in the inner temple (Leviticus 6:13):

> "Keep thy heart with all diligence; for therein lies the issues of life" (Proverbs 4:23).

Ours, brethren, is the dispensation of the Spirit. We have been ordained priests of the Spirit and not of the letter. Hence, the fire burns not physically but spiritually, in us, and on us. It is therefore not just a matter of mental assent with regards to the Gospel, but a complete transformation of our heart which is wrought by the Holy Spirit. Paul states:

> "And be not conformed to this world: but be ye transformed by the renewing of your mind, that ye may prove what is the good, acceptable, and perfect, will of God" (Romans 12:2).

This mental transformation is clearly exemplified by our Lord Jesus Himself, as He sought to empty Himself of His divinity to serve the purpose of His Father on earth as a complete human being:

> "Let this mind be in you, which was also in Christ Jesus: Who, being in the form of God, thought it not robbery to be equal with God: But made himself of no reputation, and took upon him the form of a servant, and was made in the likeness of men: And being found in the fashion of a man, humbled himself, and became obedient unto death, even the death of the cross" (Philippians 2:5-8).

Brethren, while humans focus on the outward appearance of men in their appraisal of character and personality, the Lord focuses on the heart and mind (Jeremiah 17:10; Romans 8:26-27). Jesus told Nicodemus, the Pharisee, YOU MUST BE BORN AGAIN TO SEE THE KINGDOM OF GOD! By this our Lord meant that the dead in sin's spirit of man has to be regenerated by the Holy Ghost and be brought back to life, thereby reconnecting it to God, as was originally intended: the state of man before the fall, and clothed with the spotless robes of the Lamb which is Christ Jesus, as Adam confessed at his spiritual death, when God clothed them with coats of skin, insead of leaves which is what they had earlier attempted to do themselves:

> *"I will greatly rejoice in the Lord, my soul shall be joyful in my God; for he hath clothed me with the garments of salvation, he hath covered me with the robe of righteousness, as a bridegroom decketh himself with ornaments, and as a bride adorneth herself with jewels"* (Isaiah 61:10).

Peter would later offer the right recipe for achieving maximum attention and security through the transformation of our mindset in his second epistle:

> *"And beside this, giving all diligence, add to your faith virtue; and to virtue knowledge; and to knowledge temperance; and to temperance patience; and to patience godliness; And to godliness brotherly kindness; and to brotherly kindness charity. For if these things be in you, and abound, they make you that ye shall neither be barren nor unfruitful in the knowledge of our Lord Jesus Christ. But he that lacketh these things is blind, and cannot see afar off, and hath forgotten that he was purged from his old sins. Wherefore the rather, brethren, give diligence to make your calling and election sure: for if ye do these things, ye shall never fall: for so an entrance shall be ministered unto you abundantly into the everlasting kingdom of our Lord and Saviour Jesus Christ"* (II Peter 1:5-11).

Brethren, the internalisation of the Spirit of Christ in us is about our knowledge, awareness and consciousness of this deep mystery of God which is the Gospel of Jesus Christ. Law keeping is superficial and unprofitable for doctrine. In fact, it is nothing but the old sinful nature trying in a self-righteous attitude to obey God, whereas being born of God is the new creature preordained to serve God from the standpoint of a newly obtained heart—a miraculously changed nature. God will always sanctify His elect with a new and cleansed heart, as He did to king Saul:

> *"And it was so, that when he had turned his back to go from Samuel, God gave him another heart: and all those signs came to pass that day. And when they came thither to the hill, behold, a company of prophets met him; and the Spirit of God came upon him, and he prophesied among them. and it came to pass, when all that knew him beforetime saw that, behold, he prophesied among the prophets, then people said one to another, What is this that is come unto the son of Kish? Is Saul also among the prophets? And one of the same place answered and said, But who is their father? Therefore it became a proverb, Is Saul also among the prophets? And when he had made an end to the prophesying, he came to the high place"* (I Samuel 10:9-13).

In the New Testament, Acts 16:14 states clearly that Lydia like those from Philippi and Ephesus, was a person *"whose heart the Lord opened"* to the Gospel of Jesus Christ. Thus, the heart (spirit) must be made new and restored to God's custody for it to be saved. The devil believes in Jesus but he is not saved.

Consequently, we conclude this chapter by submitting that salvation is by faith alone because Jesus Christ is enough: *"…he said, It is finished"* (John 19:30); the Apostle Paul says Jesus Christ is the only foundation, (I Corinthians 3:1-17) and that is why Jesus told Paul: *"My grace is sufficient for thee: for my strength is made perfect in weakness…"* (II Corinthians 12:9). Saving faith is a gift of God. One cannot earn it by merit. Grace is the means of salvation, and faith is the imputation of God's righteousness through our Lord Jesus Christ. Amen:

> *"Jesus saith unto him, I am the way, the truth, and the life: no one cometh unto the Father, but by me"* (John 14:6).

Chapter 3

JESUS HAS ALREADY OBTAINED ETERNAL REDEMPTION FOR YOU

"The Lord hath appeared of old unto me, saying, Yea, I have loved thee with an everlasting love: therefore with loving-kindness have I drawn thee" (Jeremiah 31:3).

Beloved in Christ, the Bible says, God is love (I John 4:7-8). The love of God or the Agape love surpasses all human understanding, transcends universal time and space and stretches into eternity:

"Therefore I say unto you, Take no thought for your life, what ye shall eat, or what ye shall drink: nor yet for your body, what ye shall put on. Is not life more than meat, and the body than raiment? Behold the fowls of the air: for they sow not, neither do they reap, nor gather into barns, yet your heavenly Father feedeth them. Are ye not much better than they? Which of you by taking thought can add one cubit unto his stature? And why take ye thought for raiment? Consider the lilies of the field, how they grow; they toil not, neither do they spin: And yet I say unto you, That even Solomon in all his glory was not arrayed like one of these. Wherefore, if God so clothe the grass of the field, which today is, and tomorrow is cast into the oven, shall he not much more clothe you, O ye of little faith? Therefore take no thought, saying, What shall we eat? Or, What shall we drink? or, Wherewithal shall we be clothed? (For after all these things do the Gentiles seek:) for your heavenly Father knoweth

> *that ye have need of all these things. But seek ye first the kingdom of God, and his righteousness; and all these things shall be added to unto you. Take therefore no thought for the morrow: for the morrow shall take thought for the things of itself. Sufficient unto the day is the evil thereof"* (Matthew 6:25-34).

Friend, the Lord is superlatively loving, merciful and kind. His kindness and love, though, is predicated on the good fortunes of helping us make heaven, which is the ultimate prize or gift from the living God. The Lord is delighted in spoiling us, but not to the extent of misleading us into living for, or even letting us take liberties in spiritual wrong doing, going on to worship material things! Just imagine what it feels like, seeing humans made in the image of the Most High, wallow inadvertently in dirt: by means of idol worship:

> *"Love not the world, neither the things that are in the world. If any man love the world, the love of the Father is not in him. For all that is in the world, the lust of the flesh, and the lust of the eyes, and the pride of life, is not of the Father, but is of the world. And the world passeth away, and the lust thereof: but he that doeth the will of God abideth for ever"* (I John 2:15-17).

Thus, aside from the works of the flesh (which has been dealt with in the first chapter), we are exhorted to ignore the lust of the eyes. Remember Adam and his wife, Eve were derailed from their principled position of preeminence, as custodians of the property of God just to stumble, thereby kicking off the earth's sinful career which ends in Revelation 20:7-15 partly because of the looks of the fruit (Genesis 3:6). Brethren, beware of the lust of the eyes! Today, we are carried by the lust for women, committing adultery, covetousness, insatiable appetite to consume, idol worshp, diverse kinds of evil acts. Worst still, besides the scourge of *the lust of the eyes* there is also the putative syndrome which is often described as *the pride of life*. Paramount on this list is self-righteousness, and the cravings for positions. Lust for power, riches, beauty, strength to war, vaulting ambition— glorying in sexual intercourse; living entirely for pleasure and the vanities of life are ways or life styles that are ultimately unbecoming in the sight of God.

Consequently, this unquestionable love-divine, loving-kindness that is expressed in our God's infinite glory, enduring mercy, unmerited grace, unshakable faithfulness, and bountiful righteousness is evident in His actions throughout scripture. The Apostle Paul outlines the characteristics of Agape love as follows:

> *"Charity (love) suffereth long, and is kind; charity envieth not; charity vaunteth not itself, is not puffed up. Doth not behave itself unseemly, seeketh not her own, is not easily provoked, thinketh no evil: Rejoiceth not in iniquity, but rejoiceth in the truth: Beareth all things, believeth all things, endureth all things"* (I Corinthians 13:5-7).

That is why Agape love is more enduring, substantial or eternal than spiritual gifts or any other talents out there. First and foremost, divine love exudes patience—love passive! It's not rushed. That is to say, true lovers are not in a haste. We are always in a hurry because of our base interest, but God is never in hurry. Suffereth long: shows forbearance, belief and hope, and ultimately enduring in every respect. God is with you for the long haul. His Spirit is with us for eternity. In agape love, there is also kindness—flowing downwards from the cognitive to the emotional, and finally to the pragmatic—kindness is love in action. God's love is made manifest by the perfect nature of His gifts—The Bible says, unto us a child is born; unto us a Son is given. Thus, as a measure of His love, God gave us His inheritance. That is to say, His most prized assest; Jesus gave us His dear life: suffered for us, died and was crucified on the cross for our sake. And the Holy Spirit agreed to serve us as Comforter and Guide throughout His entire, precious time on earth. God's love never acts rashly, inordinately or show downright insolence; it's not inconsistent, puffed up or haughty. Through the life of Jesus on earth, we can believe all the above compliments concerning God's love. Jesus was the incarnation of Jehovah's glory: the Bible says He was full of grace and truth. His full profile can be found in (Isaiah 43; Philippians 2:5-8). Furthermore, there is a clear evidence of generosity in agape love. In other words, love in competition. Hence Apostle Paul states: *"Moreover the law entered, that the offence might abound. But where sin abounded, grace did much more abound: That as sin hath reigned unto death, even so might grace reign through righteousness unto eternal life by Jesus Christ our Lord"* (Romans 5:20-21). Such a love is boundless and not restricted by jealousy or envy but rather free flowing in quantities and qualities that cannot be contained. What's more, agape love evinces uncommon humility—love in hiding! It is not paraded like a camouflage, or a flaunting charade. In fact, it is not a travesty of affection, or compassion and hence there is no room for grandstanding. It works and legitimately retires. Besides, there is courtesy in agape love that merits its place in civilised society. It can therefore be characterised, love in society! Suggesting that it meets every expectation of a civil society's code of conduct. The Bible says it does not behave unseemly; it's always polite; it's in place with all classes; never rude or discourteous towards others. Therefore, beloved, Jesus was able to associate easily with people drawn from all walks of life. Most of His disciples were illiterate Galilean fishermen who were the scum of the earth in Jewish society: rejected and shunned by many. At the same time, Jesus had disciples from the upper rung of society, such as Joseph of Arimathaea (Matthew 57-61). Also, while earthly love is egoistic, divine love, on the contrary, shows unmistakable selflessness—love in essence: a case in point is the relationship between the modern church and Jesus Christ. The Bible states that He so loved the church, He gave His life for it! Therefore, it is never self-centred, nor bitter . On the contrary, it seeks only the best for all parties, and is not revengeful. For example, it does not strive to retaliate. Peter declares Jesus as an emblem of One who suffered wrongfully, yet without any bitterness:

> *"For even hereunto were ye called: because Christ also suffered for us, leaving us an example, that ye should follow his steps: Who did no sin, neither was guile found in his mouth: Who, when he was reviled, reviled not again; when he suffered, he threatened not; but committed himself to him that judgeth righteously: Who his own self bare our sins in his body on the tree, that we, being dead to sins, should live unto righteousness: by whose stripes ye were healed. For ye were as sheep going astray; but are now returned unto the Shepherd and Bishop of your souls"* (I Peter 2:21-25).

It is meek and genuinely forgiving. In addition, agape love countenances temperateness in its disposition: it is a delight to have as company; it never portrays any form of resentment or irritation that might seek to mare a social encounter. And then there is righteousness, which is nothing other than the manifestation of excellent conduct. Hence, sinfulness is anathema! Cynical behaviour towards others' plight is not countenanced in agape love. However the joy of others is its solace; ever slow to expose to ridicule; ever eager to believe the best of others; ever hopeful, ever faithful, ever sure, and compellingly enduring. Finally, agape love professes utter sincerity. On this score, it is never arrogant nor display narrow-minded vanity. Nor is it a hypocrite. Even so, it is always honest; never pretentious or impressionistic but embraces the truth with a passion (See the parable of the Good Samaritan, where Christ juxtaposes the boring form and ritualistic arrogance of priesthood, and the ruthlessness of the intractable law of Moses which was the hallmark of the Pharisees, to contend with the spiritual depth and human compassion of the Gospel, exemplified in the deeds of the lowly Samaritan). In this wise, therefore, agape love is never blowing its own trumpet, and does not blaze out in rage, nor brood over the faults of others, but rather always elects to remain just, joyful, and truthful; understands the essence of silence; it's full of trust and ever present in times of need. Jesus has always made it clear to us that He is with us till the end of time.

Friend, like we earlier agreed, God's sacrifice of His only begotten Son on our behalf is a measure of His love towards us [*"For unto us a child is born, unto us a Son is given…"* (Isaiah 9:6-7)]. Jesus' vicarious death and the shedding of His unblemished blood upon the cross of Calvary for our sake, is a measure of His love towards us [*"Greater love hath no man than this, that a man lay down his life for his friends."* (John 15:13)]. The Holy Ghost's decision to dwell in us eternally in order to purge our consciences of dead works to serve the living God and also lead us to all truths is a measure of His love for us [*"Howbeit when he, the Spirit of truth, is come, he will guide you into all truth…"* (John 16:12-15)]. Herein lies the core message that is embedded in the Gospel:

> *"For God so loved the world, that he gave his only begotten Son, that whosoever believeth in him should not perish, but have everlasting life"* (John 3:16).

This is what many unbelievers and other law keepers tend to ignore at their own peril. God takes no prisoners when it comes to observing this divine ordinance: the just shall live by faith in Christ Jesus. The Gospel will be preached throughout every nook and cranny of this planet about the sufferings, death, and resurrection of Jesus Christ. His resurrection and subsequent glorification represent the eternal hope of the Christian faith, without which all our beliefs would be in vain. Now, those who believe it shall be saved and those who don't will be damned (Mark 16:16).

Brethren, by overcoming the world through faith in God (Revelation 3:21), Christ has set us a precedent that is affordable only through faith in Him. Salvation is a matter of choice. God's wish, beloved, as far as we are concerned, is that all of us should get to be called to salvation. He had preordained, determined, and predestined our glorification as followers of Christ; to be justified by faith in the sufferings, death and resurrection of His Son, as firstborn among many brethren (Romans 8:28-33). Only those who meet the terms of the gospel, according the purpose of His grace shall obtain glorification in the end:

> *"For Christ also hath once suffered for sins, the just for the unjust, that he might bring us to God, being put to death in the flesh, but quickened by the Spirit"* (I Peter 3:18).

Jesus has achieved for us what all the heroes of faith in the Old and New Testaments were totally unable to achieve. He is valued higher than the prophets (Hebrews 1:1-2); he is preferred to the angels in the sight of God (Hebrews 1:4); Christ is far better than Aaron. The latter's calling was ordained on a lower law. Jesus' anointing was eternal and glorious, of the highest order (Hebrews 7:19); Jesus' blood was sublime and by far superior to the sacrifices of the Old Testament priesthood (Hebrews 10:18); Christ is more precious to us than parents or any other dignified mentor (Hebrews 12:11); Christ is better than Moses, the law-giver of Israel (Hebrews 3:3); Our Saviour ranks far high than Joshua, Israel's guide to the Promised Land (Hebrews 4:14); Christ is superior to Abraham, being a member of the Godhead that made the promise to the patriarch (Hebrews 7:7). The Bible is replete with God pleading to have supreme vessels like Elijah, Moses, Aaron, Saul, David, Solomon and many other who had to struggle to keep the faith when it really mattered. Even so, few were able to see through the mission of their calling without stumbling at some crucial moment to let Him down, and it all looked awful.

Chapter 3: Jesus Has Already Obtained Eternal Redemption For You 125

This is the hopeless scenario that our Saviour Jesus Christ changed:

> *"Sacrifices and offering thou didst not desire; mine ears hast thou opened: burnt offering and sin offering hast thou not required. Then said I, Lo, I come, in the volume of the book it is written of me, I delight to do your will, O my God: yea, thy law is within my heart. I have preached righteousness in the great congregation: lo, I have not refrained my lips, O Lord, thou knowest. I have not hid thy righteousness within my heart; I have declared thy faithfulness and thy salvation: I have not concealed thy lovingkindness and thy truth from the great congregation"* (Psalm 40:6-10).

Back to the message of atonement. First off, I would like us all to be aware of the fact that the Apostle Paul was no stranger to the blessed purpose of God's grace and mercy. His holy calling was intended to epitomise the magnitude of this unconditional, unassuming, and ultimately unlimited love from the Godhead of which mankind has been beneficiary through faith in Christ Jesus. In a self-confessing epistle to Timothy, his understudy, Paul tells of the unmistakable transgression evidenced in his shameful past sinful career, literally against the church and Christians, in his native Israel:

> *"Who was before a blasphemer, and a persecutor, and injurious: but I obtained mercy, because I did it ignorantly in unbelief. And the grace of our Lord was exceeding abundant with faith and love which is in Christ Jesus. This is a faithful saying, and worthy of all acceptance, that Christ Jesus came into the world to save sinners; of which I am chief"* (I Timothy 1:13-15).

Brethren, for the man who authored more than half of the books in the New Testament, we can see clearly where his vision lay. Paul was, more than anyone else of his generation, extremely conscious and strongly aware and grateful of the abundant mercies of God on him, particularly after the mysterious encounter with Jesus Christ on the way to Damascus. Friend, the likes of Paul, like you and I can now afford to join the holy chorus and boldly declare: *"We overcame the devil by the blood of the Lamb and by the word of our testimony"* (Revelation 12:11); for it is not by might or by power, but by the Spirit of God (Zechariah 4:5-6). Brethren, saving faith comes from God.

You cannot save yourself. Humble yourself by acknowledging what Christ has already achieved with His own blood for you. No one can consciously drum up salvation through their own recognizance or good works, outside the Holy Spirit's guidance:

> *"For he hath made him to be sin for us, who knew no sin; that we might be made the righteousness of God in him"* (II Corinthians 5:21).

Brethren, long before Jesus was born, the Messiah Himself prophesied His future journey on earth which was to serve as standard for us Christians to follow. The exemplary verses were proclaimed through king David, His servant:

> *"The Lord rewarded me according to my righteousness; according to the cleanness of my hands hath he recompensed me. For I have kept the ways of the Lord, and have not wickedly departed from my God. For all his judgments were before me, and I did not put away his statutes from me. I was also upright before him, and kept myself from mine iniquity. Therefore hath the Lord recompensed me according to my righteousness, according to the cleanness of my hands in his eyesight. With the merciful thou wilt shew thyself merciful; with an upright man thou wilt shew thyself upright; With the pure thou wilt shew thyself pure; and with the froward thou wilt shew thyself froward. For thou wilt save the afflicted people; but wilt bring down high looks. For thou wilt light my candle: the Lord my God will enlighten my darkness"* (Psalm 18:20-28).

Thus, the testimony of Jesus is the Spirit of prophecy: Jesus kept the ways of the Father; He remained true to Him; He kept His Father's judgments before Him; He did not put away His laws; He walked uprightly before His Father; and kept Himself from iniquity, as a man. Beloved, as a human being, Jesus never stepped an inch away from His Father's Word (Psalm 119:99-100). But to live like this you must expect world hatred or persecution because Jesus predicted it (John 15:18-21); the world hates reproof as the evils of the world are exposed by your Christ-like life (John 3:19; Romans 12:2; Titus 2:11-12); the world is blind to the true light (II Corinthians 4:4); Christians are in the world, but not of the world (John 15:19; 17:14-16); the world is at war with Christians (John 16:33; Ephesians 6:12; I John 5:4); the king of the world is the devil who is God's sworn enemy (James 4:4; Matthew 18:7); having God's seed in you, you cannot help hating the ways of the world (I John 2:15-17); as a Christian you isolate yourself from the ways of the world (James 1:27; Romans 12:2; II Peter 2:20); the world is ignorant of the miraculous Christian experiences enshrined in Christian living (Galatians 2:20; II Corinthians 5:17); and most of all, the world is ignorant of God and the beauty and splendour of His majesty (John 15:21):

> "If the world hat you, ye know that it hated me before it hated you. If ye were of the world, the world would love his own: but because ye are not of the world, but I have chosen you out of the world, therefore the world hateth you. Remember the word that I said unto you, The servant is not greater than his lord. if they have persecuted me, they will also persecute you; if they have kept my saying, they will keep yours also. but all these things will they do unto you for my name's sake, because they know not him that sent me" (John 15:18-21).

Jesus reassures His disciples even further of the rewards of full consecration:

> "Then Peter began to say unto him, Lo, we have left all, and have followed thee. And Jesus answered and said, Verily I say unto you, There is no man that hath left house, or brethren, or sisters, or father, or mother, or wife, or children, or lands, for my sake, and the gospel's. But he shall receive an hundredfold now in this time, houses, and brethren, and sisters, and mothers, and children, and lands, with persecutions; and in the world to come eternal life. But many that are first shall be last; and the last first" (Mark 10:28-31).

Jesus consoles His sheep—LOVE, the true substance of Godliness is leveraged in (Matthew 6:25-34) passage of the Gospel.

According to those verses, beloved, the thesis of our Lord is anchored on dissuading us from the habit of fretting about the future. Suffices to submit right here that Jesus is not against you planning for your future, but rather the obsessive contemplation of future uncertainties is hopeless and ungodly. Brethren, knowing that our Lord has already secured our redemption, yet many keep being anxious over ephemeral, earthly possessions. He outlined eight reasons why we mustn't worry: First and foremost, our life—salvation is more that meat, which is only temporal. Secondly, our precious body is by far more valuable than raiment—clothes. Brethren, God made the body which cannot be duplicated. But clothes is made everywhere! Thirdly, human beings are not to be compared with materials, which are mostly not only man-made but also only temporal and earthly. Furthermore, we are greater than birds whom God feeds without any precondition, like labour. Jesus also drives home the point that it is pointless to worry, for it cannot change the body. No can any amount of our worry do anything to effect a change in our shape, form or colour. He stresses the truth that humans are superior to the gorgeous looking green plants that never bother themselves about, nor struggle with their clothing. The Messiah emphasises the truth that God's providence transcends all creation: supplying subsistence to the animal kingdom, including vilest of creatures in their ecosystem. Brethren, these creatures never trade, manufacture or engage in any systematic form of labour in exchange, but the Most High caters to their every need. The sum total of of Jesus' sermon is simple: worrying is malignant, worthless and sinful, and must be avoided at all cost.

We can now crown it all with this excerpt drawn from the book of Hebrews, talking about the Messiah's priesthood status, and especially the portraiture which sets out to present Christ as God's charismatic Broker of a new deal for all mankind:

> *"But Christ being come an high priesthood of good things to come, by a greater and more perfect tabernacle, not made with hands, that is to say, not of this building; Neither by the blood of goats and calves, but by his own blood he entered in once into the holy place, having obtained eternal redemption for us"* (Hebrews 9:11-12).

Hence, drawing inspiration from the exemplary life of Jesus Christ, Custodian of God's business on earth many lessons are easily discernible from His life experience. The book of Saint Peter (I Peter 2:21-25) lays it all bare for all to peruse. First of all the Messiah's selflessness in suffering for our sake (being the sacrificial Lamb of God) is quite commendable and unparalleled throughout Scripture. Also, we notice the sinless life style which nobody can contest. Jesus was born of the Spirit (Luke 1:26-38). This is also linked to His guilessness for the things He stood for as a man in the face of adversity (Isaiah 53). Moreover, we notice the love and gracefulness in His quiet dignity, especially when being mocked (John 1:16-18). Furthermore, Jesus had patience and endurance (long suffering), both of which constitute vital substances of the Spirit, in plenteous store. In fact, He is better than Old Testament faith heroes, for He is the Author and Finisher of our faith (Hebrews 12:1-4). Finally, His total and unconditional resignation and commitment to the cause of the Father is undeniable (John 5:19-20). He attended to His Father's business with uncommon enthusiasm and a resolve that is harder than steel (Luke 2:38-50). Therefore, we conclude that He was the incarnation of God's righteousness on earth, as stated in to the Bible.

Beloved in Christ, knowing what a High Priest we have in heaven, let us come together as one, and of one mind, as we entreat to rave onto this joy unspeakable with Apostle Paul:

> *"I beseech Euodias, and beseech Syntyche, that they be of the same mind in the joice in the Lord. And I intreat thee also, true yokefellows, help those women which laboured with me in the gospel, with Clement also, and with other my fellowlabourers, whose names are in the book of life. Rejoice in the Lord always: and again I say, Rejoice"* (Philippians 4:2-4).

Chapter 4

THERE IS NO HOPE FOR ETERNAL LIFE WITHOUT JESUS CHRIST

"Ye are from beneath; I am from above: ye are of this world; I am not of this world. I said therefore unto you, that ye shall die in your sins: for if ye believe not that I am he, ye shall die in your sins" (John 8:23-24).

Beloved in Christ, the Bible says, *"For the wages of sin is death; but the gift of God is eternal life through Jesus Christ our Lord."* Therefore, there is no neutrality in the deliverance equation: it's either you yield your body to reverence Christ in righteousness onto holiness, which is the wish of God for us all, or you err by yielding your body to condemnation which is about serving Satan in sin, whose fruit is death and damnation. If you allow sin to hold sway in your mortal body, you partake in the nocturnally raucous party of the condemned, chaired by Satan with his demons and devils in attendance. This, alas, is the dour fate of all unbelieving law-keepers. For the latter group pretend to be able to meet the expectations of God's righteousness which has been fulfilled in Jesus by their native strength, whereas all the law does is expose their shortcomings while delivering them to the slaughter slab. Brethren, our flesh; all flesh is weak, and so is fleshly law. The law is archaic and inconclusive; decrepit and abolished! Nevertheless, should you make up your mind to pursue the law of faith in Christ, then you become dead to the law of sinfulness and are resurrected by His grace to walk into the newness of life in Christ Jesus:

"But now being made free from sin, and become servants of God, ye have your fruit unto holiness, and the end everlasting life" (Romans 6:22).

Friend, God is a Master Planner. He had planned for us even before the world began. The Bible tells of two Adams. The first a living soul, and the second a quickening Spirit. Whether failure or success, the course of the Adamic stock to succeed the condemned world of Lucifer had been provided for well before hand. Consequently, the first Adam died when he sinned, according to the Word of God (See the dispensation of innocence: mankind's first test in which he failed and became a pseudo-ruler with all its perilous consequences: Genesis 2:15-17). The penalty, eternal death, took effect immediately upon the act of disobedience (Romans 5:12-21). However, *"He that is dead is free from sin."* Adam and his offsping (all of us yet unborn), got a lifeline rolled out to them by a good God whose mercy is everlasting; and his truth *edureth* through all generations. (Psalm 100:5).

Brethren, here is the mystery of God: There Bible holds that none shall be condemned without hearing the Gospel (Romans 10:9-17; Matthew 26:13; Matthew 24:14). Even Abraham to whom the promise was made had this very Gospel of Jesus Christ preached to him (Genesis 22:13-18); and the Lord's supper observed (Genesis 14:18-20). Thus, upon belief and confession is the hearer delivered into eternal salvation. But failure to do so automatically qualifies the unbeliever to eternal condemnation in hell.

Now, the Bible declares:
"And we know that all things work together for good to them that love God, to them who are the called according to his purpose. For whom he did foreknow, he also did predestinate to be conformed to the image of his Son, that he might be the firstborn among many brethren. Moreover whom he did predestinate, them he also called: and whom he called, them he also justified: and whom he justifid, them he also glorified. What shall we then say to these things? If God be for us, who can be against us?" (Romans 8:28-31).

Hence was the deal done for Adam. God cannot alter His covenant (Psalm 89:34); nor could anyone, either accidentally or by design, annul His overall purpose

(Isaiah 14:27). His prophets are all covered by this declaration revealed through David in the psalms. Here, the Word of God goes like this, *"Saying, Touch not mine anointed and do my prophets no harm"* (Psalm 105:15). As a prophet of God, Adam and his offspring (including Christ, the Seed—Genesis 3:15—benefited from His grace when he clothed us with coats of skin, symbolic of the unblemished Lamb of God (Genesis 3:21). In fact, the Holy Spirit even revealed God's emotions in the lines:

"And the Lord God said, Behold, the man is become as one of us, to know good and evil…" (Genesis 3:22).

Beloved, since Adam belonged to the dispensation of innocence, we can safely ascribe the above assertion of knowledge, awareness and total consciousness of the wisdom of God on earth to the dispensation of grace, which is that of Jesus Christ, the Omnipotent, Omniscient and Omnipresent. Beloved, the Bible says, *"Moreover the law entered, that the offence might abound. But where sin abounded, grace did much more abound. That as sin hath reigned unto death, even so might grace reign through righteousness unto eternal life by Jesus Christ our Lord"* (Romans 5:20-21). That is to say, our righteousness is predicated on the legacy of the life-giving Adam who was offered a propitiation for our sins. Brethren, the law could not bestow substantive knowledge to the children of Israel because it was only a shadow of the real thing: rather opaque and hopeless (Hebrews 4:2; 7:18-19; 10:1); whereas the Gospel has come with the shining Light that has enlightened us and made us grow and glow into bona fide ministers of God, not of the letter but of the Spirit. In fact, by His grace the veil has been torn apart in Jesus to vouchsafe our liberty, thanks to our faith (Galatians 5:1; II Corinthians 3:12-17; Hebrews 8:6). Having died to sin and resurrected by the blood of the Lamb into the newness of life in Christ Jesus, Adam's spirit, having been cleansed and sanctified in the blood of the Lamb, spoke through the Holy Ghost in the following lines:

"I will greatly rejoice in the Lord, my soul shall be joyful in my God; for he hath clothed me with the garments of salvation, he hath covered me with the robe of righteousness, as a bridegroom decketh himself with ornaments, and a as a bride adorneth herself with her jewels. For as the earth bringeth forth

her bud, and as the garden causeth the things that are sown in it to spring forth; so the Lord God will cause righteousness and praise to spring forth before all the nations" (Isaiah 61:10-11).

This is in reference to the New Covenant and all its blessings. In fact, the prophecy was again made broadcast in the book of the prophet Joel (Joel 2:28-29). Above all, beloved, the New Covenant was again explicitly proclaimed through the prophet Jeremiah:

"Behold, the days come, saith the Lord, that I will make a new covenant with the house of Israel, and with the house of Judah: Not according to the covenant that I made with their fathers in the day that I took them by the hand to bring them out of the land of Egypt; which my covenant they brake, I although I was an husband unto them, saith the Lord. But this shall be the covenant that I will make with the house of Israel; After those days, saith the Lord, I will put my law in their inward parts, and write it in their hearts; and will be their God, and they shall be my people. And they shall teach no more every man his neigbough, and every man his brother, saying, Know the Lord: for they shall all know me, from the least of them unto the greatest of them, saith the Lord: for I will forgive their iniquity, and I will remember their sin no more" (Jeremiah 31:31-34).

Brethren we say, Hosanna in the highest for the same was partly fulfilled at Pentecost, more precisely in the New Testament book—Acts of the Apostles:

"And when the day of Pentecost was fully come, they were all with one accord in one place. And sudenly there came a sound from heaven as of a rushing mighty wind, and it filled all the house where they were sitting. And there appeared unto them cloven tongues like as of fire, and it sat upon each of them. And they were all filled with the Holy Ghost, and began to speak with other tongues, as the Spirit gave them utterance. And there were dwelling at Jerusalem Jews, devout men, out of every nation under heaven. Now when this was noised abroad, the multitude came together, and were confounded, because that every man heard them speak in his own language. And they were all amazed and marvelled, saying one to another, Behold, are not all

Chapter 4: There Is No Hope For Eternal Life Without Jesus Christ   135

> *these which speak Galilaeans? And how hear we every man in our own tongue, wherein we were born? Parthians, and Medes, and Elamites, and the dwellers in Mesopotamia, and in Judaea, and Cappadoicia, in Pontus, and Asia, Phrygia, and Pamphylia, in Egypt, and in the parts of Libya about Cyrene, and strangers of Rome, Jews and proselytes, Cretes and Arabians, we do hear them speak in our tongues the wonderful works of God. And they were amazed, and were in doubt, saying one to another, What meaneth this? Others mocking said, These men are full of new wine. But Peter, standing up with the eleven, lifted up his voice, and said unto them, Ye men of Judaea, and all ye that dwell at Jerusalem, be this known unto you, and hearken to my words: For these are not drunken, as ye suppose, seeing it is but the third hour of the day.* BUT THIS IS THAT WHICH WAS SPOKEN BY THE PROPHET JOEL; AND IT SHALL COME TO PASS IN THE LAST DAYS, SAITH GOD, I WILL POUR OUT MY SPIRIT UPON ALL FLESH: AND YOUR SONS AND YOUR DAUGHTERS SHALL PROPHESY, AND YOUR YOUNG MEN SHALL SEE VISIONS, AND YOUR OLD MEN SHALL DREAM DREAMS: AND ON MY SERVANTS AND ON MY HANDMAIDENS I WILL POUR OUT IN THOSE DAYS OF MY SPIRIT; AND THEY SHALL PROPHESY" (Acts 2:1-18).

The Messiah also made proclamations regarding His earthly calling at various points in the holy Scriptures. First through king David. Here we are entreated to avail ourselves of the infinite benefits enshrined in the lesson of obedience and total submission to the will of God by the Messiah, which made the New Covenant much more superior to the previous one. Also, we are made aware of the truth: it was not God's will for animals to be offered as sacrifice for attaining our redemption, as was the case in the Old Testament (Hebrews 10:5-9). But rather, the Father required a human victim of infinite merit, such as His only begotten Son. We are also apprised of His glorious ministry: Beloved, as Jesus had internalised and assimilated the laws of His Father in His flesh, bones and blood, our Lord would go on preaching, teaching and healing all those who were held captive by the devil—Christ is therefore God's salvation to all mankind:

> "Sacrifices and offerings thou didst not desire; mine ears hast thou opened: burnt offering and sin offering hast thou not required. Then said I, Lo, I come: in the volume of the book it is written of me, I delight to do thy will, O my God: yea, thy law is within my heart. I have preached righteousness in the great congregation: lo, I have not refrained my lips, O Lord, thou knowest. I have not hid thy righteousness within my heart; I have decalred thy faithfulness and thy salvation: I have not concealed thy lovingkindness and thy truth from the great congregation" (Psalm 40:5-10).

And then through the Prophet Isaiah:

> "The Spirit of the Lord God is upon me; because the Lord hath anointed me to preach good tidings unto the meek; he hath sent me to bind up the brokenhearted, to proclaim liberty to the captives, and the opening of the prison to them that are bound; To proclaim the acceptable year of the Lord" (Isaiah 61:1-2).

The fulfilment of this prophecy was contained in Saint Peter's sermon delivered at the home of Cornelius, the centurion who happens to be the first Christian convert among the Gentiles:

> "Then Peter opened his mouth, and said, Of a truth I perceive that God is no respecter of persons: But in every nation he that feareth him, and worketh righteousness, is accepted with him. The Word which God sent unto the children of Israel, preaching peace by Jesus Christ: (he is Lord of all:) That word, I say, ye know, which was published throughout all Judaea, and began from Galilee, after the baptism which John preached; HOW GOD ANOINTED JESUS CHRIST OF NAZARETH WITH THE HOLY GHOST AND WITH POWER: WHO WENT ABOUT DOING GOOD, AND HEALING ALL THAT WERE OPPRESSED OF THE DEVIL; FOR GOD WAS WITH HIM" (Acts 10:34-38).

Brethren, going back to Adam, we were blessed when he accepted Christ by answering in the affirmative to the Most High's blessed request that he and his wife, Eve be clothed in coats of skin (with the blood of the Lamb in order to obtain a remission of their sins—Revelation 7:14); as opposed to the inferior, inadequate alternative which constituted the absurd option of harvesting leaves from a natural, season, perishable environment which forever in a state of constant decay and disintegration! Just imagine, beloved, such an act would have been an aberration of the first order which would have amounted to putting the cart before the horse: (deploying physical solutions to address a spiritual problem)! As you would clearly appreciate, Adam merely submitted a temporary proposition to an eternal question; pretty much like Nicodemus, comparing material things with spiritual. But the Lord God moved to provide His elect, even the righteous, with a perfect solution which transcended the ordinary lengths and breadths; heights and depths of the universal and proceeded towards the timeless; even providential while embracing the eternal in heavenly realms:

> *"That God of our Lord Jesus Christ, the Father of glory, may give unto you the spirit of wisdom and revelation in the knowledge of him: The eyes of your understanding being enlightened; that ye may know what is the hope of his calling, and what the riches of the glory of his inheritance in the saints, And what is the exceeding greatness of his power to us-ward who believe, according to the working of his mighty power, Which he wrought in Christ, when he raised him from the dead, and set him at his own right hand in the heavenly places. Far above all principality, and power, and might, and dominion, and every name that is named, not only in this world, but also in that which is to come: And hath put all things under his feet, and gave him to be the head over all things to the church, Which is his body, thew fulness of him that filleth all in all"* (Ephesians 1:17-23).

> *"But God who is rich in mercy, for his great love wherewith he loved us, Even when we were dead in sins, hath quickened us together with Christ, (By grace ye are saved;) And hath raised us up together, and made us sit together in heavenly places in Christ Jesus: That in the ages to come he might shew the exceeding riches of his grace in his kindness toward us through Christ Jesus"* (Galatians 2:5-7).

Finally, suffices to submit right here that king David paid tribute to this enduring mercies of God which is often manifested among God's prophets over the ages in scripture: from Adam through Abraham and David to Paul, the Apostle of Jesus Christ, as well as to those of us who happen to be of the Uncircumcision (Gentiles), who today are being called according to His holy purpose:

> *"Blessed is he whose transgression is forgiven, whose sin is covered. Blessed is the man unto whom the Lord imputeth not iniquity, and in whose spirit there is no guile"* (Psalm 32:1-2).

Brethren, to cover here means to conceal from being seen; it is about being pardoned (Romans 4:7): This pardoning is effected by God when one confesses his sins and exercises faith in the atoning blood of Jesus Christ.

In the book of Isaiah, we are taught that for those who have repented of their sinful career in sinfulness and have yielded their lives to Christ as Lord and Saviour, there is no sin so tough or thick that the blood of Jesus cannot blot out, delete or eliminate:

> *"Come now, and let us reason together, saith the Lord: though your sins be as scarlet, they shall be as white as snow; though they be red like crimson, they shall be as wool"* (Isaiah 1:18).

Indeed, all those who have put on Christ have therefore inherited His Spirit of the fear of the Lord against sinfulness:

> *"Whoever is born of God doth not commit sin; for His seed remaineth in him: and he cannot sin, because he is born of God"* (I John 3:9).

And here the benefits:

> *"But if we walk in the light, as he is in the light, we have fellowship one with another, and the blood of Jesus Christ his Son cleanses us from all sin…If we confess our sins, he is faithful and just to forgive us our sins, and to cleanse us from all unrighteousness"* (I John 1:7,9).

Beloved, Saint Paul gave a very elaborate explanation to all of the above, in his seminal missive to the Romans. Beloved, here are the fundamental precepts of the law of faith, which is about living your life according to the promptings of the Holy Ghost, so read carefully:

> "Therefore, there is now no condemnation which are in Christ Jesus, who walk not after the flesh, but after the Spirit. For the law of the Spirit of life in Christ Jesus hath made me free from the law of sin and death. For what the law could not do, in that is was weak through the flesh, God sending his own Son in the likeness of sinful flesh, and for sin, condemned sin in the flesh: That the righteousness of the law might be fulfilled in us, who walk not after the flesh, but after the Spirit. For what the law could not do, in that it was weak through the flesh, God sending his own Son in the likeness of sinful flesh, and for sin, condemned sin in the flesh: That the righteousness of the law might be fulfilled in us, who walk not after the the flesh, but after ther Spirit. For they that are after the flesh do mind the things of the flesh; but they that are after the Spirit the things of the Spirit. For to be carnally minded is death; but to be spiritually minded is life and peace. Because the carnal mind is enmity against God: for it is not subject to the law of God, neither indeed can be. So then they that are in the flesh cannot please God. But ye are not in the flesh, but in the Spirit, if so be that the Spirit of God dwell in you. Now if any man have not the Spirit of Christ, he is none of his. And if Christ be in you, the body is dead because of sin; but the Spirit is life because of righteousness. But if the Spirit of him that raised Jesus from the dead dwell in you, he that raised up Christ from the dead shall also quicken your mortal bodies by his Spirit that dwelleth in you" (Romans 8:1-11).

Good Tidings for Motivation: The Rapture

> "The Son of man shall send forth his angels, and they shall gather out of his kingdom all things that offend, and them which do iniquity; And shall cast them into a furnace of fire: there shall be wailing and gnashing of teeth" (Matthew 13:41-42).

Friend, the Gospel of Jesus Christ is about mysteries that are only revealed onto and into the spirits of the initiated by the Holy Ghost (John 16:12-15; Romans 8:14-16). There are no miracles for unbelievers. The reason for this is that if they will not believe the Word made available for understanding, chances are they wouldn't believe the evidence addressed to the senses, and might proceed to accord God's work to Satan which is a mortal sin—blasphemy. Jesus spoke in parables to solemnize this divine ordinance. The Son of man would warn against careless dispensing of sacred things:

> *"Give not that which is holy unto the dogs, neither cast ye your pearls before swine, lest they trample them under their feet, and turn again and rend you"* (Matthew 7:6).

Brethren, the image of *dogs* and *swine* here are employed to designate the fickle-minded, deceived children of God who have been lured into apostasy or unbelief through devilish platitudes and the poisonous effluvia to pollute the spiritual atmosphere by myriads of false prophets out there. The ones whom the king of this world—the devil—has prevented from catching sight of the true Light that *lighteth* all things.

The prophecy is partly aimed at confirming Deuteronomy 29:29 *"The secret things belong unto the Lord our God: but those things which are revealed belong unto us and our children for ever,..."* That is why Jehovah declared in the book of Isaiah:

> *"I will go before thee, and make the crooked places straight: I will break in pieces the gates of brass, and cut in sunder the bars of iron: And I will give thee the treasures of darkness, and hidden riches of secret places, that thou mayest know that I, the Lord, which call thee by thy name, am the God of Israel"* (Isaiah 45:2-3).

> *"Call unto me, and I will answer thee, and shew thee great and mighty things, which though knowest not" (Jeremiah 33:3).*

Chapter 4: There Is No Hope For Eternal Life Without Jesus Christ

So, brethren, deliverance is coming very soon. I say this to reassure, in particular, those defenders of the Gospel out there who are being persecuted by the world right now. But mind you, it is only going to happen in the spiritual realm, and in God's terms, not ours. This is because it is divine and not earthly. Both the second advent of Christ, and the rapture, as stated above will be spiritual events: to be revealed exclusively onto God's covenanted partners. To this effect, Jesus told many illuminating parables to project the power and wisdom of the Gospel. Beloved, resistance to the divine plea, (that is to say, failure to call on the name of Jesus: Joel 2:28; Romans 10:13) might have devastating consequences beyond the widest stretch of our imagination. Accordingly, the lines quoted from the book of Matthew 13:41-42, are quite telling: *"…all things that offend, and them which do iniquity; And shall cast them into a furnace of fire: there shall be wailing and gnashing of teeth."*

Now compare those to the following lines drawn from the book of Saint John:

> *"I am the true vine, and my Father is the husbandman. Every branch in me that beareth not fruit he taketh away: and every branch that beareth fruit, he purgeth it, that it may bring forth more fruit…Abide in me, and I in you. As the branch cannot bear fruit of itself, except ye abide in me. I am the vine, ye are the branches: He that abideth in me, and I in him, the same bringeth forth much fruit: for without me ye can do nothing. IF A MAN ABIDETH NOT IN ME, HE IS CAST FORTH AS A BRANCH, AND IS WITHERED; AND MEN GATHER THEM, AND CAST THEM INTO THE FIRE; AND THEY ARE BURNED"* (John 15:1-6).

Friend, whether you have been grafted to the universal, eternal body of Christ for righteous onto salvation; or whether you would rather have yourself embroiled in the devilish miasma and mist for sin onto damnation, the choice is yours to make. There is an expiry date for blaming others—our parents, the church and all the others—for our wrong choices. Once you have taken full control of your life to the extent of paying your rents and taxes, there will be no excuse for any delays or wrong choices. Many out there often proffer a false sense of neutrality: needless to say, their efforts are futile in the sense that in this battle, there is no room for fence-sitting. We are made in the image of

Jesus to produce great works for our God (Ephesians 2:10). This means, we are not on our own. He is the fulcrum of our ecology; much as trees are to birds or better still, just as water is the true element for the marine kingdom. As fishes and all other sea creatures flourish in their maritime environment, so do we in ours: Christ in us, the hope of glory! The Bible say in Him we are complete and have our being. Therefore Jesus is our true element, and that is why He is called the Son of man. Hence, Jesus declares Himself as the true Vine. Thus, branches that are nourished directly from the Source of life tend to produce good fruit; true tasty fruit; even righteous fruit:

> *"But the fruit of the Spirit is love, joy, peace, longsuffering, gentleness, goodness, faith, Meekness, temperance: against such there is no law"* (Galatians 5:22-23).

Their real value is determined by the quality of fruit they produce. As for those who opt to stay undecided or neutral, their portion is decidedly within the hostile camp of the enemy, the devil. Although we are made in Christ Jesus for a great and grandiose purpose of God, yet are we vulnerable to the multiple slurs, or sleight of hand and snares of Lucifer and his demons: unless we accept Christ as our Saviour; unless we let Him abide in us; unless we seek His kingdom and its righteousness we are most likely to provoke our own calamity and even risk taking the wrong path: falling pray to the multifarious woes or curses in life:

> *"Now the works of the flesh are manifest, which are these: Adultery, fornication, uncleanness, lasciviousness, Idolatory, witchcraft, hatred, variance, emulations, wrath, strife, seditions, heresies, Envyings, murders, drunkenness, revellings, and such like: of the which I tell you before, as I have also told you in time past, that they which do such things shall not inherit the kingdom of God"* (Galatians 5:19-21).

The recipe for damnation is also enlisted in the book of Revelation for those who spuriously imagine they are capable of saving themselves:

> *"But the fearful, and unbelieving, and the abominable, and murderers, and whoremongers, and sorcerers, and idolaters, and all liars, shall have their part in the lake which burneth with fire and brimstone: which is the second death"* (Revelation 21:8).

With regards to end time declarations, Jesus also made it abundantly clear to us all that there shall be resurrection of both the wicked and the righteous. By the way, death; physical death only concerns the bodies because it is only the latter that were made of dust. The souls and the spirits are never consigned to lie in dirt! Those of the righteous are taken to heaven, while those of unbelievers are commandeered to hell. Beloved, the contempt and punishment of the wicked shall be equal to the bliss of the righteous in Christ in terms of length and consciousness (Read the parable of Lazarus and the rich man: Luke 16:19-31). Consequently, at the rapture, the souls and the bodies will be retrieved from their various destinations at death, and made to reunite with their various bodies which had been buried. Like Jehovah did to the dry bones (Vision of the valley of the dry bones: Ezekiel 37), God will then resurrect them by granting them the unction to hear and respond to the call of the Son of man (John 11:43-44). The elect shall come forth to live for ever in heaven; whereas the damned will have to do the same, but, alas, in hell fire! (John 5:28-29; Daniel 12:2).

Finally, here is the full Biblical rendition of that special day of the Lord in Scripture, which also happens to mark the beginning of the second coming of the Messiah. It is the ultimate consolation to all true believers, and a nightmare to those souls that are lost in Christ:

> *"And to you who are troubled rest with us, when the Lord Jesus shall be revealed from heaven with his mighty angels, In flaming fire taking vengeance on them that know not God, and that obey not the gospel of our Lord Jesus Christ: Who shall be punished with everlasting destruction from the presence of the Lord, and from the glory of his power; When he shall come to be glorified in his saints, and to be admired in all them that believe (because our testimony among you was believed) in that day"* (II Thessalonians 1:7-10).

Friend, if you have made up your mind to be in the number when the saints go marching into the realm of eternity, in their divinity and glory with our Lord and Saviour, Jesus Christ of Nazareth, here is what you will have to comply with:

First and foremost, humble yourself and come to Jesus the Christ, Crystal and Charisma of the Almighty God of heaven and earth (John 6:37, 44, 45, 65). Secondly, having humbled yourself to believing the Gospel: eat His flesh—drink His blood. This is having total humility and communion in body, soul and spirit, as you partake in the Lord's Supper (John 6:50, 51, 53, 58). Moreover, do labour for the right cause: remember Apostle Paul's letter to the Romans, beckoning on the cosmopolitan citizens of that great city of ancient times (just like Jonah, the Old Testament prophet) to yield themselves and their bodies to Christ as it constitutes the one and only reasonable service we all have been called upon to carry out here on earth (Romans 12:1-3; John 6:27; II Timothy 2:14-16). Also, do recall that you are called through the holy calling of God in Christ Jesus to bear fruit. Therefore use the Christian power of attorney to reap and bear good fruit (John 4:35-38; 15:4-8; 15-17). Be absent with yourself, in terms of your appreciation of earthly pleasures while setting your passion on things in the heavenly sphere. Remember you are in the world, but not of the world (John 17:16; Colossians 3:3). You have been bought with a price, and your life is not yours anymore. Your deliberate absence is the token acknowledgment of the newness of life in Christ, which also guarantees you utter freedom from all earthly obligations—the chains and fetters of the old regime in sin:

> "For I through the law am dead to the law, that I might live unto God. I am crucified with Christ: nevertheless I live; yet not I, but Christ liveth in me: and the life which I now live in the flesh I live by the faith of the Son of God, who loved me, and gave himself for me. I do not frustrate the grace of God: for if righteousness come by the law, then Christ is dead in vain" (Galatians 2:19-20).

Henceforth, you have become God's goodwill ambassador, so do keep the standards of the Holy Ghost, and do not conform to the cravings of your past sinful universe (John 12:25, Colossians 3:1-3). Like king David, strive to keep a growing mindset when it comes to seeking to know more of Christ and God (John 17:2-3). Likewise, make sure to use the right gate. For example, law-keepers are all those wiseacres who are caught in the spell of their old sinful nature trying in a self-righteous way to drum up faith through their own personal obeisance. Needless to say, without Jesus theirs is only an act of spite; scornful and vainglorious (Matthew 7:13-14). Endeavour to be a peace-keeping trouble shooter: a gatherer rather than a *scatterer*; *a uniter*, and not a divider; a defender without being an offender (Matthew 18:8-9). Furthermore, brethren, see to it that you keep the commandments of God, as well as pay allegiance to the Grand Commission of Christ with due diligence (Matthew 19:17). Avoid laying your hopes on uncertain riches. The Bible says it will be easier for a hippopotamus to make heaven than a rich man. This is due to their blind attachment, even blind allegiance to the things of this world. Hence, the Bible says, forsake all of your sinful past to gain all of your righteous future (Matthew 19:27-29; Mark 10:28-30; Luke 18:28-30). Another challenge is to conduct your life free of the burden of sinfulness (Hebrews 12:14). Brethren, Jesus has not been ordained by His Father to be the minister of sinner—Come to think of it, brethren. Has Jesus been glorified in righteousness only to end up being the Minister of sinners? Has the Son of man become Defender of the offenders? God forbid! To follow Him, therefore, as the songwriter rightly says, one will have to leave the world behind them, while putting the cross and the throne of grace before them (Romans 5:21; 6:16-23; 8:1-13; Titus 2:11-14). One essential attribute of the chosen ones is their deep desire to cultivate the habit and character of well doing in every aspect of life. They are poised to seek goodwill for all and sundry; without discrimination (Romans 2:7). They are also wont to go the extra mile in order to sow to the Spirit. Brethren, we are instructed to acknowledge His presence in all our undertakings, while avoiding anything that could grieve Him. We have already seen how the elect of God tend to live according to the promptings of the Holy Ghost (Galatians 6:7-8; Romans 8:1, 14-16). Also, the holy calling is there for a sublime purpose, and not just a bed of roses. An act of faith takes courage and application. Therefore, take up the gauntlet and hit the road to fight the good fight of faith. Lay hold on to it, and remember you have been called to a battle of which you are already destined to win (I

Timothy 6:12, 19). Meantime, remember to stay focused and sober. It is more prudent to be filled with the Holy Spirit rather than with new wine. Keep your hope alive through to the end, so as to give shape to your faith (Titus 1:2; 3:7; I Peter 1:5, 9, 13; Romans 8:24). Hold your grounds against all types of trials and temptations against your faith in Christ. Resilience is the key here. Upgrade your knowledge of Him every day. And do not relent in your strive to aim high. Do not give up; never give up. Rather learn from it, since it might turn out to be a blessing in disguise, often the richest source of testimony for Christians (James 1:12). Moreover, hold firmly onto the promise of salvation, and let it remain in you richly, even as you grow in the Lord and Christ (I John 2:24-25; 5:11-20; John 15:4-6). Finally, remember the old adage: like-pairs tend to attract each other. Brethren, if the Bible says, *"God is love,"* this clearly suggests that to be like Him one needs to strive as much as possible to be in love with everybody (I John 3:14-15). Apart from loving all human beings, strengthen your love of God Himself, like king David, looking for eternal life just as the deer panteth for water (Jude 20-24). Be determined to overcome evil with good in order to completely obscure any appearance of sinfulness or transgression in your life (Revelation 2:7, 11; 17, 26; 3:5, 12, 21:14-15). Additionally, the Bible says we all are appointed to die (Hebrews 9:27). Therefore, like our Lord Jesus, be courageous and faithful onto death. In fact, for the believer dying in faith itself is great gain (Revelation 2:10; Hebrews 12:14-15). Of course, before we round up, beloved, do not hesitate to do the obvious which is to believe and obey the Gospel of Jesus Christ:

> *"And that from a child thou hast known the holy scriptures, which are able to make thee wise unto salvation through faith which is in Christ Jesus. All scripture is given by inspiration of God, and is profitable for doctrine, for reproof, for correction, for instruction in righteousnes: that the man of God may be perfect, throughly furnished unto all good works"*
> (II Timothy 3:15-17).

To crown it all, be born again, hear Christ, and follow Him (John 3; 10:27-29). Brethren, if you can imbibe the above points, you will undoubtedly be able to get hold of eternal life and keep it forever. Mind you, however, that this precious gift does not become an *unforfeitable* eternal personal property until you literally *"enter into"* it (Matthew 7:13; 18:8-9; 19:17; Romans 6:22); *"receive"* it (Romans 6:23; James 1:12; I Peter 1:13; Revelation 2:10); *"reap"* it (Galatians 6:7-8); and *"inherit"* it in the world to come (Matthew Matthew 19:27-29; Mark 10:28-30; Luke 18:28-30), at the *"end"* of this life (Romans 6:22). Brethren, one last word: as the incarnation of the Word, Jesus is life. Life is eternal, and remains thus, whether or not we enter or possess it , AND IT IS ONLY IN JESUS CHRIST. AMEN.

Book The Third

THE HOLY SPIRIT AND OUR RESTITUTION AND RESTORATION

Introduction

Jesus Christ of Nazareth is the greatest heritage of God to humanity. As a result, He has become the most precious gift ever made to mankind with regards to deliverance from evil and other hardships on earth (Genesis 3:15; John 3:16). The Messiah's life and works is a testimony of the works and power of the Holy Spirit. Nobody can question the divinity of Jesus Christ:

> *"But thou, Bethlehem Ephratah, though thou be little among the thousands of Judah, yet out of thee shall he come forth unto me that is to be ruler in Israel; whose goings forth have been from of old, from everlasting"*
> (Micah 5:2).

Even so, on earth He had completely emptied Himself of all His divine power to enable Him accomplish His earthly mission which was to make manifest God's gracefulness and blessings by His personal appearance on earth. Jesus Christ abolished death; brought life through the Gospel, and brought immortality through the Gospel. His testimony is the Spirit of prophecy:

> *"The Spirit of the Lord is upon me, because he hath anointed me to preach the gospel to the poor; he hath sent me to heal the brokenhearted, to preach deliverance to the captives, and recovering of sight to the blind, to set at*

liberty them that are bruised, To preach the acceptable year of the Lord" (Luke 4:18).

He deployed His twelve disciples to the field with strict commission as to what to preach and to do:

> *"And as ye go, preach, saying, The kingdom of heaven is at hand. Heal the sick, cleanse the lepers, raise the dead, cast out devils: freely ye have received, freely give"* (Matthew 10:7-8).

Therefore, being vulnerable in an evil world after His *"kenosis"*: relinquishing divine power so as to be able to experience human suffering (Philippians 2:5-8), He had to be strengthened through the Holy Spirit anointing and with power that went beyond any set limit—past or present:

> *"For he whom God hath speaketh the words of God: for God giveth not the Spirit by measure unto him"* (John 3:34).

Also in Peter's maiden sermon onto the Gentiles, (Acts 10:38) we get the Spirit and power of the anointing that was unrestricted, unlike those given to previous vessels in the past who were granted the anointing merely to perform specific tasks, and it was especially limited to the Jewish commonwealth. In particular, the first mission field of His disciples was a case in point:

> *"These twelve Jesus sent forth, and commanded them, saying, Go not into the way of the Gentiles, and into any city of the Samaritans enter ye not: But go rather to the lost sheep of the house of Israel"* (Matthew 10:5-6).

But Christ came as a far more superior and perfect tabernacle; even the Lamb of God that reflects the beauty, splendour, grace, wisdom and eternal excellency of God in all its glory, who went on to receive the anointing of the glory that *excelleth* and was over and above all human understanding:

> *"And Jesus being full of the Holy Ghost returned from Jordan, and was led by the Spirit into the wilderness"* (Luke 4:1).

"And Jesus returned in the power of the Spirit into Galilee: and there went out a fame of him through all the region round about" (Luke 4:14).

"And Jesus went about all Galilee, teaching in their synagogues, and preaching the gospel of the kingdom, and healing all manner of disease among the people. And his fame went throughout all Syria: and they brought unto him all sick people that were taken with diverse diseases and torments, and those which were possessed with devils, and those which were lunatick, and those that had the palsy (to be paralysed); and he healed them. And there followed him great multitudes of people from Galilee, and from Decapolis, and from Jerusalem, and from Judaea, and from beyond Jordan" (Matthew 4:23-25).

Jesus' deity designated is in His ultimate glory: the purpose of the second advent (I Colossians 15:24-28).

"Which in his times he shall shew, who is the blessed and the only Potentate, the King of kings, and Lord of lords; Who only hath immortality, dwelling in the light which no man can approach unto; whom no man hath seen, nor can see: to whom be honour and power everlasting. Amen"
(I Timothy 6:15-16).

So Jesus was truly a mega phenomenon. His global fame was unmistakable in every aspect which bears all the hallmarks of the works of the living God through the blessed Holy Ghost. What is more, Christ's second appearing will make known the only Potentate—Mighty Prince, a Ruler of all the earth. Like His Father, Jehovah, both are great Potentates and ultimate Kings and prime source of immortality. God's infinite glory lies beyond the glare of natural eyes (John 4:24). No human being can nor has ever beheld this infinite glory, except when He opts out of it. He is able to manifest in different ways in the physical realm, such as a cloud, an angel, a star etc. But His infinite glory is only accessible through faith in Christ. For example, when Moses made his solemn request, the law-giver of Israel was only granted the back parts, on condition that he stands upon the rock, which represents the Gospel of Jesus Christ, in the Spirit. However, before that time, there are Scriptural records that testify Moses talked with God face to face as if speaking with a friend. But this was after God had stepped out of His eternal glory (Exodus 33:11-23). Hence, without the Holy Spirit, no man can see God. He is the Guarantor and Purveyor of our spirituality.

Chapter 1

LESSONS ON THE HOLY SPIRIT

Who Is The Holy Spirit?

1. He is God. The Holy Spirit is One of the three **Persons making up the Godhead:**

Beloved friend, no singular passage in the whole Scripture so succinctly captures and seeks to demonstrate, in stark reality, the professed deity of the Holy Spirit as God than this incident of the unfortunate couple that attempted woefully to test His mettle when they transgressed against the apostolic church, having succumbed to the pressures, driven by their carnal appetites in self-preservation and greed. Coming as it did, at the inception of the Christian church, God was bent on setting a precedent for future would-be blasphemers to take heed of themselves. Before this unfortunate episode, the early church was firmly in the hands of God, as they genuinely exhibited uncommon unity of place, spirit, and soul, and therefore were anointed, and became blessed recipients of the baptism of the Spirit together as one body in Christ Jesus (Acts 2:1-13):

> *"And the multitude of them that believed were of one heart and and of one soul: neither said any of them that ought of things which he possessed was his own; but they had all things common. And with great power gave the*

> *apostles witness of the resurrection of the Lord Jesus: and great grace was upon them all. Neither was there any among them that lacked: for as many as were possessors of lands or houses sold them, and brought the prices of the things that were sold, And laid them down at the apostles' feet: and distribution was made unto every man according as he had need. And Joses, who by the apostles was surnamed Barnabas, (which is, being interpreted, The son of consolation,) a Levite, and and of the country of Cyprus, Having land, sold it, and brought the money, and laid it at the apostles' feet"* (Acts 32:37).

> *"But a certain man named Ananias, with Sapphira his wife, sold a possession, And kept back part of the price, his wife also being privy to it, and brought a certain part, and laid it at the apostles' feet. But Peter said, Ananias, why hath Satan filled thine heart to lie to the Holy Ghost, and to keep back part of the price of the land? Whilst it remained, was it not thine own? and after it was sold, was it not in thine own power? why hast thou conceived this thing in thine heart? thou hast not lied unto men, but unto God. And Ananias hearing these words fell down, and gave up the ghost: and great fear came on all them that heard these things"* (Acts 5:1-5).

Hence, Peter's indictment against the unrighteous couple lends credence to the truth that the Apostle of Jesus Christ believed the Holy Ghost is God.

Also, alluding to the power behind His *"Grand Commission"* at the end of the Gospel according to Saint Matthew, Jesus invoked the name of the Holy Spirit to buttress His authority:

> *"All power has been given unto me in heaven and in earth. Go ye therefore, and teach all nations, baptizing them in the name of the Father, and of the Son, and of the Holy Ghost: Teaching them to observe all things whatsoever I have commanded you: and, lo, I am with you always, even unto the end of the world. Amen"* (Matthew 28:18-20).

2. He Is Omnipotent; Omniscient; Omnipresent:

The *omnipotence* of the Holy Spirit is clearly stated in the opening verses of the historic book of Saint Luke when the angel was assigned from heaven to deliver the prophecy of the Messiah's birth on earth through Mary:

> *"And the angel answered and said unto her, The Holy Ghost shall come upon thee, and the power of the Highest shall overshadow thee: therefore also that Holy thing which shall be born of thee shall be called the Son of God"* (Luke 1:35).

This constitutes one of the most powerful mysteries of the Bible in the sense that Mary had not known any man before she became pregnant of her first Son. The Word had been given in Genesis 3:15, and confirmed from generation to generation by various anointed vessels of God. These Spirit-filled declarations concerning the Messiah's coming are what the Holy Spirit used to impregnate Mary to birth our Saviour:

> *"Therefore the Lord himself shall give you a sign; Behold, a virgin shall conceive, and bear a son, and shall his name Immanuel"* (Isaiah 7:14).

> *"And she shall bring forth a son, and thou shalt call his name JESUS: for he shall save his people from their sins"* (Matthew 1:21).

> *"For unto us a child is born, unto us a son is given: and the government shall be upon his shoulder: and his name shall be called Wonderful, Counsellor, The mighty God, The everlasting Father, The Prince of Peace"* (Isaiah 9:6).

It is those testimonies that overcame the world to bring forth this joy unspeakable. Thus, Jesus was birthed and revealed only by the Holy Spirit:

> *"Whom having not seen, ye love; in whom, though now ye see him not, yet believing, ye rejoice with joy unspeakable and full of glory: Receiving the end of your faith, even the salvation of your souls. Of which salvation the prophets have enquired and searched diligently, who prophesied of the grace*

> *that should come unto you: Searching what, or what manner of the Spirit of Christ which was in them did signify, when it testified beforehand the sufferings of Christ, and the glory that should follow. Unto whom it was revealed, that not unto themselves, but unto us they did minister the things, which are now reported unto you by them that have preached the gospel unto you with the Holy Ghost sent down from heaven; which things the angels desire to look into…Forasmuch as ye know that ye were not redeemed with corruptible things, as silver and gold, from your vain conversation received by tradition from your fathers; But with the precious blood of Christ, as of a Lamb without blemish and without spot: Who verily was foreordained before the foundation of the world, but was manifest in these last times for you, Who by him do believe in God, that raised him up from the dead, and gave him glory; that your faith and hope might be in God. Seeing ye have purified your souls in obeying the truth through the Spirit unto feigned love of the brethren, see that ye love one another with a pure heart fervently: Being born again, not of corruptible seed, but of incorruptible, by the word of God, which liveth and abideth for ever"* (I Peter 1:8-12,23).

Greatly beloved in Christ, according to Elihu, Job's friend, we are all made by the Holy Spirit, formed in the womb of the mother, which is the centre of the human body, and given life by the Almighty:

> *"The Spirit of God hath made me, and the breath of the Almighty hath given me life"* (Job. 33:4).

The psalmist appraises His wondrous works in no uncertain terms. The eulogistic poem is pitched in unrestrained admiration, which is also an index to His omnipotence, when looking at the the intricate embroidery of our very different and varied members to form a complete whole. It is definitely amazing to observe the gradual growth from conception of all our variegated, woven parts—from conception to the full development of the perfect child:

> *"I will praise thee; for I am fearfully made: marvellous are thy works; and that my soul knoweth right well. My substance was not hid from thee, when I made in secret, and curiously wrought in the lowest parts of the earth.*

Chapter 1: Lessons on the Holy Spirit 159

> *Thine eyes did see my substance, yet being unperfect; and in thy book all my members were written, which in continuance were fashioned, when as yet there was none of them. How precious also are thy thoughts unto me, O God! how great is the sum of them! If I should count them, they are more than the sand: when I awake, I am still with thee"* (Psalm 139:14-18).

Beloved, the *omnipotence* of the Holy Spirit means that we can only achieve the following through yieldingness to Him: purity of soul (Hebrews 9:14); obedience to the truth (John 16:12-15); love without hypocrisy (Romans 5:5); love with fervency (v 22); purity of heart (v 22); the new birth by the Word (v 23; John 3:5). In fact, Jesus Himself was begotten through the Holy Spirit (Matthew 1:18-25; Luke 1:35); trained (Isaiah 50:4; Luke 2:40, 52); tested (Matthew 4:1; Luke 4:1); worked (Matthew 12:28; Luke 4:14-21; Acts 10:38; Isaiah 11:1-2; 42:1-7; 61:1-2); offered self a sacrifice (Hebrews 9:14); was resurrected (Romans 8:11); justified (I Timothy 3:16).

The Holy Spirit's *omniscience* is evident in the doctrine Paul, the apostle of Jesus Christ in his maiden epistle to the Corinthians, depicting the authority of the Holy Spirit as a Revealer and Teacher of the deep secrets of God unto, and into the spirits of those human beings who are covenanted to God:

> *"But as it is written, Eye hath not seen, nor ear heard, neither have entered into the heart of man, the things which God hath prepared for them that love him. But God hath revealed them unto us by his Spirit: for the Spirit searcheth all things, yea, the deep things of God. For what man knoweth the things of a man, save the spirit of man which is in him? even so the things of God knoweth no man, but the Spirit of God. Now we have received, not the spirit of the world, but the Spirit which is of God; that we might know that are freely given to us of God. Which things also we speak, not in the words which man's wisdom teacheth, but which the Holy Gost teacheth; comparing spiritual things with spiritual. But the natural man receiveth not the things of the Spirit of God: for they are foolishness unto him: neither can he know them, because they are spiritually discerned. But he that is spiritual judgeth all things, yet he himself is judged of no man. For who hath known the mind*

of the Lord, that he may instruct him? But we have the mind of Christ"
(I Corinthians 2:9-16).

King David also prophesied on the tenfold omniscience of God's operations in His Spirit; namely, our ante-natal preparation in the Spirit, which is the Power of His Might and Might of His Power:

"O Lord, thou hast searched me, and known me. Thou knowest my downsitting and mine uprising, thou understandest my thought afar off. Thou compassest my path and my lying down, and art acquainted with all my ways. For there is not a word in my tongue, but, lo, O Lord, thou knowest it altogether. Thou hast beset me behind and before, and laid thine hand upon me. Such knowledge is too wonderful for me; it is high, I cannot attain unto it"
(Psalm 139:1-6).

3. The Holy Spirit is The Creator. He is The Creative Power of God: The God of God

We have already seen how the Son of God was manifested on earth through the intermediary of the Spirit of God. Now let us proceed to explore the latter's contribution in the perfect creation of heaven, as well as the recreation of the earth, in perfection, by God:

"In the beginning God created the heaven and the earth. And the earth was without form, and void; and darkness was upon the face of the deep. And the Spirit of God moved upon the face of the waters. And God said, Let there be light: and there was light" (Galatians 1:1-3).

Clearly, therefore, brethren, it was the Spirit of God that orchestrated the manifestation of the spoken Word on earth, so one could actually see the realisation of God's glorious purpose on earth through His Word. Beloved in Christ, it is the Spirit-filled Word that makes all the difference. The Holy Spirit is the Spirit of truth. Therefore, Jehovah's Word was filled with truth, and hence its manifestation through the Spirit of testimony. The Psalmist praises Him as follows:

Chapter 1: Lessons on the Holy Spirit 161

> *"For the word of the Lord is right; and all his works are done in truth. He loveth righteousness and judgment: the earth is full of the goodness of the Lord. By the word of the Lord were the heavens made; and all the host of them by the breath of his mouth. He gathereth the waters of the sea together as an heap: he layeth up the depth in storehouses. Let all the earth fear the Lord: let all the inhabitants of the world stand in awe of him"*
> (Psalm 33:4-8).

The current world is sustained by the same Spirit-filled Word. Without the Word of truth, this world would not be able to sustain. Jesus incarnates that Word, and the Bible says the Lord is now the Spirit (II Corinthians 3:17). Saint Peter, the Apostle of Jesus highlights this dramatic influence and power of the Holy Spirit-Word on earth today, as he warns scoffers who have chosen to remain ignorant of the Perfect Law:

> *"For this they willingly are ignorant of, that by the word of God the heavens were of old, and the earth standing out of the water and in the water: Whereby the world that then was, being overflowed with water, perished: But the heavens and the earth, which are now, by the same word are kept in store, reserved unto fire against the day of judgement and perdition of ungodly men"* (II Peter 3:5-7).

Thus, through the Spirit-filled Word of God, the new earth was created. Brethren, our God is always creating new things. He is a God of restoration, renewal, and re-awakening: *"Remember ye not the former things, neither consider the things of old. Behold, I will do a new thing; now it shall spring forth; shall ye not know it? I will even make a way in the wilderness, and rivers in the desert"* (Isaiah 43:18-19). God's creative genius is leveraged onto and into the spirit of the true believer through the Holy Spirit: revealing the secret of the transition from the first Adam, who was a living soul; onto the second Adam, Who is a quickening Spirit; the mystery of the first son who was that of a bond woman (Hagar), whereas it was the second son that was to be appointed heir, for he (Isaac) was born of the free woman (Sarah). The first son (Ishmael) had to be cast away: done away with, in the manner of the abolished laws (the Old Testament, without faith); whereas the second Adam, like Isaac, is the covenanted son, and therefore is associated with (the Gospel of Jesus Christ which is mixed with faith). Brethren, it was Isaac, not Ishmail, who inherited the covenant granted to Abraham, His father (Genesis 22:15-18; Galatians 4:21-31). Friend, having been born by the free woman, we are heirs of the Father; we are the offspring of the second Adam who is a quickening Spirit: Having been baptized in Jesus, we are born of the Holy Spirit—descendants of the free woman:

> *"For as many as are led by the Spirit of God, they are the sons of God. For we have not received the spirit of bondage again to fear; but we have received the Spirit of Adoption whereby we cry, Abba, Father. The Spirit itself beareth witness with our spirit, that we are the children of God: And if children, then heirs of God, and join heirs with Christ; if so be that we suffer with him, that we may be also glorified together"* (Romans 8:14-17).

And today, chosen one, beloved brethren, the spirit of the Lord is with you, for you, on you, in you. He operates through you, as temple of God! In fact, as a result, all His goodness, loving kindness, gracefulness and tender mercies shall never depart from you. The Holy Ghost will secure your JUBILEE! And you shall see the manifest glory of God in the land of the living, and not of the dead, for you serve a Living God! Thus, the heaviness shall be replaced with the garment of praise. And in this garment is the beauty and splendour of the kingdom which embodies our salvation in the Holy Spirit:

> *"To appoint unto them that mourn in Zion, to give unto them beauty for ashes, the oil of joy for mourning, the garment of praise for the spirit of heaviness; that they might be called trees of righteousness, the planting of the Lord, that he might be gloried"* (Isaiah 61:3).

Well, friend, apart from manifesting the power of the Word to those followers of Christ, who worship the Almighty in Spirit and in truth, it is worth mentioning here that the self-same Spirit of God is a complete, bona fide human being with all the attributes of a person displayed in the following verses:

> *"Likewise the Spirit also helpeth our infirmities: for we know not what we should pray for as we ought: but the Spirit itself maketh intercession for us*

Chapter 1: Lessons on the Holy Spirit 163

> *with groanings which cannot be uttered. And he that searcheth the hearts knoweth what is the mind of the Spirit, because he maketh intercession for the saints according to the will of God"* (Romans 8:26-27).

Brethren, the Greek word for *help* here is sunantilambanomai, meaning *joint help*. That is to say, the assistance afforded by any two persons to each other, who mutually bear the same burden or support it between them. It might also be helpful to draw your attention to the fact that the infirmities alluded to here include the sum total of our physical, mental, or moral weaknesses or flaws—feebleness of mind and body, malady, frailty, disease, sickness. All of which Christ bore on the cross in the the great exchange in fulfilment of Isaiah 53. Not every infirmity is a disease or sickness but all these are infirmities (Luke 5:15; 7:21; 8:2; 13:11-12; John 5:5). Having been conceived and born into sin and or have sinned (Psalm 51:1-5; Isaiah 53:6; Psalm 14:2-6; Romans 3:23), we all display weaknesses of diverse sort. The Old Testament priests, for example, had infirmities which were not necessarily diseases or physical imperfections (Hebrews 5:2; 7:28) since they had to be cleared of their physical fitness prior to their ordination (Leviticus 21:17-24). As expressed in the Biblical reference above, saints also have infirmities or weaknesses of various kinds. However, our weaknesses may not actually have to do with sicknesses and/or diseases (Romans 14:1-2; 15:1). Apostle Paul tells of the weaknesses and infirmities of his body which were due to the sufferings of II Corinthians 11:24-30; 12:5-10; Galatians 4:13, but there is no evidence to prove he suffered from sicknesses and diseases thanks to the great exchange on the cross of Calvary. The thorn to his flesh, though, was "a messenger (angel) of Satan" who was the brain behind these tortures and stoning that marked his days of persecution (II Corinthians 12:7). In short, any weaknesses in body, soul, spirit, faith, and ability, especially that needed to enable us work the works of God to the full can be ascribed to this category of infirmities as prescribed above.

The other point is that we cannot pray effectively without the Holy Spirit: *"for we know not what we should pray for as we ought."* Hence, if the Spirit were not there to inspire us with appropriate desires and support us in the fulfilment of those desires according to the will of God the Father, we would ultimately falter.

Also notice the use of the personal pronoun, *itself*, meaning Himself, for He is a person—having a spirit body, and soul like any other person. He undertakes to help us spiritually in a very generous and human way: He pleads our case (intercede) by groaning or gushing of the heart before God the Father. He acts as an agent or manager in all phases of salvation and dealings with God on our behalf (John 3:5; 14:16-17, 26; 15:7-13, 25-26; I Corinthians 12).

(Brethren, we are going to go deeper into His functions later on in our discourse). What is more, there is an implication of His interaction with Jesus in this endeavour, through the *he* in Romans 8:27 above. This is no doubt Jesus who knows the mind of the Spirit, as it would seem unlikely that the Spirit would seek to know His own mind. Friend, all three persons of the Trinity search hearts: God the Father (Chronicles 28:9; Jeremiah 17:10); the Son (Revelation 2:23); and the Spirit (I Corinthians 2:10).

Greatly beloved, one other factor that clearly sets the Holy Ghost aside, as a person, is the fact He has got emotions, and can therefore be grieved by our moral lapses:

> *"And grieve not the Holy Spirit of God, whereby ye are sealed unto the day of redemption"* (Ephesians 4:30).

These moral lapses include walking out there in the vanity of your depraved mind: thinking of yourself more highly than you ought; having the eyes of your understanding blindfolded by the god of this world that has bewitched the children of disobedience, preventing them from uncovering the exquisite taste and majesty of the kingdom of light in our Lord and Saviour Jesus Christ; effectively alienating yourself from the abundance of God's life brought to the world by the Gospel of Jesus Christ; unwittingly electing to stay ignorant of God:

> *"Wherefore remember, that ye being in time past Gentiles in the flesh, who are called Uncircumcision by that which is called Circumcision in the flesh made by hands; That at the time ye were without Christ, being aliens from the commonwealth of Israel, and strangers from the covenants of promise, having no hope, and without God in the world"* (Ephesians 2:11-12).

Chapter 1: Lessons on the Holy Spirit 165

This alienation has also caused your heart to become immune and unfeeling to the weightier issues of life such as salvation through the Gospel of Jesus Christ; all the inglorious details of the past: yielding readily to, or succumbing totally to the filthy habits of lasciviousness and various works of uncleanness and untold greed; we let our bodies be easily consumed as we fall prey to the works of the flesh: adultery, fornication, idolatry, witchcraft, hatred, variance, emulations, envy, indignation, wrath or fierce anger, strife or vain disputes, contention arising from a cantankerous spirit, sedition, heresies, murders, drunkenness, and finally, the tendency to revel, which, as explained in the previous books, are a kind of riotous or boisterous feasting, resulting from addiction to extreme social indulgences.

We can therefore avoid a crisis with our Maker by keeping away from all the above acts of moral, spiritual and physical malpractice.

Lastly, the Holy Spirit is a person thanks to the Biblical revelation which clearly states that He accords spiritual gifts to various members of the body of Christ according to His own volition:

> *"But all these worketh that one and the selfsame Spirit, dividing to every man severally as he will"* (I Corinthians 12:11).

Also, the trait of the Holy Spirit as a person is clearly discernible as Apostle Paul testifies of his consecration to suffer, contained in the volumes of the book of Acts. It proves the Holy Ghost's prescience—pretty much like God the Father's (Isaiah 46:10; Daniel 2:19-23), and Jesus' (119:99-100). All Paul needed to do to accomplish his mission into the various cities was engaged in during his ministry, is to acknowledge the presence, protection and guidance of the Holy Ghost, prior to his journey.

> *"And now, behold, I go bound in the spirit unto Jerusalem, not knowing the things that shall befall me there: Save that the Holy Ghost witnesseth in every city, saying that bonds and afflictions abide me. But none of these things move me, neither count I my life dear unto myself, so that I might finish my*

course with joy, and the ministry, which I have received of the Lord Jesus, to testify the gospel of the grace of God" (Acts 20:22-24).

Dear reader, details of the gifts will be fully explained in our next chapter which delves deeper into the functions of the Holy Ghost.

Chapter 2

THE HOLY SPIRIT IS THE POWER OF GOD'S MIGHT, AND THE MIGHT OF HIS POWER

Beloved one, the anointed son/daughter in Christ, at several instances in the Bible, there are references of God exhorting and empowering His people to rise to the occasion, make good use of our mighty gifts to carry out great exploits for a good purpose: undoubtedly, therefore, the Lord shall reward everybody according to their works (Matthew 16:27; John 14:12; Revelation 2:23). In fact, according to the the book of James, faith without works is like the body without the spirit, which literally means is very dead!(James 2:14-26) Suffices for us to understand that the works being referred to here are not those which are done outside the realms of the Spirit of God. Brethren, any work, which is driven by human wisdom or ego, regardless of its purpose, quality or quantity is anathema at the sight of God. What God means by works can only be understood through revelation from the Gospel of Jesus Christ. That is to say, the born-again Christian who is led by the Holy Spirit will go on to do or perform great exploits, as revealed in the book of (Daniel 11:32 or Ephesians 2:10). Great works follow if we acknowledge Jesus as our Lord and Saviour (John 15; II Corinthians 5:17; Ephesians 1:3, 2:4-7), and the Holy Spirit descends upon us to birth Jesus in us. Hence we become full of, and filled in with Jesus, making our bodies the temple of God:

"Until the spirit be poured upon us from on high, and the wilderness be a fruitful field, and the fruitful field be counted for a forest" (Isaiah 32:15).

Beloved friend in Christ, it is the Apostle Paul's fervent wish to the Philippians, that: *"Only let your conversation be as it becometh the gospel of Christ: that whether I come and see you, or else be absent, I may hear of your affairs, that ye stand fast in one spirit, with one mind striving together for the faith of the gospel"*. Thus, it is possible to be led by the Spirit and to gain His anointing on corporate terms if only you are able stick together, especially in spirit. Let your minds be saturated with the truth of the Gospel of Jesus, which is food for the soul. You stir up the powerful Spirit in you, as you enhance your divine essence in spirit and substance. As models, Jesus and the Holy Ghost never depart from the Father in all their activities and exploits. And Jesus Himself knew jolly well, as He told His disciples, *"Howbeit when he, the Spirit of truth, is come, he will guide you into all truth: for he shall not speak of himself: but whatsoever he shall hear, that shall he speak: and he will shew you things to come"* (John 16:13). Therefore, Jesus has come to baptize us with the Holy Spirit and with power. Brethren, as He is with us, then do we receive His anointing on us, which is also in us and works through us and will always be there for us. The unction does not come to us as some left-over peanuts from heaven, and is not doled out on a top-down basis: namely, some meagre welfare grants which is distributed on a carefully regulated doses by mundane despots from above, but it is rather given freely granted, bountifully and without measure, by a better and enduring substance in heaven: namely, the One who is holy; the One who is harmless; the One who is undefiled or untainted; the One who is separate from sinners; the One who is upon the heavens, where no man has seen nor can see, and which is sealed and/or confirmed by the Father Himself (John 3:30-36; Acts 10:38):

"Labour not for the meat which perisheth, but for that meat which endureth unto everlasting life, which the Son of man shall give unto you: for him hath God the Father sealed" (John 6:27).

That is why upon His ascension onto heaven, to be glorified by the Father, the Son of man commanded His disciples to tarry in Jerusalem until they be imbued with the supernatural power from on high, in order for them to have

Chapter 2: The Holy Spirit Is the Power of God's Might, and the Might of His Power 169

the competence and authority to work the works of God (Acts 1:8; Luke 24:49). But the Old Testament book of Zechariah spells it out quite clearly what the works in the Bible are all about—that any such great works are not meant to stir up primitive instincts, puffed up from our carnal minds to foster interest out of our thinly disguised vainglorious egos, but to give all the glory where it is due—onto God the Father and our Lord and Saviour Jesus Christ, for all such magnificent works are made manifest only through the Spirit, that proceeds from the Father, sent in Jesus' name:

> *"Then the angel that talked with me answered and said unto me, Knowest thou not what these be? And I said, No, my lord. Then he answered and spake unto me, saying, This is the word of the Lord unto Zerubbabel, saying, Not by might, nor by power, but by my spirit, saith the Lord of hosts. Who art thou, O great mountain? before Zerubbabel thou shalt become a plain: and he shall bring forth the headstone therefore with shoutings, crying, Grace, grace unto it"* (Zechariah 4:5-7).

Brethren, if you are anointed like Zerubbabel with the Spirit and power, there will be no obstacles to your efforts toward achieving you goals: *"Who are you, O great moutntain? You will become a plain before Zerubbabel"*; You shall bring forth the headstone thereof with shouting of Grace, grace—which is the dispensation of the Messiah, the Headcorner Stone. This is important in the sense that the Bible says: *"Except the Lord build the house, they labour in vain that build it"* (Psalm 127:1. You will finish your work like Zerubbabel. God is a Finisher— *"It is finished:"* (John19:30)—just as Jesus planned, prepared and implemented the working scheme, content and purpose of His Father's project, so shall you see all your efforts come to a fruitful end, for that is the purpose of God in your life (Jeremiah 29:11). Brethren, it is, in fact, God's wish to grant you the Messianic mantle. Only make sure you are as meek and humble as the Messiah Himself was (Matthew 17:20, 18:18, 21:22; Mark 9:23; John 14:12; 15:5, 16; 20:23; Luke 10:19, 24:49; Acts 1:8; I Corinthians 12:7-11). Read these verses extracted from the book of Isaiah:

> *"Then I said, I have laboured in vain, I have spent my strength for nought, and in vain: yet surely my judgment is with the Lord, and my work with*

> *my God. And now, saith the Lord that formed me from the womb to be his servant, to bring Jacob again to him, Though Israel be not gathered, yet shall I be glorious in the eyes of the Lord, and my God shall be my strength. And he said, It is a light thing that thou shouldest be my servant to raise up the tribes of Jacob, and to restore the preserved of Israel: I will also give thee for a light to the Gentiles, that thou mayest be my salvation unto the ends of the earth"* (Isaiah 49:4-6).

Brethren, through the quality of your work, you will be able to recognise and acknowledge the arm of God as it is revealed in the course of your struggles to fulfil your God-given mandate. Finally, you shall rejoice, and shall see the plummet in your blessed hands, like Zerubbabel's, with those seven lamps, which are the eyes of the Lord running to and fro, through the whole earth (Zechariah 4:10). The Lord routinely searches the earth to bless the works of the righteous. He rewards the proud doer, against their lousy, plaintive counterpart—that is, His favour is only with those doers whose works are sanctioned by the Holy Spirit: Doers of the Perfect Law of Peace: (Psalm 31:23; James 1:20-25).

> *"Then said they unto him, What shall we do, that we might work the works of God?" (John 6:28)*

Beloved in Christ, we Christians are always eager to demonstrate our good works for people to see and glorify our God (Mark 5:16), and to demonstrate the expanse of our faith by works as demanded of us in James 1:22-27. Furthermore, the Bible stipulates that people zealous of good works are the only type that are redeemed (Titus 2:11-14). That is what makes this a time-honoured, and an essential FAQ in Christendom. In a general sense though, a desire to perform miracles through Christ is holy, only if there are no ulterior motives to which we all are often prone. There is a plethora of examples in the Bible showing great visionary works that were done with the wrong motives: Lucifer (Isaiah 14:12-14); Adam and his descendants (Genesis 3:1-14; 11:1-4). All harboured a lofty desire to be like God, or rather sought to arrogate God's glory onto themselves to no avail, since their motives and methods were not Holy Spirit driven; theirs was not wisdom from on high, but earthly, sensual and devilish (James 3:15). The Holy Spirit is the Supernatural Power in the Word.

Chapter 2: The Holy Spirit Is the Power of God's Might, and the Might of His Power

He is the Might of God, and also the Power of His Might! For Jesus once told His disciples that the words he spoke were not actual words, but spirit and life. Therefore, it is the Holy Spirit Himself who sets the tone that underpins the great exploits of God on earth; He sanctions the standards in kingdom righteousness, and drives excellence in human performance by paying massive attention to detail, even as He undertakes to ensure close supervision and sanctification of the works of divine vessels:

> *"Thus, saith the Lord, thy redeemer, and he that formed thee from the womb, I am the Lord that maketh all things; that stretcheth forth the heavens alone; that spreadeth abroad the earth by myself; That frustrateth the tokens of liars, and maketh diviners mad; that turneth wise men backward, and maketh their knowledge foolish; That confirmeth the word of his servant, and performeth the counsel of his messengers; that saith to Jerusalem, Thou shalt be inhabited; and to the cities of Judah, Ye shall be built, and I will raise up the decayed places thereof: That saith to the deep, Be dry, and I will dry up thy rivers: That saith to Cyrus, He is my shepherd, and shall perform all my pleasure: even saying to Jerusalem, Thou shalt be built; and to the temple, Thy foundation shall be laid"* (Isaiah 44:24-28).

Dearly beloved in Christ, the Bible says, those who do business in great waters, see the glory of God (See the deliverance song of the mariners: Psalm 107:21-30). Consequently, all those who claim to be wise or scheme to use magic for dubious motives must come under the curse of the Most High, as expressed in the verses above. This is because, you see, friend, all work in the Holy Spirit is holy. True achievement comes from God. All great assignments to enhance services or production in different ministries, authorities or organisations on earth must proceed from the throne of grace and be sanctioned by the Holy Spirit before they can see the light of day. In an interview, Bill Gates, founder of Microsoft acknowledged that till date he simply cannot get himself to understand, let alone explain to the world the real reasons for failure of the earlier products that preceded Microsoft's Windows 95! It goes without saying, therefore, that God is firmly in control. Windows 95 succeeded thanks to the spiritual significance of the 5 in 95, which stands for *"grace"*. After 30 years of concerted effort, it was time for his works to be rewarded. And that all inventions tend to fall into place, in accordance with God's timing and purpose, for our use. That is the more reason why one should desire this (the Word) more than the actual food for nutritive purposes (John 4:31-34). After all, the Bible says, man shall not live on bread alone, but by every word that proceed from the mouth of God shall man live (Matthew 4:4). Thus, to this end, and even to proceed through greater works, the approach has to be based on the example set by Jesus Christ Himself—that is, by emptying yourself to be refilled with the Spirit for greater works (Philippians 2:5-11; John 14:12).

What is even more interesting here, friend, is the fact that even though Jesus saw into the smokescreen of selfishness and greed that smeared the legitimacy of these Jewish impostors, who were only out for gleaming power to show off and grandstand their egos, He did not rebuke them, but went ahead to give them the one answer that is the whole truth:

> *"Jesus answered and said unto them, This is the work of God, that ye believe on him whom he hath sent"* (John 6:29).

Brethren, there is no better way to achieve landmark, sustained success in the vineyard of God, other than what Christ prescribes to these people. Indeed, it constitutes the sum total of all answers to this question. Some limit its meaning to only faith and forgiveness from the Son of God which is only a part of the whole range of impact of this answer. As a matter of fact, although faith and forgiveness are implied here, but the crux of the matter is about receiving the endowment of power from on high, through the Holy Ghost to work the works of God (Mark 16:15-20; Luke 24:49; John 14:12).

Therefore, the prime contribution of the Holy Ghost as far as we are concerned, is that He brings the presence of God into our lives (Matthew 6:33; Romans 14:17). The kingdom of God dwells in the Holy Spirit so His presence on earth and in us actually restores, or restitutes the precious atmosphere of heaven as it was in the days before the fall of Adam and Eve:

> *"And it shall come to pass that I will pour out my spirit upon all flesh; and your sons and your daughters shall prophesy, your old men shall dream*

dreams, your young men shall see visions: And also upon the servants and upon the housemaids in those days will I pour out my spirit" (Joel 2:28-29).

Brethren, the realisation of this prophecy commences with the baptism of Jesus Christ by the prophet, John the Baptist:

"And Jesus, when he was baptized, went straightway out of the water: and, lo, the heavens were opened unto him, and he saw the Spirit of God descending like a dove, and lighting upon him: And lo a voice from heaven, saying, This is my beloved Son, in whom I am well pleased" (Matthew 3:16-17).

Beloved, this was the restoration of the heavenly atmosphere upon the Messiah, and consequently upon all those who believe in Him, and have put on Christ as Son of God, and to whom have been granted faith to have peace with God. It is also the restitution that has come onto those who have received God's grace through faith in Christ, and which enables them to hope in God's glory through the Holy Spirit. The self-same prophecy was later manifested on the day of Pentecost and many years following this day (Acts 2:1-28:31); during the future tribulation (Acts 2:16-21); during the Millennium (Isaiah 32:15; 44:3; Eze. 36:26-27; 39:29; Zechariah 12:10).

Thus, it is quite accurate and appropriate for the Apostle Paul to remind us:

"Know ye not that ye are the temple of God, and that the Spirit of God dwelleth in you? If any man defile the temple of God, him shall God destroy; for the temple of God is holy, which temple ye are" (I Corinthians 3:16-17).

"What? know ye not that your body is the temple of the Holy Ghost which is in you, which ye have of God, and ye are not your own? For ye are bought with a price: therefore, glorify God with your body, and in your spirit, which are God's" (I Corinthians 6:19-20).

The other good news regarding the Holy Ghost's contribution to our divinity is His authorship and authentication of the holy Scriptures. Brethren, it is the Holy Spirit of God who inspired, supplied, powered and actually sanctified the capacities of the various prophets of God to make the Bible possible, as the Apostle Paul testifies in this letter to Timothy:

> *"And that from a child thou hast known the holy scriptures, which are able to make thee wise unto salvation through faith which is in Christ Jesus. All scripture is given by inspiration of God, and is profitable for doctrine, for reproof, for correction, for instruction in righteousness: that the man of God may be perfect, thoroughly furnished unto all good works"*
> (II Timothy 3:15-17).

Aside from writing the Bible, it is the self-same Spirit that revealed and birthed the church of Jesus Christ, even as the Messiah Himself acknowledged in the book of Jehovah's King:

> *"When Jesus came into the coasts of Caesarea Philippi, he asked his disciples, saying, Whom do men say that I the Son of man am? And they said, Some say, that thou art John the Baptist: some, Elias; and others, Jeremias, or one of the prophets. He saith unto them, But whom say ye that I am? And Simon Peter answered and said, Thou ar the Christ, the Son of the living God. And Jesus answered and said unto him, Blessed art thou, Simon Barjona: for flesh and blood hath not revealed it unto thee, but my Father which is in heaven. And I say unto thee, That thou art Peter, and upon this rock I will build my church; and the gates of hell shall not prevail against it"*
> (Matthew 16:13-18).

Hence the first mention of the New Testament church. It was this revelation by the Spirit of God into and onto the spirit of the initiated that would go on to proclaim its existence on earth. The Lord will never act on earth without the consent of His covenant partners (Amos 3:7; Job 22:28; Isaiah 44:26). Having declared it, the Christian church saw its manifestation after the resurrection and glorification of Jesus Christ at Pentecost:

> *"But ye shall receive power, after that the Holy Ghost is come upon you: and ye shall be witnesses unto me both in Jerusalem, and in all Judaea, and in Samaria, and unto the uttermost part of the earth"* (Acts 1:8).

Chapter 2: The Holy Spirit Is the Power of God's Might, and the Might of His Power

And here comes its final manifestation:

> *"And when the day of Pentecost was fully come, they were all with one accord in one place. And suddenly there came a sound from heaven as of a rushing mighty wind, and it filled all the house where they were sitting. And there appeared unto them cloven tongues like as of fire, and it sat upon each of them. And they were all filled with the Holy Ghost, and began to speak with other tongues, as the Spirit gave them utterance. And there were dwelling at Jerusalem Jews, devout men, out of every nation under heaven. Now when this was noised abroad, the multitude came together, and were confounded, because that every man heard them speak in his own language. And they were all amazed and marvelled, saying one to another, Behold, are not all these which speak Galilaeans? And how hear we every man in our own tongue, wherein we were born? Parthians, and Medes, and Elamites, and the dwellers in Mesopotamia, and in Judaea, and Cappadocia, in Pontus, and Asia, Phrygia, and Pamphylia, in Egypt, and in parts of Libya about Cyrene, and strangers of Rome, Jews and proselytes, Cretes and Arabians, we do hear them speak in our tongues the wonderful works of God. And they were all amazed, and were in doubt, saying one to another, What meaneth this? Other mocking said, These men are full of new wine. But Peter standing up with the eleven, lifted up his voice, and said unto them, Ye men of Judaea, and all ye that dwell at Jerusalem, be this known unto you, and hearken to my words: For these are not drunken, as ye suppose, seeing it is but the third hour of the day. But this is that which was spoken by the prophet Joel"* (Acts 2:1-16).

Thus, from the very outset, the veil of Moses had been torn apart by the powerful, overwhelming and irresistible anointing on Jesus Christ (John 3:34), and there was to be henceforth no division based on race or geneology: we have become one in the body of Christ: whether we are of the Circumcision or Uncircumcision; Jew or Greek; male or female, bond or free, Hallelujah!

Furthermore, the Holy Spirit is the great Revealer of truth. Beloved, truth is one, indivisible and universal. What is true today, is true for all time. Truth is valid eternally, in time and space, and it is indelible and/or indestructible. For example, the church of Christ that was revealed through Peter, in spite of stiff resistance and persecutions from the early years on, has become a reality throughout the whole world and will last till the second millennium of the Messiah. That is the true church. All fake churches and religions shall come and go like the Amalekites, Jebusites, Hittites and all the bulk of other extinct pagan tribes and human cultures of yore. Hence the need to venerate the Holy Spirit. Brethren, the Old Testament law failed to deliver us from sin because men were compelled by law to do the work of God without putting on Christ! Thus, as mostly natural beings, people we were obliged to interpret and observe the subtle, nitty-gritty of spiritual ordinances which were against our nature, and contrary to our fleshly spirits (Colossians 2:14). Nevertheless, having been wholly converted into bona fide Christian believers, Jesus said we have become friends and no longer wanted to countenance a master-servant relationship with us, (like Moses engendered with the children of Israel) and that is why He evolved a brand new relationship based on mutual friendship. According to Jesus, therefore, in the former relationship, the master does not have to reveal all truth to the servant, and therefore, He had us imbued with the Holy Spirit:

> *"I have yet many things to say unto you, but ye cannot bear them now. Howbeit when he, the Spirit of truth, is come, he will guide you into all truth: for he shall not speak of himself; but whatsoever he shall hear, that shall he speak: and he will shew you things to come. He shall glorify me: for he shall receive of mine, and shall shew it unto you. All things that the Father hath are mine: therefore said I, that he shall take of mine, and shall shew it unto you"*
> (John 16:12-15).

Consequently, It was now possible for human beings to operate exclusively in the Spirit like Jesus told Nicodemus (John 3:5-12). Beloved in Christ, Saint John the divine, who authored the book of Revelation, for example, was in the Spirit: that is to say, he was in consecration with Jesus, in the Spirit, to perform the will and/or purpose of God regarding the future of mankind in the end times:

> *"The Revelation of Jesus Christ, which God gave unto him, to shew unto his servants things which must shortly come to pass; and he sent and signified it by his angel unto his servant John: Who bare record of the Word of God, and*

> *of the testimony of Jesus Christ, and of all things that he saw…I John, who also am your brother, and companion in tribulation, and in the kingdom and patience of Jesus Christ, was in the isle that is called Patmos, for the word of God, and for the testimony of Jesus Christ. I was in the Spirit on the Lord's day, and heard behind me a great voice, as of a trumpet, Saying, I am the Alpha and Omega, the first and the last: and, What thou seest, write in a book, and send it unto the seven churches which are in Asia; unto Ephesus, and unto Smyrna, and unto Pergamos, and unto Thyatira, and unto Sardis, and unto Philadelphia, and unto Laodicea"* (Revelation 1:1-2, 9-11).

Saint John the divine was thus led to the truth, being in communion with the Holy Ghost. All such great works could and shall only happen through total submission or surrender of our self-throne to the Spirit of truth and revelation. As a man, Jesus did it likewise to prove that it is possible for those who believe in Him to carry on His work through their consecration with the Holy Ghost:

> *"God is a Spirit: and they that worship him must worship him in spirit and in truth"* (John 4:24).

The Holy Spirit As Sole Custodian of the Glory of God:

The next significant contribution of the Holy Ghost is that of teaching: The Holy Ghost Is My Teacher! Friend, you cannot understand the dimensions of the Word of God without acknowledging the power of the Holy Spirit. To date, many preachers interpret the Scriptures in default of official requirements. As well as the Holy Spirit, Jesus never used His sole imagination or personal initiative whilst preaching the Gospel—in doing the works of His Father:

> *"Believe thou not that I am in the Father, and the Father in me? the words that I speak unto you I speak not of myself: but the Father that dwelleth in me, he doeth the works"* (John 14:10).

> *"Then answered Jesus and said unto them, Verily, verily, I say unto you, The Son can do nothing of himself, but what he seeth the Father do: for what things soever he doeth, these also doeth the Son likewise"* (John 5:19).

> *"Turn you at my reproof: behold, I will pour out my spirit unto you, I will make known my words unto you"* (Proverbs 1:23).

In the same vein, we are warned against undue reliance on uncertain human wisdom, knowledge and understanding at several instances in Scripture (Proverbs 3:5-7). In particular, the Apostle Paul upbraids preachers and other popular orators cautioning them to heed the power of the Gospel which is enshrined in the wisdom of God—the wisdom of God, the Gospel of Jesus Christ was hidden from great kings, princes and prophets of old, up to the time of its revelation, and which God ordained before this age for us. Thus, end time evangelists, teachers, prophets, apostles, pastors and bishops must resist the temptation of employing persuasive doctrine drawn from human philosophy, which is a method often resorted to by some popular orators, to sway men. Henceforth, they must transmit the oracles of God under the anointing and power of the Spirit which is always confirmed with signs and wonders and miracles (Romans 15:18-19, 29; Acts 19:11):

> *"And I, brethren, when I came to you, came not with excellency of speech or of wisdom, declaring unto you the testimony of God. For I determined not to know any thing among you, save Jesus Christ, and him crucified. And I was with you in weakness, and in fear, and in much trembling. And my speech and my preaching was not with enticing words of man's wisdom, but in demonstration of the Spirit of power. That your faith should not stand in the wisdom of men, but in the power of God. Howbeit we speak wisdom among them that are perfect: yet not the wisdom of this world, nor of the princes of this world, that come to nought. But we speak the wisdom of God in a mystery, even the hidden wisdom, which God ordained before the world unto our glory: Which none of the princes of this world knew: for had they known it, they would not have crucified the Lord of glory"* (I Corinthians 2:1-8).

> *"Trust in the Lord with all thine heart; and lean not unto thine own understanding. In all thy ways acknowledge him, and he shall direct your paths"* (Proverbs 3:5-6).

Chapter 2: The Holy Spirit Is the Power of God's Might, and the Might of His Power

It is vain for us to rely on our own wisdom, knowledge, understanding or sheer native strengthen for self-defence or martial assault, since we do not fight against flesh and blood, but against principalities and powers, as well as spiritually wicked forces in high places. Brethren, at this time and age, the use of material weaponry in spiritual warfare is inconsequential. Hence the Bible says:

> *"For though we walk in the flesh, we do not war after the flesh: (For the weapons of our warfare are not carnal, but mighty through God to the pulling down of strong holds;) Casting down imaginations, and every high thing that exhaulteth itself against the knowledge of God, and bringing into captivity every thought to the obedience of Christ"* (II Corinthians 10:3-5).

Hence, we cannot afford to employ carnal weapons to destroy the depraved reasoning of apostate scholars and/or the satanic dogmas which have been churned up nightly through the ages by reprobate philosophers bent on nullifying or contradicting the Word of God and the truth and grace of the Gospel of Jesus Christ. Rather, we must strive to pull down these fortifications and bring them to utter ruin. We must put on Christ through the Spirit that raised Him from the dead to enable us defeat the demon powers and alien armies, and bring them to condemnation. We must raise the banner of the cross high on the battle field. Beloved, we are called to demolish all these theories, paradigms. In short, any high ethical, religious, metaphysical, or philosophical system or set of notions that, either inadvertently, or by design is set to defy the knowledge of God in us, and in the world, must not survive our demolishing campaign. On this score, all the false gods, lords, sacrificial and meditating creeds for yogis and yoga, itself must fall like Dagon, the god of the Philistines of old, before the Gospel. What is more, all the high-sounding phrases of renown philosphers and spiritualists like Plato, Aristotle, the Stoics, Sir Isaac Newton, Friedrich Nitzsche, Thomas Hardy, Charles Darwin and Darwinism, Buddha and Buddhism, Judaism, Confucius, Muhammad, the Dalai Lama, Bahaullah, Baha'i, Abdul Baha, Shoghi Effendi, Scientology, Illuminati, Freemasonry, Mormon, Joseph Smith, idolaters, Rosicrucian movements, to name just a few. In a nutshell, any secret society with an agenda to wield power furtively, through various forms of occult knowledge and commanding mighty power by professing esoteric religious paradigms; all intellectual works of global import, and/or of international stature must be rendered inadequate and be exposed to appear wanting before the ultimate power of Jesus, our Lord and Saviour, the Crucified and Resurrected Christ, the only Potentate: King of kings and Lord of lords—the SOURCE of ALL KNOWLEDGE, and the FOUNTAIN of ALL LIFE forms. There is no other faith, no surreptitious knowledge other than His. He is the Author and the Finisher of All the we need to know about our spirituality. Amen and Amen. Consequently, anybody or institutional authority, such as the Rosicrucian Order or Ancient Mystic Order *Rosae Crucis* must be discarded and binned until the coming of our Lord Jesus Christ. Amen. Henceforth, it is the duty of the militant Christian to arrest every dubious thought process of blasphemous undertones, and subdue it: channelizing it into the realm of captivity , in the obedience of Christ—vile thoughts such as lasciviousness: vain, and wicked thoughts of insidious or invidious intent must be brought down and be made subject to the Perfect Law of Christ. Friend, Christ's, way indeed, must be our perspective.

Robbers In Paradise: Destiniy Dealers

"The thief cometh not, but for to steal, and to kill, and to destroy" (John 10:10):

Greatly beloved, there is hardly any other verse in Scripture which is being vastly misunderstood, misinterpreted, undervalued and even abused by carnal speakers in various Christian denominations. Very often, the *"thief"* in this context is used to merely designate the devil, which is not far from the mark. But in actual fact, the verse's overall meaning embraces all workers of iniquity who are agents of Lucifer: either directly or indirectly—all those whose spirits are still under captivity by the so-called *old man,* and who do live, act and arrange their lives, beings, thought patterns and daily routines in accordance with the rebellious purpose of the transgressor; all those who do operate firmly under the influence of Lucifer himself effectively constitute an integral part of the evil empire:

> *"For rebellion is as the sin of witchcraft, and stubbornness is as iniquity and idolatry. Because thou hast rejected the word of the Lord, he hath also rejected thee from being king"* (I Samuel 15:23).

Friend, to demonstrate the devil's sophistication and high sense of organisation, let me make it crystal clear, right away, that the various demonic agents on the face of this earth can be subsumed under four different categories of evil-doers, the first of which are witches/wizards, and spiritual gurus, plying their pernicious trade mostly in mainland Asia. They are seducers who rebel against the word of God, claiming to be in a position to tell the truth, but are in fact, charlatans of the first order. Witches and wizards are spiritual crooks who tap into the power of God for a living, but without the least intention to submit to His will or purpose. Thus they take delight in swindling divine power and using it to subsidise mercantile supplies. The ilk bunch can be classified into two major groups: namely, the traditional *voudou* priests, the shifty traditional healers or herbalists, the inglorious marabouts—made up chiefly of local medicine men and women, marauding the pristine landscapes of tropical Africa and the Caribbean to hoodwink unwary peasants and choke it in the folds of idols—diminutive, marionette gods that have eyes, but cannot see; man-made gods that have hands, but cannot handle; puppet gods that have mouths but cannot speak. A parallel in the Old Testament would be the prophets of Baal, all of whom Elijah slew at the brook *Kishon* (I Kings 18:30-40). In Israel, at the time, witchcraft was not condoned, and witches and wizards were not allowed to live, by law, as the source of their power was demonic:

"Thou shalt not suffer a witch to live" (Exodus 22:18).

This exposes one of the short-comings of the Mosaic laws: comparing things of the flesh with things of the spirit. Otherwise, of what earthly use is it to ask men to kill spirits? Is the devil human? Definitely, not. Consequently, Elijah's killing of the many prophets of Baal, as well as all his fire miracles had no effect on the queen, Jezebel who was determined to take revenge on the Prophet of God, for having humbled her god, defeated his prophets and had them slain mercilessly. Therefore, not being able to command the requisite dosage of faith, Elijah fled for his life (I Kings 19:1-3). What an interesting turn of fortune for this mighty man of God! Nevertheless brethren, in today's dispensation of the Spirit, we do not need to go after our enemies with carnal weapons. Like David told the embattled Goliath, as soon as the encounter took a spiritual twist:

"And the Philistine said unto David, Am I a dog, that that thou comest to me with stave? And the Philistine cursed David by his gods. And the Philistine said to David, Come to me, and I will give thy flesh unto the fowls of the air, and to the beasts of the field. Then said David to the Philistine, Thou comest to me with a sword, and with a spear, and with a shield: but I come to thee in the name of the Lord of hosts, the God of the armies of Israel, whom thou hast defied. This day will the Lord deliver thee into mine hands; and I will smite thee, and take thine head from thee; and I will give the carcases of the host of the Philistines this day unto the fowls of the air, and to the wild beasts of the earth; that all the earth may know that there is a God in Israel. AND ALL THIS ASSEMBLY SHALL KNOW THAT THE LORD SAVETH NOT WITH SWORD AND SPEAR: FOR THE BATTLE IS THE LORD'S, AND HE WILL GIVE YOU INTO OUR HANDS" (I Samuel 17:43-47).

Friend, this is straight-forward stuff. Christianity is a very practical religion. We have nothing to hide, even as we use the utmost clarity of speech to reach out or minister to our congregation and other interested parties, say, during evangelistic missions. Having said that, it is also fair to state that in the current ministry of the Spirit we must strive to be Spirit-led; we must learn to confront the forces of the darkness of this world solely with the sword of the Spirit, which is the Word of God—the Name of Jesus who is the incarnation of the Word; His unblemished blood. (see more on this under The Holy Spirit—Custodian of the Glory of God).

On the other hand, there are the scientific, modern organisations, such secret societies or occultist groups like Scientology, Illuminati, or Ancient Mystic-Order-Rosae-Crucis, aka, Roscicrucian Order. These are cryptic, even blood-thirsty movements whose only design is to misdirect God's people to hell. Brethren, their solace is spilling blood for fun. They claim to have power that they can never obtain nor wield in good faith. In fact, secret societies strike a historical precedent in the evil designs that informed the actions of the conceptual engineers who were masterminds of ill-fated Tower of Babel (Genesis 11:1-9). I have often taught that any work without the authority or guardianship of the Holy Spirit is despicable in the sight of God. but this ilk claim to command demonic powers, which is a monumental hoax, as all power originates from the Most High. Therefore, they are shenanigans of ill-gotten power wielded about impetuously for motiveless malignity. Most of these organisations are centred in the Western hemisphere where they flourish due to a preponderance of descendants of unbelieving traditionally Catholic cultures. It also fair to admit that the failure of several Christian denominations over the years have created a spiritual vacuum in Continental Europe, that is being exploited by the better part of these desperate cults.

Brethren, after diviners, witches and wizards, bush-doctors, marabouts, and/or other spiritualists like the traditional herbalists, gurus and their ilk black magic charlatans, including several modern secret societies operating in the West, the next group to worry about as a militant Christian are apostates. The Oxford English Dictionary defines apostasy simply as the desertion of a belief or principle, which makes these knaves worse than common backsliders, who are mostly a confused and demented lot.

Friend, false prophets are essentially manipulators like the notorious American religious leader, Jim Warren Jones who caused havoc in his temples, and was not only an outlaw, a hardened criminal, but a particularly demonic instrument under the employ of the devil, to be transformed into true weapon of mass destruction. You can google that name to acquaint yourself with the atrocities perpetrated by this reprobate clergyman. That is why *the thief*, as applied in John 10:10, must be interpreted to refer to crook who exploits his or her position behind the pulpit in order to surreptitiously tap into the power of God, without readily submitting to His will and purpose. No wonder the Bible finds an excellent congruence between a *thief* and a *witch*, for both are rebelling against the authority of God. The Bible is replete with instances of falsehood perpetrated by men of God. To the extent that any degree of disobedience or transgression against the Word of God should be considered sinful, the act of apostasy must therefore be ascribed to the category of false prophets. Beloved in Christ, faithfulness in God, just like His glory, is in diverse levels or dimensions of consecration and sanctification in the Spirit: ranging from His permissive will, and stretches all the way: culminating in that which is considered absolute perfection:

> *"And be not conformed to this world: but be ye transformed by the renewing of your mind, that ye may prove what is that GOOD, ACCEPTABLE, AND PERFECT, WILL OF GOD"* (Romans 12:2).

Dear chosen one, just as the devil used the word of God to challenge Jesus Christ (Matthew 4:1-11), so do false prophets to all born-again Christians nowadays. They are out and out to tease the devout Christian believer, frustrate their efforts and tarnish their reputation in the sight of God. In fact, they exist for the singular purpose of stealing, killing and carrying out mass destruction in Christian communities. As Saint Peter testifies, many contemporary preachers, who, like Balaam, for selfish reasons, scheme to compromise the truth by carving out portions of the Bible with a view to swindling hard-earned collections from their congregations are like witches, and shall endure the ire of God, sooner or later. In his case, Balaam's divine instruction was twofold: firstly, what to tell the princes of Moab sent by Balak, and secondly, not to go with them:

> *"And God said unto Balaam, Thou shalt not go with them; thou shalt not curse the people: for they are blessed"* (Numbers 22:12).

But when Balak mounted pressure, offering assurances of even greater largesse, Balaam yielded: (*"For I will promote thee unto very great honour, and I will do whatsoever thou sayest unto me: come therefore, I pray thee, curse me this people"* v 17). Therefore, Balaam pleaded God to let him, at least go with the princes of Moab, although he was certainly not going to defy God with regards to the issue of pronouncing a curse against Israel (v 19-21). Thus, Balaam pushed God into granting His permissive will. Eventually, the Most High, having seen that Balaam struggled desperately with his faith in view of the prevailing circumstances, and possibly knowing that he would at last go regardless of the outcome, consented to His servant's pleas, and finally granted Balaam permission to go with the provisos:

1. That the men would come and call him while he was resting that night (v 20).
2. That he would speak the words which Jehovah would command him.

Chapter 2: The Holy Spirit Is the Power of God's Might, and the Might of His Power

Beloved in Christ, the bad news is that Many churches today have been so weak as to succumb to the unyielding urge of apostasy. They have decided to settle for second-best, which is the hallmark of spiritual delirium; like mendicants, coming cap-in-hand before the throne of grace and begging for the permissive will of God, rather than striving to achieve His perfect glory in Christ Jesus (Philippians 4:13-14). They have all gone astray: all have given up on pursuing the course for greater works as prophesied by Jesus Christ in John 14:12, and later fulfilled by the early church in the book of Acts (Acts 5:12-16, 19:11-12). To all intents and purposes, friend, this proclivity does not bode well at all for the prospects of the rapture. The Apostle Peter, in his second letter to the church in Asia, warned against Christians falling prey to false, apostate teachers like Balaam in time to come, which is now:

> *"But chiefly them that walk after the flesh in the lust of uncleanness, and despise government. Presumptuous are they, self-willed, they are not afraid to speak evil of dignities. Whereas angels, which are greater in power and might, bring not railing accusation against them before the Lord. But these, as natural brute beasts, made to be taken and destroyed, speak evil of the things that they understand not; and shall utterly perish in their own corruption; And shall receive the reward of unrighteousness, as thy that count it pleasure to riot in the day time. Spots they are and blemishes, sporting themselves with their own deceivings while they feast with you; Having eyes full of adultery, and that cannot cease from sin; beguiling unstabel souls: an heart they have exercised with covetous practices; cursed children: Which have forsaken the right way, and are going astray, following the way of Balaam the son of Bosor, who loved the wages of unrighteousness; But was rebuked for his iniquity: the dumb ass speaking with man's voice forbad the madness of the prophet. THESE ARE WELLS WITHOUT WATER, CLOUDS THAT ARE CARRIED WITH A TEMPEST; TO WHOM THE MIST OF DARKNESS IS RESERVED FOR EVER. For when they speak great swelling words of vanity, they allure through the lusts of the flesh, through much wantonness, those that were clean escaped from them who live in error. While they promise them liberty, they themselves are the servants of corruption: for of whom a man is overcome, of the same is he brought in bondage. For if after they have escaped the pollutions of the world through the knowledge of the Lord*

and Saviour Jesus Christ, they are again entangled therein, and overcome, the latter end is worse with them than the beginning. For it had been better for them not to have known the way of righteousness, than, after they have known it, to turn from the holy commandment delivered unto them. But it is happened unto them according to the true proverb, The dog is returned to his own vomit again; and the sow that was washed to her wallowing in the mire" (II Peter 2:10-22).

Greatly beloved, the final classes of demonic agents that can cause the devout Spirit-filled believer to lose weight are none other than fornicators and racists. Both are pernicious to the human soul, especially because they occur at a very personal level. Most sins happen outside of our bodies, and are usually perpetrated by extraneous forces other than ourselves, such masterminds as false prophets or some *voudou* priests or spiritual gurus whom we must have hired or fall victim to. Even so, sex-related sins such as adultery, bigamy, prostitution, homosexuality, lesbianism or fornication all take place within us. Sex abuse is also connected to gluttony, sodomy and alcoholism. As you would appreciate, dear reader, these crimes or sins are interrelated. Addictions of any kind are exploited by the devil as conduits for the proliferation of wrongful deeds in humans societies. Adam lost charge of himself once his beautiful wife, Eve, presented him with the appealing fruit. Similarly, the Bible says that from the times Cain, when mankind founded the first civilisation (Genesis 4:16-19), up until the times of Noah (Genesis 8-10), people led a very licentious way of life, to the extent their daughters were seduced by fallen angels. Both Cain and Noah were hedonistic. And in actual fact, once Noah resumed his career of licentiousness, all sense of decency and morality flew through the window, and he was effectively abused by his own very son, the cursed Ham, father of Canaan (Genesis 9:22-23). Brethren, inappropriate sensual behavioural patterns die hard, and without the indwelling of the Spirit, it must have been even harder for these people to escape. Without the Spirit of God in us, all flesh is weak, and subject to the senses. No amount of emotional intelligence can help you out of the grip of the evil spirit behind licentious, sinful proclivities. That is why Joseph, when he became a target of the sexual assaults of Potiphar's wife, had not other option, but to make use of his legs—Joseph ran! But king David was not quite as smart, and he succumbed to the sex appeal of Bathsheba, Uriah's wife (II Samuel 11-12).

Brethren, these sins defile not only our bodies, but also condemn our souls due to the close physical as well as spiritual fusion of the the various members of our separate bodies, caught in the act of abusive sexual intercourse. As a result, the Bible takes no prisoners as concerns spelling out the mortal consequence of our nefarious act:

> *"To deliver thee from the strange woman, even from the stranger which flattereth with her words; Which forsaketh the guide of her youth, and forgetteth the covenant of her God. For her house inclineth unto death, and her paths unto the dead. None that go unto her return again, neither take they hold of the paths of life"* (Proverbs 2:16-19).

Thus, the sins of prostitution are outlines as follows:

First of all, they are branded as flatterers or damned liars. Secondly, they abhor parental guidance which makes them utterly unruly children. Worst still, they deliberately forget God's covenant, which is the first commandment— renounce true religion or marriage vows. As a result their life span is seriously contracted, and they do all in their power to lure others to their doomed estate in hell. They destroy men utterly, and misguide them to their permanent ruin. Friend, this might sound like jazz to you, coming as it does from the Old Testament book of Proverbs. Nevertheless, I stand to testify that in my country, Cameroon, some twenty years ago, stories like these formed part of many private conversations. It was pretty awful.

In the ensuing extract, dear reader, the Bible provides us with at least fifteen reasons to stay clear of the injurious consequences often incurred at brothels. And the warning goes out there to all those men and women who get embroiled in dubious sexual relationships outside their marital homes:

> *"My son, attend unto my wisdom, and bow thine ear to my understanding: That thou mayest regard discretion, and that thy lips may keep knowledge. For the lips of a strange woman drop as an honeycomb, and her mouth is smoother than oil: But her end is bitter as wormwood, sharp as a twoedged sword. Her feet go down to death; her steps take hold on hell. Lest thou*

shouldest ponder the path of life, her ways are moveable, that thou canst not know them. Hear me now therefore, O ye children, and depart not from the words of my mouth. Remove thy way far from her, and come not nigh the door of her house: Lest thou give thine honour unto others, and thy years unto the cruel: Lest strangers be filled with thy wealth; and thy labours be in the house of a stranger; And thou mourn at the last, when thy flesh and thy body are consumed, And say, How have I hated instruction, and my heart despised reproof; And have not obeyed the voice of my teachers, nor inclined mine ear to them that instructed me! I was almost in all evil in the midst of the congregation and assembly. Drink waters out of thine own cistern, and running water out of thine own well. Let thy fountains be dispersed abroad, and rivers of waters in the streets. Let them be only thine own, and not strangers' with thee. Let thy fountain be blessed: and rejoice with the wife of thy youth. Let her be as the loving hind and pleasant roe; let her breasts satisfy thee at all times; and be thou ravished always with her love. And why wilt thou, my son, be ravished with a strange woman, and embrace the bosom of a stranger? For the ways of man are before the eyes of the Lord, and he pondereth all his goings. His own iniquities shall take the wicked himself, and he shall be holden with cords of his sins. He shall die without instruction; and in the greatness of his folly he shall go astray" (Proverbs 5).

Thus, the fifth chapter of the book of Proverbs educates us on the virtues of pursuing a legitimate marital life and raise cheerful children with the pride of being offspring of a legitimate union, instead of bastards. From the outset in verse three, the Bible stigmatises the prostitute as an apostate, meaning she is idolatrous—flirting with unknown gods. Also, she is considered deceptive—showing a complete lack of integrity by telling half truth in order to hoodwink her lover, and lure them into hell fire. Hence, her solace is flattery, blended with lies bent on ingratiating her insatiable carnal appetites. In the next verse, we are plunged into the consequence of dealing with such an unholy relationship—its end is as bitter as *wormwoood,* literally postulating the alternative experience derived in a life style conceived outside the sound, powerful and loving counsel of the Holy Spirit. It is therefore a life style associated with epithets of utter destruction. In verse five we are told that, *her feet go down to death,* which reminds us of the last lines of the second chapter in the book of James: *"For as the*

Chapter 2: The Holy Spirit Is the Power of God's Might, and the Might of His Power 189

body without the spirit is dead, so faith without works is dead also." (James 2:26): meaning—just as surely as the spirit departs from the body at physical death, so faith without works is separated from the Source of all power, which is the Spirit-filled inner man in fusion with the Holy Spirit. Such a person is inexorably bound to hell. Furthermore, we apprised of the standards of a whore—she is predictably unpredictable. And her waywardness is informed by her furtive agenda to eschew or divert sound attention or reflection on her sordid predisposition. In verse nine, it becomes obvious that anybody embroiled in such a complicated sexual partner is bound to bring their whole reputation into complete ruin. As a matter of fact, your yearning for peace and tranquility will be transformed into a misguided foray into the camp of the devil, fool of trouble and sorrow. Moreover, verse ten lets us know that your whole financial standing shall be seriously tempered with by this super-subtle rogue of a woman. Consequently, your mental troubles will affect your health, even as material torture will aggravate into a mental health disorder. She will orchestrate a wickedness that will engender eternal ruin to your existence.

Greatly beloved in Christ if you are being tempted by the any of the spirits behind the following soul-damning sins you had better run. Otherwise, you will be accused of theft or robbery, because:

"Ye are bought with a price; be not ye servants of men" (I Corinthians 7:23). The said sins are outlined by the Apostle Paul as follows:

> *"know ye not that the unrighteous shall not inherit the kingdom of God? Be not deceived: neither fornicators, nor idolaters, nor adulterers, nor effeminate, nor abusers of themselves with mankind, Nor thieves, nor covetous, nor drunkards, nor revilers, nor extortioners, shall inherit the kingdom of God"* (I Corinthians 6:9-10).

Therefore, if you happen to fall prey to any of the above spirits, you have erred, and are badly in need of repentance before it is too late. You see, the price at Calvary of the blood of the Lamb, although revealed in the New Testament—at the Messiah's first advent, had actually been paid by our heavenly Father way back in time, even before the world began:

> "For as much as ye know that ye were not redeemed with corruptible things, as silver and gold, from your vain conversation received by tradition from your fathers; But with the precious blood of Christ, as of a lamb without blemish and without spot: Who verily was foreordained before the foundation of the world, but was made manifest in the last times for you"
> (I Peter 1:18-19).

Thus, the Almighty God did not establish His temple in you, as well as made you a royal priesthood, a peculiar person and a chosen one on the cheap! He paid a huge price for it. That is why it behoves each and every one of us to do his or her utmost to keep it holy and and acceptable unto God, which is our only reasonable service on earth:

> "What? Know ye not that your body is the temple of the Holy Ghost which is in you, which ye have of God, and ye are not your own? For ye are bought with a price: therefore glorify God in your body, and in your spirit, which are God's" (I Corinthians 6:19-20).

> "Know ye not that ye are the temple of God, and that the Spirit of God dwelleth in you? If any man defile the temple of God, him shall God destroy; for the temple of God is holy, which temple ye are" (I Corinthians 3:16-17).

And Paul continues:

> "Meats for the belly, and the belly for meats: but God shall destroy both it and them. Now the body is not for fornication, but for the Lord; and the Lord for the body. And God hath both raised up the Lord, and will also raise up us by his own power. Know ye not that your bodies are members of Christ? shall I then take the members of Christ, and make them members of an harlot? God forbid. What? Know ye not that he which is joined to an harlot is one body? for two, saith he, shall be one flesh. But he that is joined unto the Lord is one spirit. Flee fornication. Every sin that a man doeth is without the body; but he that committeth fornication sinneth against his own body" (I Corinthians 6:13-18).

Chapter 2: The Holy Spirit Is the Power of God's Might, and the Might of His Power

Dear reader, Paul even went further to leverage his argument for abstinence from acts of sexual misdemeanour by quoting from the incident in Numbers 25:1, where obsession with, or indulgence in such sensual excesses as fornication and adultery provoked the wrath of God which fell upon the children of Israel in the wilderness, slaying them in their thousands: 24,000, including the many leaders whose heads were hung up before the Lord, and 23,000 who died in the plague. Saint Paul issues a warning to all Christians *thieves*, who like the Jeshuruns of old, yearn for power in the Lord with wavering faith:

> *"But with many of them God was not pleased: for they were overthrown in the wilderness. Now these things are our examples, to the intent we should not lust after evil things, as they also lusted. Neither be ye idolaters, as were some of them; as it is written, The people sat down to eat and drink, and rose up to play. Neither let us commit fornication, as some of them committed, and fell in one day three and twenty thousand. Neither let us tempt Christ, as some of them, as some of them also tempted, and were destroyed of the destroyer. Now all these things happened unto them for ensamples: and they are written for our admonition, upon whom the ends of the world are come"* (I Corinthians 10:5-11).

Hence, the warning is not only relevant for sinning sinners, but is also vital for sinning saints. God id no respecter of persons. According to Saint Peter, whoever fears Him and worketh righteousness is worthy of Him, and will be reworded bountifully at His appointed time. However, His anger is usually directed at those who:

1. **Murmur**—brethren, murmuring is the same as being anxious. Those who murmur are considered frozen in faith, and are not worthy of His grace. The same are more likely to end up as thieves of the spirit, because they lack the courage to express their concerns before the throne of grace, and reason with the Lord on righteous terms (Exodus 17:2).

2. **Unbelief** (Exodus 17:7). This is a typical characteristic of real and potential thieves. Many preachers are found wanting in the area of

financial propriety and moral rectitude due to an inadequate expanse of faith. The Bible says, without faith it is impossible to please God (Hebrews 11:6), and unbelievers should therefore find themselves in a position, impossible for them to seek His help, even through prayers (Hebrews 4:1-11).

3. **Rebellion** is one of those sins that are in Scripture, often likened to theft (Numbers 14:22; 21:1-9). Particularly, the Prophet Samuel rightly compared Saul's rebellious act against Jehovah to witchcraft. And, brethren, all witches and wizard are common spiritual thieves, for they claim to do what they cannot afford—they are charlatans.

4. **Provoking God** (Psalm 78:17-18, 56). This is a satanic spirit that derives from our earthly, sensual, and devilish proclivities (James 3). Taking delight in human wisdom, or philosophy while misleading many into bondage—brethren, you can only give what you have, but false teachers keep promising what they themselves do not possess. Hence, they steal by amassing platitudes that only add to their licentious and lustful predilection, which is anathema to God:

"For when they speak great swelling words of vanity, they allure through the lusts of the flesh, through much wantonness, those that were clean escaped from them who live in error. While they promise them liberty, they themselves are the servants of corruption; for of whom a man is overcome, of the same is he brought in bondage" (II Peter 2:18-19).

Many false prophets, in the tradition of Balaam, son of Bosor, claim to know bettter, and are in a better position to address earthly concerns, as well as having what it takes to appreciate life's pleasures better than the Holy Spirit, sent by God to assist us in our earthly journey. Therefore, only the meek and the righteous saints in Christ will inherit it (Isaiah 40:17-31).

5. **Backsliding/apostasy** is the destination of all who are embroiled in the nasty chores of false prophetic dealing, and are caught in the act,

in spiritual soul-condemnation, like lost violent souls in the devil's demonic inferno. According to Apostle Peter, apostates have gone past any signpost of hope or salvation, on the fairway to perdition:

"For if after they have escaped the pollutions of the world through the knowledge of the Lord and Saviour Jesus Christ, they are again entangled therein, and overcome, the latter end is worse with them than the beginning. For it had been better for them not to know the way of righteousness, than, after they have known it, to turn from the holy commandment delivered unto them. But it is happened unto them according to the true proverb, The dog is turned to his own vomit again; and the sow that was washed to her wallowing in the mire" (II Peter 2:20-22).

6. **Hardening of the heart** (Psalm 95:8-99. Brethren, our hearts are hardened over the years, from serfdom in the kingdom of darkness: even as we were being led by the spirit of oppression and fear. We departed in all our ways from illusions self delusion, and from vainglory to self-deception. Repentance and Holy Spirit cleansing is what we need to render ourselves valuable servants of the Most High. Enter Jesus:

"No man putteth a piece of new cloth unto an old garment, for that which is put in to fill it up taketh from the garment, and the rent is made worse. Neither do men put new wine into old bottles: else the bottles break, and the wine runneth out, and the bottles perish: but they put new wine into new bottles, and both are preserved" (Matthew 9:16-17).

Friend, old habits die hard. In other words, any fundamental effort towards change must be executed from within. This is because of our dual status of existence: as we are both spiritual and physical beings. Ordinarily, also, you cannot find any farmer who goes to plant fresh seeds in due season, and expecting a rich harvest without having ploughed the earth on which the planting is to be done. Psalm 23 tells us:

"The Lord is my shepherd I shall not want.
He maketh me to lie down in green pastures..." (Psalm 23:1-2)

Here king David is evoking all the harshness and hard work involved, undertaken by Jehovah in ploughing the arid physical landscape of Palestine in order to transform them, and render them arable enough, fit for producing quality pasture for grazers. This is the work of the Holy Spirit, who has come to convict our souls of sin, so we achieve redemption through repentance in Christ. The heart is the temple of the Holy Spirit, and must be kept with all diligence. Thus, our Lord Jesus Christ was revealing the deep secrets, padlocked in the mysteries of the Gospel to the children of Israel. Friend, just as old wine skins were unfit for liquids, especially for wine to ferment in, because the violence of the fermentation would burst them, so are our old, derelict heart of spiritual and faithful wantonness. We need a revival Spirit. The Lord provides us with the Spirit of re-awakening like we have never had before. The Apostle Paul makes it abundantly clear that we have been given a Spirit of power, love and of a sound mind. That is why King Saul and Lydia were given a new heart, at the commencement of their ministration, to suit their new status and function, as servants of the true God. Also, the Bible declares: *"He that believeth on me, as the scripture hath said, out of his belly shall flow rivers of living water."* (John 7:38). Therefore, old wine skins to hold wine must be soaked in water to soften them. Then they must be greased with oil to prevent licking or evaporation. Similarly, for anybody to aspire to attain the kingdom of God, they must be born again with water and with the Spirit. Brethren, for us, the oil and the water represent the Holy Spirit baptism and anointing. You can neither understand, nor retain the contents of the Gospel without the agency of the Holy Ghost in you. Back then, men only put newly made wine in renewed wine skins and both are preserved. Thus, the image of heart hardening means we are in dire need of a complete renewal (Matthew 9:10-13; II Corinthians 5:17-18; Ephesians 4:23-24; Colossians 3:10; Romans 12:2). Brethren, the old covenant and the new cannot co-exist. Similarity is not sameness. What is letter is letter, and what is spirit is spirit. The Bible says, the letter killeth,whereas the spirit giveth life, hence the difference: life and death are not the same. Therefore, any attempt to patch the old with the new would only make things worse. Ishmael and Isaac can never live together. In the same wavelength, old Jewish customs of law keeping, as well as the traditional rites and rituals of old Gentile cultures can never live side by side with true Christianity (Matthew 26:28; Romans 3:24; 5:9; Ephesians 1:7; 2:13; Hebrews 9:14;

Chapter 2: The Holy Spirit Is the Power of God's Might, and the Might of His Power 195

10:1-19; I John 1:7; Revelation 1:5; I Peter 1:18-20). Worse still, to combine both would lead to chaos and utter destruction. The old covenant must give way for the new, but the new cannot be made part of the old because of the new life and freedom impossible with the old (Acts 15:24; Galatians 3:10-15; 5:1; Hebrews 7:11-10:18). The sinner is not outwardly reformed, neither are the old law-abiding Jewish customs, as well as the other traditional Gentile customs merely given a new dress or container by Christianity. Both are new things. The sinner (container) has been transformed into a new creature and Christianity (the new wine) is a new religion altogether (Colossians 2:14-17). Finally, it is fair to postulate from the point of view of the Spirit of God, right here, that anyone who schemes to mix them up is a thief. The thief will then proceed to deliver you to the devil, who is no other than the wolf:

> *"But he that is an hireling, and not the shepherd, whose own the sheep are not, seeth the wolf coming, and leaveth the sheep, and fleeth: and the wolf catcheth them, and scattereth the sheep. The hireling fleeth, because he is an hireling, and careth not for the sheep"* (John 10:12-13).

Another area of the Gospel that has generated much controversy lately happens to be passage in the book of the Prophet Malachi that explicitly talks about church workers robbing God. Even as I write, many churches out there have throwing this divine indictmen at members of the congregation who are routinely being accused of robbing God because they categorically refuse to christen their donation or offering as *tithes!* Brethren, this is a major apostolic fallacy that has plagued the church for generations unend. Thankfully, the Lord has imbued me with the anointing set things right and restitute the heaven state of divine truth with regards to the mystery behind these verses:

> *"Will a man rob God? Yet ye have robbed me. But ye say, Wherein have we robbed thee? In the tithes and offerings. Ye are cursed with a curse: for ye have robbed me, even this whole nation. Bring ye all the tithes into the storehouse, that there may be meat in mine house, and prove me now herewith, saith the Lord of hosts, if I will not open you the windows of heaven, and pour you out a blessing, that there shall not be room enough to receive it. And I will rebuke the devourer for your sakes, and he shall not destroy the*

fruits of your ground; neither shall your vine cast her fruit before the time in the field, saith the Lord of hosts. And all nations shall call you blessed: for ye shall be a delightsome land, saith the Lord of hosts" (Malachi 3:8-12).

Dear reader, first of all I would like to spell it out clearly that I do not intend to focus, at this juncture, entirely on the issue of offering and thanksgiving in the New Testament. My aim is to deflate the false assumptions or doctrines that are being preached by many a false prophet in many church to the indignation of my Lord Jesus Christ many of His sheep who are crying out for justice to hold sway, for justice delayed is justice denied.

Without much ado, peerhaps it would be sensible to commence with the tithe palaver. Suffices to state right here, that if there are any born-again Christians out there who are still buttressing their hope on the premise of tithing—saving 10% of your proceeds to God, then you are living in the distant past. In fact, it is amazing how bad habits die hard! Imagine that the very laws which our forefathers were unable to keep for donkey years; for innumerable generations, blessed with so many perceptive or visual evidence in terms of miracles, yet the Bible says, *"All we like sheep have gone astray; we have turned every one to his own way; and the Lord hath laid on him the iniquity of us all"* (Isaiah 53:6). So, wait a minute, brethren, are these tithe-payers or law-keepers insinuating that they are once again, after the ultimate sacrifice on the cross at Calvary of our Lord and Saviour Jesus Christ, that they are qualified and prepared turn on its head this might offering from God? God forbid:

"Behold, the days come, saith the Lord, that I will make a new covenant with the house of Israel, and with the house of Judah: Not according to the covenant that I made with their fathers in the day that I took them by the hand to bring them out of the land of Egypt; which my covenant they brake, although I was an husband unto them, saith the Lord: But this shall be the covenant that I will make with the house of Israel; After those days, saith the Lord, I will put my law in their inward parts, and write it in their hearts; and will be their God, and they shall be my people. And they shall teach no more every man his neighbour, and every man his brother, saying, Know

> *the Lord: for they shall all know me, from the least of them, saith the Lord: for I will forgive their iniquity, and I will remember their sins no more"* (Jeremiah 31:31-34).

Thus, if our forefathers (the houses of Israel and Judah) were not able to keep the laws of Moses without Jesus Christ, it is unlikely that your flirting with it once again shall yield any dividend whatsoever. No wonder the Apostle Paul warns the Galatians to:

> *"Stand fast therefore in the liberty wherewith Christ hath made us free, and be not not entangled again with the yoke of bondage"* (Galatians 5:1).

Beloved in Christ, Paul's wartime command to the saints is to the effect of: Stand fast in the faith (Philippians 1:27; 4:1; I Thessalonians 3:8; II Thessalonians 2:15). Keep rank. Do not be disorderly or reatreat. Keep unity of mind, soul and spirit. Let nothing divide you so that Satan—the wolf can devour you raw. Yet, a people who have been so blessed with the anointing of Jesus Christ (John 3:34; Ephesians 1:3; 2:4-7,10), are headed backwards to a redundant unction of obsolescence aspect. In his second letter to the Corinthians, the Apostle paul attempts a comparison of the times before and that after the first coming of Christ:

> *"Who also hath made us able ministers of the new testament; not of the letter, but the spirit: for the letter killeth, but the spirit giveth life. But if the ministration of death, written and engraved in stones, was glorious, so that the children of Israel could not stedfastly behold the face of Moses for the glory of his countenance; which glory was to be done away: How shall not the ministration of the spirit be rather glorious? For if the ministration of condemnation be glory, much more doth the ministration of righteousness exceed in glory. For even that which was made glorious had no glory in this respect, by reason of the glory that excelleth. For if that which is done away was glorious, much more that which remaineth is glorious"* (II Corinthians 3:11).

A Scriptural parallel of this would be those Jews of old, who having seen all the miracles of Jesus Christ, still persisted in following John the Baptist, despite the Prophet's advice to the contrary. In John 19:30, the Messiah declared: *"It is finished!"* Yet we keep enslaving ourselves with the primitive laws of Moses (Colossians 2:14-17; Psalm 40:6-10).

This is what the Bible tells us about the Messiah's first coming, regarding offerings:

1. Because the New Covenant sacrifices brought eternal redemption (Hebrews 7:27; 9:15; 10:10-23):

   "But Christ being come an high priest of good things to come, by a greater and more perfect tabernacle, not made with hands, that is to say, not of this building; Neither by the blood of goats and calves, but by his own blood he entered in once into the holy place, having obtained eternal redemption for us" (Hebrews 9:11-12).

2. Because the Old Covenant sacrifices could not remit one sin (Hebrews 10:4), but the blood of Christ does (Matthew 26:28; Romans 3:25; 5:9; Ephesians 1:7; 2:13; Hebrews 10:19; I John 1:7; I Peter 1:18; Revelation 1:5; 59):

   "For if the blood of bulls and goats, and the ashes of an heifer sprinkling the unclean, sanctifieth to the purifying of the flesh: How much more shall the blood of Christ, who through the eternal Spirit offered himself without spot to God, purge your conscience from dead works to serve the living God? And for this cause he is the mediator of the new testament, that by means of death, for the redemption of the transgressions that were under the first testament, they which are called might receive the promise of eternal inheritance" (Hebrews 9:13-15).

3. Because the death of Christ was necessary to make the New Covenant (Matthew 26:28; I Peter 2:24):

   "For where a testament is, there must also of necessity be the death of the testator. For a testament is of force after men are dead: otherwise it is of no strength at all while the testator liveth" (Hebrews 9:16-17).

4. Because the Old Covenant was only a shadow of the realities of the New Covenant (Colossians 2:14-17):
"For the law having a shadow of good things to come, and not the very image of the things, can never with those sacrifices which they offered year by year continually make the comers thereunto perfect. For then would they not have ceased to be offered? because that the worshippers once purged should have no more conscience of sins. But in those sacrifices there is a remebrance again made of sins every year. For it is not possible that the blood of bulls and of goats should take away sins" (Hebrews 10:1-4).

5. Because Christ abolished the Old Covenant (Galatians 4:21):
"Wherefore when he cometh into the world, he saith, Sacrifice and offering thou wouldest not, but a body hast thou prepared me: In burnt offerings and sacrifices for sin thou hast had no pleasure. Then said I, Lo, I come (in the volume of the book it is written of me,) to do thy will, O God. Above when he said, Sacrifices and offering and burnt offerings and offering for sin thou wouldest not, neither hadst pleasure therein; which are offered by the law; Then said he, Lo, I come to thy will, O God. He taketh away the first, that he may establish the second" (Hebrews 10:5-9).

6. Because the Old Covenant sacrifices were powerless but the New Covenant one is eternally efficacious (Colossians 2:14-17; I Peter 2:24):
"By the which will we are sanctified through the offering of the body of Jesus Christ once and for all. And every priest standeth daily ministering and offering oftentimes the same sacrifices, which can never take away sins: But this man, after he had offered one sacrifice for sins for ever, sat down on the right hand of God; From henceforth expecting till his enemies be made his footstool. For by one offering he hath perfected for ever them that are sanctified. Whereof the Holy Ghost also is a witness to us: for after that he had said, This is the covenant that I will make with them after those days, saith the Lord, I will put my laws into their hearts, and in their minds will I write them; And their sins and iniquities will I remember no more. Now where remission of these is, there is no more offering for sin" (Hebrews 10:10-18).

7. Because every believer is a priest and is exhorted to enter the holiest and enjoy his full rights in Christ (Hebrews 4:14-16; Ephesians 1:3, 14; 2:14-22):

"Having therefore, brethren, boldness to enter into the holiest by the blood of Jesus, By a new and living way, which he hath consecrated for us, through the veil, that is to say, his flesh; And having an high priest over the house of God; Let us draw near with true heart in full assurance of faith, having our hearts sprinkled from an evil conscience, and our bodies washed with pure water. Let us hold fast the profession without wavering; (for he is faithful that promised;)" (Hebrews 10:19-23).

Ergo, we are no longer in the dispensation of the flesh or letter which killeth. Christ died for us, not in vein but for a sublime purpose! His death ushered in a completely different perception of godliness and apostolic resplendence far from the opaque, repellent and/or mortar and brick fiat that constituted the Mosaic divine volumes. Brethren, we have been shown love beyond measure (John 3:16; 15:9-14; 16:12-15); we have been given power beyond measure (Matthew 18:18; Luke 10:19; Luke 24:49; Matthew 10:7-8; Mark 16:17-18; Acts 1:4-8; John 14:12; John 1:12): Brethren, this show of love is unprecedented, and the demonstration of power has no parallel in Scripture, how then can we justify our perseverance with the derelict Mosaic ordinances?

Precious one of God, the New Testament is not the same as the Old Testament. In other words, the Old Testament is revealed in the Old Testament. Furthermore, the Bible holds that Christ is the end of the law unto righteousness. Brethren, as ministers in the vineyard, we walk in faith, *"Casting down imaginations, and every high thing that exalteth itself against the knowledge of God, and bringing into captivity every thought to the obedience of Christ."* (II Corinthians 10:5). Consequently, we conclude that the meat that was collected from the congregation in the Old Testament, and that was used to support the priesthood in those days was overthrown by Jesus Christ, who inaugurated the individual church: with a royal priesthood, from a chosen generation and all for the benefit of a peculiar people. Not only was Jesus of Nazareth not drawn from the traditional Levites blood line, but He was also ordained in heaven, and prophesied on earth (Psalm 110:4; Hebrews 5:6; 6:20). Brethren, the individual church (where our bodies have all

Chapter 2: The Holy Spirit Is the Power of God's Might, and the Might of His Power 201

been spiritually transformed into becoming living temples of God: I Corinthians 3:16-17; 6:13-20; Romans 8:1-13; 12:1-2; II Corinthians 7:1; Galatians 5:24) is a divine modification of the Mosaic tabernacles that were ostensibly hand-made. Solomon's temple that was destroyed due to transgression was basically a human construct. With the coming of the Messiah, the power of attorney inherent in the name of Jesus was invested in humans, tranfering authority, responsibility and power onto all of us who are divinely called to carry out the work of God in Christ Jesus (John 15:15-17; Mark 16:15-18; Matthew 28:18-20; 1:4-8; Luke 24:46-49).

In the dispensation of the Spirit, the aforementioned events have overtaken the purpose for which the tithes (10%) of Christian earnings or substance collected to support a group of church workers anointed to carry out the work of God. The supreme purpose for this development has to do with the fact that the heaven's gate to priesthood has been opened and made accessible to all interested parties (Matthew 7:7-11; 11:12-13). Jesus has therefore demystified priesthood:

> *"Blotting out the handwriting of ordinances that was against us, which was contrary to us, and took it out of the way, nailing it to his cross; And having spoiled principalities and powers, he made a show of them openly triumphing over them in it. Let no man therefore judge you in meat, or in drink, or in respect of an holyday, or of the new moon, or of the sabbath days: Which are a shaddow of things to come; but the body is of Christ"*
> (Colossians 2:14-17).

Brethren, this was the death knell of the culture of formalised giving or carnal offering in churches, and the Messiah Himself epitomised this spiritual overthrow by operating tithless ministry. He issued a caveat as He rebuked the motive of the mixed multitude:

> *"Jesus answered them and said, Verily, verily, I say unto you, Ye seek me, not because ye saw the miracles, but because ye did eat of the loaves, and were filled. Labour not for the meat which perisheth, but for the meat which endureth unto everlasting life, which the Son of man shall give unto you: for him hath God the Father sealed"* (John 6:26-27).

Herein lies the mystery in the *meat!* Brethren, herein lies the revelation of God! Herein lies the power in the Gospel of Jesus Christ! There the verse in Malachi: *"Bring ye all the tithes into the storehouse, that there may be meat in mine house"* (Malachi 3:10), is about the communion of saints unto the edification of the body of Christ! The meat to pursue here is what lies in us, through Christ: confirmed by giving Him the Holy Spirit without measure (John 3:33-34). Brethren, with Christ in us, on us, for us, with us, and as us, we are anointed as flames of fire or royal priests to do greater works, which by implication is also a huge burden! We therefore bear the responsibility, both individually as well as collectively, to deliver the goods and to keep blazing the messianic trail (Ephesians 2:10; Romans 8:28-33).

The Apostle Paul firmly captured the vision of this dispensation when he writes:

> *"For the kingdom of God is not meat and drink; but righteousness, and peace, and joy in the Holy Ghost. For he that in these things serveth Christ is acceptable to God, and approved of men. Let us therefore follow after the things which make for peace, and things wherewith one may edify another"* (Romans 14:17-19).

Thus, for all the fuss, even frenzied bargaining going on in churches over prescribed or mercantile donations, as if in a bazaar or fairground, the Bible holds that the kingdom of God is not about all those substances such as meat, drink, and/or residue of carnal religion. He lists three things: Righteousness (Romans 3:21-31; 4:1-25; 8:4). Peace (Romans 2:10; 5:1; 8:6; 10:15); and Joy (5:11; Galatians 5:22; I Peter 1:8). According to Paul, anybody who possess these three qualities also commands three other blessings in the Holy Ghost: He is a true servant of Christ (Romans 14:18). He is also acceptable with God (Romans 14:18). He is approved of men (Romans 14:18). In order to have all of the above, we must follow whatever brings them about. All bickering over *meats* (obsession with material things), drinks sabbaths, and doubtful things which only serve to destroy the soul must be stopped, and that which edifies the others must be taught (Romans 14:19). Accordingly, he teaches that it is better to deny self to personal pleasures than to cause brethren to apostatise (Romans 14:21; Matthew 18:6-10; I Corinthians 8:7-13;

10:23-31). Alas, in churches across the globe, there is hardly any virtue that is more needed that the selflessness regarding the equitable dispensation of church income.

> "And I will rebuke the devourer for your sakes, and he shall not destroy the fruits of your ground; neither shall your vine cast her fruit before the time in the field, saith the Lord of hosts" (Malachi 3:11).

Beloved in Christ, the devourer in the above verse is none else but the devil and his agents who operate in darkness to usurp our inheritance. Like all who are familiar with details of the Scripture, the devils knows what we possess in Christ Jesus (Ephesians 2:10; Genesis 3:15; I John 3:5-10). The incarnation of the Word, Jesus explained this supernatural phenomenon with attention to detail after having narrated them to His disciples through parables (Matthew 13). Most notably, the parable of the sower tells of what became of the various categories of seeds that fell on the different surfaces on the face of a cursed earth. Brethren, the Bible tells us that the Word became flesh and lived amongst men (John 1:12-14), that through faith in Him we may gain our divine inheritance. Brethren, in the New Testament, all Scripture must be made subject to the power of this great inhetitance of ours (Isaiah 9:6-7). Thus, the Lord our God plants the Seed in us which is made manifest through the Holy Ghost of truth, and birthed through our faith in Christ Jesus:

> "I am the true vine, and my Father is the husband man " (John 15:1).

> "Abide in me, and I in you. As the branch cannot bear fruit, except it abide in the vine; no more can ye, except ye abide in me. I an the vine, ye are the branches: He that abideth in me, and I in him, the same bringeth forth much fruit: for without me ye can do nothing. If a man abide not in me, he is cast forth as a branch, and is withered; and men gather them, and cast them into the fire, and they are burned. If ye abide in me, and my words abide in you, ye shall ask what ye will, and it shall be done unto you. Herein is my Father glorified, that ye bear much fruit; so shall ye be my disciples" (John 15:4-8).

> "Ye have not chosen me, but I have chosen you, and ordained you, that ye should go and bring forth fruit, and that your fruit should remain: that whatsoever ye shall ask of the Father in my name, he may give it you. These things I command you, that ye love one another" (John 15:16-17).

The Bible also gives a vivid description of the fruit of the Spirit:
> "But the fruit of the Spirit is love, joy, peace, longsuffering, gentleness, goodness, faith, Meekness, temperance: against such there is no law."

Hence the very substance of godliness. Beloved in Christ, the fruit of the Spirit which derives from agape love, is shared abroad in our hearts through the Holy Spirit that is given onto us (Romans 5:5; I Corinthians 12-13). No wonder Jesus went on to illustrate in this uncanny love in the Gospel. Brethren, I hereby provide the verses for your perusal:

> "Therefore I say unto you, Take no thought for your life, what ye shall eat, or what ye shall drink; nor yet for your body, what ye shall put on. Is not the life more than meat, and the body than raiment? Behold the fowls of the air; for they sow not, neither do they reap, nor gather into barns; yet your heavenly Father feedeth them. Are ye not much better than they? Which of you by taking thought can add one cubit unto his stature? And why take ye thought for raiment? Consider the lilies of the field, how they grow, they toil not, neither do they spin: And yet I say unto you, That even Solomon in all his glory was not arrayed like one of these. Wherefore, if God so clothed the grass of the field, which today is, and to morrow is cast into the oven, shall he not much more clothe you, O ye of little faith? Therefore take no thought, saying, What shall we eat? or What shall we drink? (For after all these things do the Gentiles seek:) for your heavenly Father knoweth that ye have need of all these things. But seek ye first the kingdom of God, and his righteousness; and all these things shall be added unto you" (Matthew 6:25-33).

That is why we are exhorted by the Messiah to emulate the love and compassion of the heavenly Father, by eschewing worry while embracing continued worship, prayer and supplication in the love of God, as well as for one another through the unrestrained Holy Spirit anointing on us:

> *"As the Father hath loved me, so have I loved you: continue ye in my love. If ye keep my commandments, ye shall abide in my love; even as I have kept my Father's commandments, and abide in his love. These things have I spoken unto you, that my joy might remain in you, and that your joy might be full. This is my commandment, That ye love one another, as I have loved you. Greater love hath no man that this, that a man lay down his life for his friends. Ye are my friends, if ye do whatsoever I command you"* (John 15:9-14).

Brethren, as the disciples of the first century such as Simon Peter were transformed from being mere fishermen into becoming fishers of souls for Christ, so have we been restored and promoted upwards from our erstwhile vile or lowly estate, as local farmers and harvesters of earthly fruit, into the honourable position of managers in the spiritual real of the Most High, in the garden of Eden (Genesis 2:15-17; Isaiah 61:4-11):

> *"Say not ye, There are yet four months, and then cometh harvest? behold, I say unto you, Lift up your eyes, and look on the fields; for they are white already to harvest. And he that reapeth receiveth wages, and gathereth fruit unto life eternal: that both he that soweth and he that reapeth may rjoice together. And herein is the saying true, One soweth, and another reapeth. I sent you to reap that whereon ye bestow no labour: other men laboured, and ye are entered into their labour"* (John 4:35-38).

Thus, the disciples, just like us will have to benefit from the work of those who commenced well in advance of our labour: The coming of Christ, for example, had been preached and prayed by the prophets long before the advent of messianic discipleship in Israel. In fact, John had already begun the dispensation of the Spirit before Christ came into the scene in person. Also, before the disciples, Jesus and John had preached, baptised and healed so many well before the disciples were asigned to undertake their first apostolic mission (Matthew 10; Luke 9; 10; John 4:2). For example, Christ had sown the seed in the Samaritan woman already, and received wages of gratification of saving souls. He had sown and gathered fruit unto life eternal that very day, hence, the sower and the reaper, who in this case (John 4) were one and the same person, rejoiced over the harvest of that day (I Corinthians 3:6-9).

Therefore, like His disciples, Christ has sent us out to reap benefits of the labours, and to carry on the work of the prophets and others before them, including Himself, the Holy Spirit, and the Prophet John the Baptist. This is the fruit talked about in the book of Malachi, not money or other material emolument to buy favours from the pastors.

To round up this section of spiritual theft, it would be fair to state that all spiritualist media must be discarded by Christians (I Corinthians 12:3; I John 4:1-3). They are like false prophets who are also evil seducers, claiming to reveal hidden secrets through the sanctified medium with God and the invisible world, whereas their prime concern is to make sure people are turned away from Him, and commandeered into perdition. Hence, the curse lashes out at anyone who, either consciously or by default, elects to preach the Gospel by stubbornly relying on his own carnal wisdom or worldly philosophy, thereby failing to bring out the full range of meaning from the coded verses—Christ in us, with us, for us, through us and as us; anyone eligible for divine calling, but is still resisting overtures to listen to, and be led by the Holy Spirit; or for that matter, turning down requests from Jesus and His servants, to hear the Gospel or acknowledge Jesus Christ of Nazareth as Lord and Saviour, falls within this despicable bracket

How To Triumph Through The Spirit of God

> *"The fear of the Lord is the beginning of knowledge: but fools despise wisdom and instruction"* (Proverbs 1:7).

Brethren, Jesus as man, was equipped with the seven spirits of God as follows:

> *"And the spirit of the Lord shall rest upon him, the spirit of wisdom and understanding, the spirit of counsel and might, the spirit of knowledge and of the fear of the Lord"* (Isaiah 11:2).

Jesus' profile, as enunciated through the revelation penned by the Apostle Paul in Scripture represents, succinctly, the heavenly ordained posture for our spiritual warfare:

Chapter 2: The Holy Spirit Is the Power of God's Might, and the Might of His Power

> "*10 Finally, my brethren, be strong in the Lord, and in the power of his might. 11 Put on the whole armour of God, that ye may be able to stand against the wiles of the devil. 12 For we wrestle not against flesh and blood, but against principalities, against powers, against the rulers of the darkness of this world, against spiritual wickedness in high places. 13 Wherefore take unto you the whole armour of God, that ye may be able to withstand in the evil day, and having done all to stand. 14 Stand therefore, having your loins girt about with truth, and having on the breastplate of righteousness; 15 And your feet shod with the preparation of the gospel of peace; 16 Above all, taking the shield of faith, wherewith ye shall be able to quench all the fiery darts of the wicked. 17 And take the helmet of salvation, and the sword of the Spirit, which is the word of God: Praying always with all prayer and supplication in the Spirit, and watching thereunto with all perseverance and supplication for all saints*" (Ephesians 6:10-17).

Accordingly brethren, the Apostle Paul developed his thesis in three varying dimensions of meaning. At the outset—from v. 10, he sets out to proffer the great power behind those Christians who truly have faith in Christ. He hereby recalls the psalmist's rhyme: "*He that dwelleth in the secret place of the most High shall abide under the shadow of the Almighty*"-Meaning, in this spiritual warfare, the Holy Spirit is the Power of God's Might, as well as the Might of His Power. He is the God of God. Thereafter, precisely, from v. 11-12, Paul went on to uncover the believers' enemies in the spiritual realm. And finally, from v. 13-17, the reader is brought up to speed on the weapons Jesus has put at the disposal of the believer. The superpower status of Jesus' anointing means that all His followers are duly equipped with enough firepower to overcome their enemies, as opposed to the Old Testament heroes who were usually anointed to address specific tasks, particularly meant to serve the purpose of the state of Israel. However, with Christ's anointing, the Spirit moves in extraordinary dimensions to enable the believer stand against all the enemies (v. 11-14); withstand all attacks (v. 13); and quench every satanic fiery dart (v. 16). But they will have to put up with twelve prophetic commands to make these happen. First of all, they will have to be strong in the Lord, which means in the power of His Might—Holy Ghost fire! There should be no wavering, doubt or fear (v 10). Jesus was anointed with the Holy Ghost and with power (v. 10; Acts 10:38). Thirdly, they have to put on the complete package, dwelling under the shadow of the Almighty—the whole armour of God (v. 11). Having done that they should be able to stand firm against any fiendish threats from the enemy (v. 13-14). Further, they must have their loins girt with truth. This is because the Holy Ghost only responds to the truth of the Gospel of Jesus Christ (v. 14). They are also required to put on the breastplate of righteousness. That is to say, their hearts have to encompass man-made greatness, they have to countenance all the virtues of the kingdom—put on the breastplate of righteousness (v. 14)—*"But seek ye first the kingdom of God and its righteousness and all other things shall be added unto you"* (Matthew 6:33). Moreover, believers must *ask, seek and knock* from within, not without (Matthew 7:7)! Christians must avoid keeping company with unbelievers. They must not be unduly yoked with unbelievers or apostates—But rather strive to have their feet shod with the preparation of the Gospel of peace (v. 15), which denotes the standard which is recognised and defended by the Holy Spirit (Psalm 1:1; Isaiah 59:19). In addition, The Apostle Paul recommends the shield of faith, which symbolises the strength and working of our faith in Christ (Hebrews 11:6; I John 5:4-5), which is what has overcome the world, and granted the believer access to His grace and peace in heavenly places, where they can afford to hope for His glory through our Lord Jesus Christ. Also, taking the helmet of salvation, (v 17) to protect their minds from unholy impressions or getting pretty much indulged in things mundane, which has the potential to undermine the prospect of setting their minds on things above, where Christ is seated at the right hand of God (Colossians 3:1-3). And they should be bold to take up the sword of the Spirit (v 17), which is the word of God to which the Spirit of God responds (John 1:1; Psalm 129-130; Matthew 4:4-11). Finally, all militant believers are recommended to cultivate the habit of prayer and endurance in the Spirit, being watchful of signs and wonders from the God that made the heaven and the earth. All in all, suffices to say it is impossible to achieve all this without the Holy Spirit (John 3:5). Spiritual warfare is the singular domain and/or prerogative of the Spirit of God: for the battle is not ours, but God's.

Chapter 2: The Holy Spirit Is the Power of God's Might, and the Might of His Power

The Holy Spirit is the Ultimate Encoder And Decoder of Divine Wisdom

Thus, when the Lord God laments, as He does in Hosea 4:6, saying my people perish for lack of knowledge many are those who quickly jump to the conclusion, and even start thinking that the Most High is alluding to human cognitive values, but there is nothing further away from the truth, as God's ways are higher than man's and His thoughts are higher than man's (Isaiah 55:8-9). If king David who was also a prophet of God, says *"The Lord is my shepherd..."* it is because of the sum total of the testimonies of divine interventions in his life, especially vivid memories of his experiences, when he used to toil in the wilderness as a shepherd boy. The Bible says, those who do business in great waters, they see the glory of God (see God's work of deliverance: The mariners' song—Psalm 107:19-30). Friend, Christ is therefore the wisdom of God according to the Scriptures: *"He shall see of the travail of his soul, and shall be satisfied: by his knowledge shall my righteous servant justify many; for he shall bear their iniquities"* (Isaiah 53:11).

Oh, chosen one of God, I am here to let you know, your heavenly Father's knowledge is unsearchable, and His understanding is beyond human comprehension. No human being can manipulate God into acting awkwardly, or influencing His judgment, either for or against you. The nurturing and sustenance of your relationship with Jesus Christ, is the exclusive preserve of the Holy Spirit. Those kings and prophets in Old Testament times who tried in their own power, using human knowledge, to do the works of God without His Spirit's consent all failed. We know of Moses, for example, who was so impatient with his mission to save his people—the children of Israel from the fangs of slavery in Egypt that he had to commit murder, and was forced to flee. In the same vein, when Joseph's brothers tried to put an end to his dreams, by implementing their wicked plans against him, the whole move was counterproductive. In fact, they invariably helped to precipitate its final outcome. The Bible also states that if only the judges and executioners of the Messiah had caught the vision, they would not have proceeded with their devilish designs to persecute the Prince of Peace, which action actually became crucial for the fulfilment of the prophecy (Colossians 2:14-15). But those who are humble and patient to wait for their God and seek the face of

His Counsellor, who is the Holy Spirit, will always be successful in life, and their actions will forever be counted as valuable and significant by everybody in every age, place and time:

> *"Why sayest thou, O Jacob, and speakest, O Israel, My way is hid from the Lord, and my judgment is passed over from my God? Hast thou not known? hast thou not heard, that the everlasting God, the Lord, the Creator of the ends of the earth, fainteth not, neither is weary? there is no searching of his understanding. He giveth power to the faint; and to them that have no might he increaseth strength. Even the youths shall faint and be weary, and the young men shall utterly fall: But they that wait upon the Lord shall renew their strength; they shall mount up with wings as eagles; they shall run, and not be weary; and they shall walk, and not faint"* (Isaiah 40:27-31).

This knowledge, wisdom and understanding is passed onto us through the agency of the Holy Spirit, by His grace, should we have faith in Christ, as Apostle Paul explains to the Ephesians:

> *"Blessed be the Lord God and Father of our Lord Jesus Christ, who hath blessed us with all spiritual blessings in heavenly places in Christ: According as he hath chosen us in him before the foundation of the world, that we should be holy and without blame before him in love: Having predestined us unto the adoption of children by Jesus Christ to himself, according to the good pleasure of his will, To the praise of the glory of his grace, wherein he hath made us accepted in the beloved. In whom we have redemption through his blood, the forgiveness of sins, according to the riches of his grace; Wherein he hath abounded toward us in all wisdom and prudence; Having made known unto us the mystery of his will, according to his good pleasure which he hath purposed in himself: That in the dispensation of the fulness of times he might gather together in one all things in Christ, both which are in heaven , and which are on earth; even in him: In whom also we have obtained an inheritance, being predestinated according to the purpose of him who worketh all things after the counsel of his own will: that we should be to the praise of his glory, who first trusted in Christ. In whom ye also trusted, after that ye heard the word of truth, the gospel of your salvation: in whom also after that ye believed, ye were*

> *sealed with the holy Spirit of promise, Which is the earnest of our inheritance until the redemption of the purchased possession, unto the praise of his glory. Wherefore I also, after I heard of your faith in the Lord Jesus, and love unto all the saints, Cease not to give thanks for you, making mention of you in my prayers; That the God of our Lord Jesus Christ, the Father of glory, may give unto you the spirit of wisdom and revelation in the knowledge of him: The eyes of your understanding being enlightened; that ye may know what is the hope of his calling, and what the riches of the glory of his inheritance in the saints, And what is the exceeding greatness of his power to us-ward who believe, according to the working of his mighty power, Which he wrought in Christ, when he raised him from the dead, and set him at his right hand in the heavenly places, Far above all principalitity, and power, and might, and dominion, and every name that is named, not only in this world, but also in that which is to come: And hath put all things under his feet, and gave him to be the head over all things to the church, Which is his body, the fulness of him that filleth all in all"* (Ephesians 1:3-23).

Brethren, now we are heirs of the kingdom of God. Joint-heirs with our Lord Jesus Christ through whom we have been blessed with all spiritual blessings in heavenly places, and which includes all the seven spirits of God in Jesus Christ. Herein lies the thesis of our overwhelming blessing. This is the joy unspeakable! That is why we are more than conquerors through the love of God in Christ Jesus. We possess the Excellent Spirit, to unlock the warehouses of God's mysteries, in excess of which Old Testament prophets only had in carefully regulated doses or quantities. Joseph and Daniel, for example, were able to interpret dreams to the letter and spirit, and Solomon had wisdom more that any previous royal due to this self-same Spirit of Excellence. That Spirit that revealed the kings' matters, be it Pharaoh's or Nebuchadnezzar's, now dwells in us fine and well. He is with us, in all, and in full glory. The Bible says, the Lord (Jesus Christ) is now that Spirit (II Corinthians 3:17).

Finally, as Revealer of all truth, operating in the name of our Lord Jesus, the Holy Ghost has also come to glorify our Saviour. He has come to glorify the One who, through the power of the Holy Ghost, has made the gracefulness and the glory of God to resonate and dwell on earth, during His lifetime as a man. So, now brethren, if you ask me, who has seen the glory of the Lord? I will answer: I have seen His glory; Jesus is the glory of the Lord! Is that not a miracle?

It definitely is, for the Apostle Paul also submits:

> *"For without controversy great is the mystery (wisdom) of godliness in the bible: God is manifested in the flesh; justified in the Spirit, seen of angels; preached onto the Gentiles, is believed on in the world and received up in glory"* (I Timothy 3:16).

The Holy Spirit as Comforter and Intercessor

Our God is quite magnificent at trouble shooting. He is the ultimate disturbance-Handler, as well as Provider and Caterer to our basic needs, interests, rights, well-being and aspirations. He consciously and consistently insists on making our lives special (III Jn.2). We must also bear in mind that humankind is not the only purpose of God. Oh chosen one, SO dearly as you are appreciated in His holy heart, yet your heavenly Father has multiple functions and prerogative outside his prime concern of making our lives unique (read his arguments with Job in chapterss. 38-42). That is why He had had to take time off His busy schedule to plan for us well before the world began. For example, after making Adam, He gave it a thought, and worked out that his creature might need company to keep going, so He went ahead and created Eve. When the first couple fell from grace to grass through sin, He stepped up in time to restored their inheritance by making His only Son a ransom for their sins. And how beautiful are those lines when the Bible says: *"And the Word became flesh and dwelt among us, (and we beheld his glory, the glory as of the only begotten of the Father,) full of grace and truth"* (John 1:14).

Even so, upon His departure for heaven, our Lord Jesus Christ made and kept His promise, of being determined, never to leave us destitute. He insisted He would not leave us comfortless:

"But when the Comforter is come, whom I will send unto you from the Father, even the Spirit of truth, which proceedeth from the Father, he shall testify of me: And ye also shall bear witness, because ye have been with me from the beginning" (John 15:26-27).

Again He spoke about the Holy Ghost to boost our morale and strengthen our resolve to keep holding until His second advent:

"Nevertheless, I tell you the truth; it is expedient for you that I go away: for if I go not away, the Comforter will not come unto you; but if I depart, I will send him unto you" (John 16:7).

Jesus rightly thought it expedient to send us the Holy Spirit for He is not merely a Comforter but most especially an Intercessor! Beloved, we have seen that God's foolishness is wiser than man, and His weakness is stronger or greater than man. For example, Jesus declared that of all who are born of the flesh, there is none like John the Baptist, but even the least person from the kingdom is greater than him. Hence, we are badly in need of spiritual support, just as Jesus had also had to rely on, during His time on earth. The blessed Apostle Paul spelt out a rather gradual, evolutionary perspective of our spiritual development:

"For we know in part, and we prophesy in part. But when that which is perfect is come, then that which is in part shall be done away. When I was a child, I spake as a child, I understood as a child, I thought as a child: but when I became a man, I put away all childish things" (I Corinthians 13:9-11).

Beloved in Christ, we are in dire need of an Intercessor, if we are to experience any measure of growth in the vineyard of the Most High. And if we are to be weaned off the childish, breast-feeding stage and proceed to that at which we feel comfortable, helping ourselves and others—living significantly: chewing real meat like reliable adults in the house of the Father, and not passively being spoon-fed on *Bebelac* milk, then we simply need to court the total and unequivocal assistance of the Spirit of God, because, after all, the battle truly is not ours, but the Lord's. We do have a justified belief in the resolve of our

God, as the Apostle Paul did plead our case before the Throne of Grace, by outlining the basis of our faith in divine intervention which is supposed to serve as a Scriptural guide to all believers in Christ who are hot on God:

"What shall we then say to these things? If God be for us, who can be against us? He that spared not his own Son, but delivered him up for us all, how shall he not with him also freely give us all things? Who shall lay any thing to the charge of God's elect? It is God that justifieth. Who is he that condemneth? It is Christ that died, yea rather, that is risen again, who is even at the right hand of God, who also maketh intercession for us. Who shall separate us from the love of Christ? shall tribulation, or distress, or persecution, or famine, or nakedness, or peril, or sword? As it is written, For thy sake we are killed all the day long; we are accounted as sheep for the slaughter. Nay, in all these things we are more than conquerors through him that loved us. For I am persuaded, that neither death, nor life, nor angels, nor principalities, nor powers, nor things present, nor things to come, Nor height, nor depth, nor any other creature, shall be able to separate us from from the love of God, which is in Christ Jesus our Lord" (Romans 8:34-39).

And beloved son, beloved daughter, know this: You are the apple of the eyes of your heavenly Father who shall keep you under the shadow of His wings. The Holy Ghost as Comforter means, the devil cannot render you comfortless. Therefore, brethren, as you would appreciate, getting any reasonable job done here, in the spiritual realm will normally require the full attention of the Holy Ghost as Comforter and Intercessor on your side. We must henceforth bear in mind that, at least from Saint Paul's doctrine, God is for us and will freely give us all things; and that He alone is our Judge; that Christ and the Holy Spirit are there to help us; that nothing can separate us from the love of Christ, and that is why we are more than conquerors over our enemies through Christ Jesus our Lord. In fact, except we backslide, our security in Christ is perfectly guaranteed by the Holy Spirit. Thus, one who lives and walks in the Spirit, will never be separated by any of the 17 things mentioned in v35-v39, unless he or she elects to commit the 17 things of Galatians 5:19-21. Therefore, the key to victory and blessed assurance for the believer resides in their ability to stick to the law of faith as outlined by Saint Paul in Romans 6:14-23; 8:1-13; Galatians 5:16-26.

Chapter 2: The Holy Spirit Is the Power of God's Might, and the Might of His Power

The Holy Ghost As Originator of Our Re-awakening; The Spirit of Revival:

Brethren, the Holy Ghost is at the centre of this new birth operation which the Apostle Paul so elaborately preached in his second apostolic missive addressed to the Corinthians:

> *"Wherefore henceforth know we no man after the flesh: yea, though we have known Christ after the flesh, yet now henceforth know we him no more. Therefore if any man be in Christ, he is a new creature: old things are passed away; behold, all things are become new"* (II Corinthians 5:16-17).

According to this doctrine, therefore, it is absolutely vain for any man to profess relationship with Christ in terms of the flesh. That is to say, without a genuine change of heart and mind or without being dead in sins and trespasses. That is why we do not know any man after the flesh, not even Jesus Christ! Beloved, this new heart is essential to assimilating the details of, as well as dispensing with the mystical power involved in decoding the mysteries embedded in the Gospel of Jesus Christ. No fleshly minded person can afford this onerous task by themselves, but by the Spirit of God, who the Might of His Power and the Power of His Might. In fact, all the Old Testament High Priests, Pharisees, Saddusees, Scribes or Sanhedrins were oftentimes at pains trying to follow the sermons of Jesus in the synagogues as they were still saddled with all the vestiges pertaining to the curse of the Mosaic veil. However, the bona fide born-again Christian who has died and resurrected with Christ through the power of the Gospel and the water baptism mystery has obtain the Spirit by grace, through faith. This then affords us the authority to unveil, and key into three essential functions of the Holy Spirit, as prescribed below:

> *"And I will pray the Father, and he shall give you another Comforter, that he may abide with you for ever; Even the Spirit of truth; whom the world cannot receive, because it seeth him not, neither knoweth him: but ye know him; for he dwelleth with you, and shall be in you"* (John 14:16-17).

Hallelujah! Hallelujah! Hallelujah!!!

> *"And when he is come, he will reprove the world of sin, and of righteousness, and of judgment: Of sin, because they believe not on me; Of righteousness, because I go to my Father, and ye see me no more; Of judgment, because the prince of this world is judged"* (John 16:8-11).

According to the Scriptures, therefore, it is the duty of the Holy Ghost to expose or bring to shame, anyone trying to conceal their sinfulness either by keeping it top secret or masking it in tradition, like the hypocritical Scribes, Pharisees and Saddusees of the first century. Jesus told the Pharisee Jews that He had not come to judge anybody, (John 8:15), but the Words (meaning, the Holy Spirit) that He spoke would judge them in the end. Due to the illusory power of of man-made traditional beliefs, many are not even aware of their acts as sin, unless it is totally unmasked by the Spirit of truth. For example, in the Western hemisphere there is the institutionalised hoax sanctioned by church authorities to compose songs of worship for, and even reverence the Tennenbaum (Christmas Tree); Father Christmas or Santa Claus—Nikolaus. All of which are demonic practices initiated by fleshly-minded ecclesiastic workers to quench the fire of Christmas. What is more, it is fast becoming endemic, often taken to grassroots levels, as the unlearned and worst still, little children are being raised and indoctrinated to perpetrate the heathen spirit, in the unholy culture of idolatry—worshiping the virgin Mary, and angels that are meant to serve them! What a pity! Turning the holy Christmas ritual on its head! So much with the encroachment of tradition into sacred history of the Nativity. Nevertheless, This function of soul-conviction by the Holy Spirit is global, and is embedded within the unction of Christ which is all-embracing, and not limited to the Jews. The Holy Spirit also convicts your heart to prove that sinfulness is the product of unbelief. The latter is therefore the source of our ignorance which births every transgression that will eventually damn the soul. Secondly, the Holy Ghost judges the world (all mankind) of righteousness due to the fact that our righteousness is an illusion in the face of the Lord (I Corinthians 1:30). Thus, it is only by Jesus alone, and by faith in His atonement that we will be able to obtain righteousness (Romans 3:22-25; 4:1-22; II Corinthians 5:14-21). As earlier mentioned, the Holy Spirit's earthly ministry comes under the authority of Jesus Christ. Hence, He does all this due to the absence of Jesus Christ, the Son of man. Remember God made the heaven and the earth. He rules in heaven, but the earth has He given to the children of men, of which Jesus is the firstborn. (Psalm 115:16; Romans 8:29-30). The Holy Spirit does all this while Jesus is at His Father's. It is expedient for us because, as Jesus Himself states (John 14:12); and as the Apostle Paul re-iterates (Hebrews 8:1; 10:19-23), He is in the secret place, at the throne of grace, at the right-hand side of His Father, to intercede for us. Above all, the Holy Ghost executes judgment so that all those who believe in Christ can escape the judgment of damnation through repentance (John 3:15-20; 5:24)—that all who refuse to believe will be damned with Satan (Matthew 25:41; John 3:36; Revelation 20:11-15; 21:8). Lucifer is referred to here as "the prince of this world". Therefore, all unbelievers are guaranteed judgment here, given that the devil himself has not been able to escape the long arm of God's divine justice system. Consequently, in the mighty name of Jesus, the Holy Ghost has also come to destroy all the works of the devil:

> *"And it shall come to pass in that day, that the remnant of Israel, and such as are escaped of the house of Jacob, shall no more again stay upon him that smote them; but shall stay upon the Lord, the Holy One of Israel, in truth. The remnant shall return, even the remnant of Jacob, unto the mighty God. For though thy people Israel be as the sand of the sea, yet a remnant of them shall return: the consumption decreed shall overflow with righteousness. For the Lord God of hosts shall make a consumption, even determined, in the midst of all the land. Therefore thus saith the Lord God of hosts, O my people that dwelleth in Zion, be not afraid of the Assyrian: he shall smite thee with a rod, and shall lift up his staff against thee, after the manner of Egypt. For yet a very little while, and the indignation shall cease, and mine anger in their destruction. And the Lord of hosts shall stir up a scourge for him according to the slaughter of Midian at the rock of Oreb: and as his rod was upon the sea, so shall he lift it up after the manner of Egypt. And it shall come to pass in that day, that his burden shall be taken away from off thy shoulder, and his yoke from off thy neck, and the yoke shall be destroyed because of the anointing"* (Isaiah 10:20-27).

Beloved in Christ, the above prophetic passage drawn from the Old Testament tells of the future victory of the Messiah over the Antichrist, and the restoration and restitution of the state of Israel in God's kingdom and righteousness through the power of the Holy Spirit. The point here is for all believers to consider themselves as bona fide members of *the house of Jacob*, a term frequently employed in the Old Testament to designate all of God's elect in Christ. The word rod is used here to denote the actions and authoritative power of the Holy Ghost upon the Messiah at His second coming. Once gathered and returned to Israel, the elect of the Most High will have to undergo chastening and tribulation, a battle that they are destined to win! The tribulation is therefore expected to last for a very brief while. Also, the Messiah will be God's scourge assigned to annihilate the Antichrist, even as Gideon was Jehovah's scourge in the day of Midian. As surely as God supernaturally parted the waters of the Red sea to preserve Israel, and destroyed Pharaoh in the midst of the sea, so will He supernaturally destroy the Antichrist and his armies. The Bible clearly states that come that day of the Lord, the yoke and burden which the Antichrist will have put upon Israel will be broken and destroyed because of the anointing on Jesus Christ, which is nothing else, but the power of the Holy Ghost.

Lastly, thanks to the anointing of the Holy Ghost who is the Power that proceeds from His Father, the Messiah will be able to redeem Israel at His second advent and establish a covenant with the house of Jacob—today, this group has been expanded and will include all God's covenanted people, taking on board those Jews and Gentiles who are in Christ Jesus our Lord:

> *"And he saw that there was no man, and wondered that there was no intercessor: therefore his arm brought salvation unto him; and his righteousness, it sustained him. For he put on righteousness as a breastplate, and an helmet of salvation upon his head; and he put on the garment of vengeance for clothing, and was clad with zeal as a cloke. According to their deeds, accordingly he will repay, fury to his adversaries, recompence to his enemies; to the islands he will repay recompence. So shall they fear the name of the Lord from the west, and his glory from the rising of the sun. When the enemy shall come in like a flood, the Spirit of the Lord shall lift up a standard against him. And the Redeemer shall come to Zion, and unto them that turn from transgression in Jacob, saith the Lord. As for me, this is my covenant with*

them, saith the Lord; My spirit that is upon thee, and my words which I have put in thy mouth, shall not depart out of thy mouth, nor out of the mouth of thy seed, nor out of the mouth of thy seed's seed, saith the Lord, from henceforth and for ever" (Isaiah 59:16-21).

The passage basically dramatises the struggles against satanic powers, but will assume a literal meaning when Christ will return in the power of the Holy Spirit to claim His authority over all principalities and dominions on earth by setting up His kingdom in Jerusalem which must be done at the expense of all opposing forces under the evil empire of the Antichrist, sweeping in from Palestine. The name of the famous battle is know in Christendom as the battle of Armageddon.

To sum up this section brethren, methinks it is fair and very much in place to submit that the Holy Spirit has come to help us hit the bull's eye of success in our spiritual battles. The ultimate Armageddon may not have occurred yet, but each and every one of us has got their respective Armageddons on a personal or collective basis, to prepare us for the final rout of the enemy. Nevertheless, the Spirit has come to intercede for us by helping us pray according to the graceful will and purpose of God, in Jesus' name.

The Holy Spirit Distributes Spiritual Gifts: Why The Gifts?

1. God's wish for us is that every believer should stay and operate within their gifts (*"Let every man abide in the same calling wherein he was called"* (I Corinthians 7:20).

2. He has also called upon His elect to eagerly pursue spiritual gifts (*"Follow after charity, and desire spiritual gifts, but rather that ye may prophesy"* (I Corinthians 14:1).

3. God grants the gifts for the general good. – *"For the perfecting of the saints, for the work of the ministry, for the edifying of the body of Christ: Till we all come in the unity of the faith, and of the knowledge of the Son of God, unto a perfect man, unto the measure of the stat-*

ure of the fulness of Christ: That we henceforth be no more children, tossed to and fro, and carried about with every wind of doctrine, by the sleight of men, and cunning craftiness, whereby they lie in wait to deceive; But speaking the truth in love, may grow into him in all things, which is the head, even Christ: From whom the whole body fitly joint together and compacted by that which every joint supplieth, according to the effectual working in the measure of every part, maketh increase of the body unto the edifying of itself in love" (Ephesians 4:12-16).

4. Finally, the gifts are given to empower the saints, enabling them live supernaturally through the promptings of the Holy Ghost— *"There is therefore now no condemnation to them which are in Christ Jesus, who walk not after the flesh, but after the Spirit"*(Romans 8:1).

Dear reader, this topic will be further consolidated in the next chapter. God bless you as you read on.

Chapter 3

PRESENTATION OF THE GIFTS (I CORINTHIANS CHAPTER 12)

"Now concerning spiritual gifts, brethren, I would not have you ignorant. Ye know that ye were Gentiles, carried away unto these dumb idols, even as ye were led. Wherefore I give you to understand, that no man speaking by the Spirit of God calleth Jesus accursed: and that no man can say that Jesus is the Lord, but by the Holy Ghost. Now there are diversities of gifts, but the same Spirit. And there are differences of administrations, but the same Lord. And there are diversities of operations, but it is the same God which worketh all in all. But the manifestation of the Spirit is given to every man to profit withal. For to one is given by the Spirit the word of wisdom; to another the word of knowledge by the same Spirit; To another faith by the same Spirit; to another the gifts of healing by the same Spirit; To another the working of miracles; to another prophecy; to another discerning of spirits; to another diverse kinds of tongues; to another thr interpretation of tongues: But all these worketh that one and the same Spirit, dividing to every man severally as he will" (I Corinthians 12:1-11).

Friend, the Apostle Paul opens his letter to the Corinthians by reminding them of the truth that Gentiles have been delivered from darkness by the power of the Holy Spirit, and that not by themselves or their works, but by the unmerited favour, mercy and grace of God. This gospel truth holds water here, because the Bible also says, nobody calls Jesus Lord but by the

Holy Spirit. Therefore the power of attorney which used to be the exclusive preserve of the Jews has become a common inheritance among both Jewish and Gentile believers of the Gospel of Jesus Christ. The first part of his letter also highlights the diversities of the gifts, their purpose and how they are distributed.

> *"For as the body is one, and hath many members, and all the members of that one body, being many, are one body: so also is Chrsit. For by one Spirit are we all baptized into one body, whether we be Jews or Gentiles, whether we be bond or free; and have been all made to drink into one Spirit. For the body is not one member, but many. If the foot shall say, Because I am not the hand, I am not of the body; is it therefore not of the body? And if the ear shall say, Because I am not the eye, I am not of the body; is it therefore not of the body? If the whole body were an eye, where were the hearing? If the whole were hearing, where were the smelling? But now hath God set the members every one of them in the body, as it hath pleased him. And if they were all one member, where were the body? But now are they many members, yet but one body. And the eye cannot say unto the hand, I have no need of thee: nor again the head to the feet, I have no need of you. Nay, much more those members of the body, which seem to be more feeble, are necessary: And those members of the body, which we think to be less honourabel, upon these we bestow more abundant honour; and an uncomely parts have more abundant comeliness. For our comely parts have no need: but God hath tempered the body together, having given more abundant honour to that part which lacked: That there should be no schism in the body; but that the members should have the same care one for another. And whether one member suffer, all the members suffer with it; or one member be honoured, all the members rejoice with it"* (I Corinthians 1212-26).

With a touch of genius, Paul evokes a verisimilitude between the usefulness and functionality of the various gifts to those of the different members that constitute the human body, and in this case, the body of Christ, in the second segment of his letter. The letter is also a showcase of the author's in-depth knowledge and sound understanding of the human anatomy. The body parts are used as spiritual conceits or metaphors to break the allegorical logjam contained in the mysteries of the Gospel of Jesus Christ. Paul maintains that Jews and Gentiles are now in the same body, and that as the human body is one and has many members, so the body of Christ is one and has many members who have been born again and who live godly consecrated lives:

> "When ye have lifted up the Son of man, then shall ye know that I am he, and that I do nothing of myself: but as my Father hath taught me, I speak these things. And he that sent me is with me: the Father hath not let me alone; for I do always those things that please him" (John 8:28-29).

In the latter part of his thesis, Paul argues that should Christians seek to please God with their attitudes, actions and life styles, then whatever part they play in the pecking order would only result in resounding success, and there would be no strife or confusion for positions and ranking as concerns their different offices:

> "Jesus answered them, and said, My doctrine is not mine, but his that sent me. If any man will do his will, he shall know of the doctrine, whether it be of God, or whether I speak of myself. He that speaketh of himself seeketh his own glory: but he that seeketh his glory that sent him, the same is true, and no unrighteousness is in him" (John 7:16-18).

Friend, here is the truth; here is the very mystery behind the righteousness in service to God and man: the man of God dissects the hidden truth to unearth the paradox that such inner members of the body as the liver, stomach, kidney, lungs or heart which we do not see and are therefore less honourable, delicate and feeble, tend to be those we not only cover, but have them well protected and preserved by the outward parts which make our physical structure, and upon which we are wont to bestow much honour and respect. Brethren, the paradox here is that while we apparently assume that life depends, for the most part, upon the functioning of the outward parts which we acknowledge, but still, we tend to inadvertently grant special care and attention to those members of our body which we apparently value less. This balances the equation of God's infallible sense of justice, namely that our limbs, feet, eyes, mouth, ears, noses and mouths which are the outer parts get the acclaim as they are physically attestable, while the hidden parts gain greater care and protection from being surrounded by those members that are visible. This itself, is a metaphor for the dichotomy between the value and importance of what is spiritual (not seen); and that which are material (seen). Paul makes it clear that the former are more enduring than the latter. Hence, the comely (graceful or good bearing) parts are beautiful enough in themselves, and as such have no special need to be highlighted for our attention or honour. To the uncomely (unseemly; shapeless) parts, we bestow more abundant elegance and grace as we cherish good looks in our outward appearance. Paul goes on to teach that the Almighty, in His infinite wisdom, has constituted and compounded the body together, rendering more special dignity to the inferior parts; making sure there is no independent and unnecessary segment to the body, and hence to see to it that every part contributes perfectly for the good of the human body as a whole. Friend, God's superior sense of justice means that at the final verdict, there are no complete losers or complete winners. All believers are winners! And this regardless of their various positions or abilities. Even today, many a clergyman out there are still in the throes of emulating the unwitting acts of the wicked servant whose insatiable greed and misconduct caused him to undermine the benevolent overtures of his Master to the extent of burying his talent in the rotting earth, an act that broke the heart of the former. Pretty much unbeknownst to him at the time of reception though, His Master had given him opportunity that matched his abilities, but he woefully lacked the Spirit of recognition which is vital for spiritual sustenance. Brethren, here is why we need the Holy Spirit to open the spiritual eyes of our understanding:

> *"Now ye are the body of Christ, and members in particular. And God hath set some in the church, first apostles, secondarily prophets, thirdly teachers, after that miracles, then gifts of healing, helps, governments, diversities of tongues. Are all apostles? are all prophets? are all teachers? are all workers of miracles? Have all the gifts of healing? do all speak with tongues? do all interpret? But covet earnestly the best gifts: and yet shew I unto you a more excellent way"* (I Corinthians 12:27-31).

The closing segment of Saint Paul's letter sets out to designate what exactly amounts to the making of the body of Christ, which is the church. He concludes that Christians—Christlike people who assume different functions actually sum up the argument of what is collectively known today as the church of Jesus Christ. He sets out to name the various classes of devout men and women who are legitimate vessels of providence, in the house of God. What we should never lose sight of is the fact that we cannot assume any position without the support of the Holy Spirit. He made us in His image, after His likeness and thus remains the corner-stone of our ecosystem. In hierarchical order, therefore, the offices are named as follows:

Apostles: The name is derived from the Greek *apostolos*, meaning delegate, one assigned with the complete power of attorney to represent or act in someone else stead, with the original person staying readily in the background to provide any necessary support to that effect. In Christianity, this means God grants His vessels the unction to perform certain important tasks on His behalf—what He would do if He were to be there in person. It is sometimes referred to as either *messenger or he that is sent*, at various intervals in the Bible. Jesus had many apostles: the three (Matthew 17:2; Mark 9:2); the twelve (Matthew 10:2); and the seventy (Luke 10:17) and many others (Joseph of Arimathaea Matthew 27:57; Ananias Acts 9:10-16; Paul I Corinthians 1:1).

Prophets: Next in line are the prophets. Prophets are the mouth-piece of God (Amos 3:7). They are preachers primarily preachers of righteousness, but are also equipped with the unction to predict the future. Therefore, prophecy is one of the important gifts of the Spirit (I Corinthians 12:4-11,28). Prophets are the ones who are endowed with this gift. Paul gave directions as to how this gift should be exercised in I Corinthians 14.

Teachers: The third office of the apostolic hierarchy is that of teaching. The word *"teacher"* is derived from its Greek etymology, *didaskalos* which is often translated as Master. In fact, most of the first century Scribes, Pharisees and Sanhedrins were teachers. Jesus addressed Nicodemus as master, meaning *"teacher"* which often carried both religious as well as administrative overtones: *"Jesus answered and said unto him, Art thou master of Israel, and knowest not these things?"*(John 3:10). Of course as a *"teacher"*, Jesus expected him to know more about spiritual matters than he actually displayed in his reaction to those questions. Thus, teaching is one of the important gifts of the Spirit.

Miracles: miracle workers fall just under teachers in terms of hierarchical significance. The Greek word for miracle is semeion, which stands for a sign or token by which something is known; a token of confirmation to prove a divine work or calling. It is sometimes also translated to mean wonders. All in all, the term is used to designate all the miracles and wonders wrought by supreme vessels of God to demonstrate their acknowledgment of the power of the Holy Ghost to their call and mission from God. More than any other gifts of the Spirit, this particular one happens to be the most abused of all. It is often used of the power by which false teachers show their sleight of hand to exploit the simple piety of the congregation, even as they hoodwink them into believing their fallacies to have come from God: *"Verily, verily, I say unto thee, We speak that we do know, and we testify that we have seen; and ye receive not our witness."*(John 3:11). Brethren, as the above Scripture teaches, and as the Prophet Isaiah asked the question: *"Who hath believed our report? And to whom is the arm of the Lord revealed?"* (Isaiah 53:1), Nicodemus did not believe in the testimonies of Jesus, at least not at this point in time. Hence the hopelessness of performing miracles to unbelievers. For the Holy Spirit, therefore, miracles are intended to manifest the power of the Gospel of Jesus Christ onto those who believe. As a matter of fact, those whose hearts are hardened against the Word will also not accept the evidence that is addressed to the senses, otherwise they might proceed to blaspheme: according the work of God to Satan thereby committing a mortal sin.

Healing: Friend, the gift of healing is by no means insignificant. In fact, it is one of the most important gifts of the Spirit of God because it is the first sign or token of salvation. That is why the Messiah made it one of the prime concerns of His three-and-the-half-year ministry: *"How God anointed Jesus Christ of Nazareth with the Holy Ghost and with power: who went about doing good, and healing all that were oppressed of the devil; for God was with him."* (Acts 10:38).

> *"But he was wounded for our transgressions, he was bruised for our iniquities: the chastisement of our peace was upon him; and with his stripes we are healed"* (Isaiah 53:5).

Hence, talking about the Holy Ghost and restoration or restitution normally centres pretty much on mending, curing, repairing: in a nutshell, it is simply a matter of carrying on the works of the Messiah which is all about making whole a world that has fallen short of the glory of God; a people that have descended so low into the worst squalor of irreparable self-ruin and moral decadence due to their sinfulness, iniquities and transgressions, having elected to pursue a life of rebellion against their God: *"All we like sheep have gone astray; and the Lord hath laid on him the iniquity of us all"* (Isaiah 53:6).

Hence the need for the Holy Spirit to impart the gift of healing for the restoration and restitution of the saints in terms of spiritual and clinical health care.

Helps: The Greek derivative is *antilepsis*, a support; succor; an aid. Greatly beloved in Christ, this refers to the different types of assistance God sets at the disposal of the church. This is not limited to the service rendered by the presbytery: elders, deacons and deaconesses, for there is usually other helps besides these. For example, when Solomon was building the Lord's Temple in the Old Testament times the Bible says he was supplied with a number of skilled and unskilled workers, by the Spirit of God. In total, there were 153,600 foreigners involved in the project, at various levels of construction and production—70,000 men to bear burdens; 80,000 men to hew wood and stone; 3,600 overseers. Besides them were 30,000 Israelites who served: 10,000 each month (I Kings 5:13-18). However, the gift of help is not limited to persons only, but to the various spiritual gifts which endue men with power to offer help. It is mentioned as a centre piece to the functions of the Spirit as Comforter—in the midst of references to certain gifts.

Governments. The church is also equipped with believers who possess extraordinary leadership skills, which is what governments are all about. The Greek equivalent for governments is *kubernisis*, meaning to steer or guide; pilotage. In short, this term as employed in this context is meant to designate all the means of guidance made available to the church by the power of the the Holy Spirit. Without necessarily alluding to the power of patronage, yet it implies to rally, at least in nomenclature, the collective effort of the distinguished men and women of valour, and in command of great wisdom, with a track record of proven ability and in-depth knowledge. People blessed with expertise in various areas of proficiency to fulfil the apostolic as well as administrative, and organisational requirements in the house of the living God: men and women whose business acumen and political clout puts them heads and shoulders above the average member, all constitute a resourceful pull of endless know-how for the ministry's daily upkeep. Moreover, the church is supplied with talented members possessing deep understanding, and sound counsel, and who are there primarily to help the church excel in matters such as conflict management and decision-making. The Spirit sets aside believers with the spiritual might to discern and guide the church along the narrow paths of God's will and kingdom values in righteousness.

Diversities of Tongues: Being the last mentioned, but by no means the least of the gifts of the Holy Spirit to believers in Christ, this is ideally demonstrated by God in the Scriptures of (Acts 2:5-13). It involves believers so imbued to supernaturally communicate with other languages which are, otherwise, totally unknown to them. It is one of the powerful ways to keep the devil at bay through the obscure utterances (especially during prayers and praises), by the believer who must worship God in spirit and in truth: *"God is a Spirit: and they that worship him must worship him in spirit and in truth."* (John 4:24). Therefore we conclude that diversities of tongues is nothing but the divinely ordained vehicle for channelizing the truth. Hence the Bible declares: *"Out of the mouth of babes and sucklings hast thou ordained strength because of the enemies, that thou mightest still the enemy and the avenger."* (Psalm 8:2). It is the language of salvation granted by the Holy Spirit: *"Jesus saith unto them, Did ye never read in the scriptures, The stone which the builders rejected, the same is become the head of the corner: this is the Lord's doing, and it is marvellous in our eyes?"* (Matthew 21:42).

Chapter 4

HOW THE GIFTS ARE CATEGORISED

Spiritual gifts can be subsumed under three different classes:

Subliminal Gifts or Gifts of Mental Transformation

The word of wisdom. The recipient is supernaturally imbued with insight intended to reveal the divine will and purpose, enabling them to solve any complex problems that may occur (Matthew 2:20; Luke 22:10-12; John 2:22-24; 4:16-19; I Kings 3:16-28; Acts 26:16; 27:21-25; I Corinthians 5).

The word of knowledge. That is not ordinary knowledge, but a heavenly initiative to supernaturally instruct the vessel by revealing details from the divine realm; insight into the mind of the Most High, about His plan, or that of another that His vessel cannot easily gain access to (Matthew 16:16; John 1:1-3; Genesis 1:1-2:25; I Samuel 3:7-15; II Kings 6:8-12; Acts 9:11-12; Acts 5:3-4; 21:11; Ephesians 3).

Discerning of spirits. This grants the believer full insight and understanding, by revelation, into the surreal world of the spirit. By this power, the servant of God will be able to survey the mindset and plans of men (Matthew 9:4; Luke 13:16; John 2:25; Acts 13:9-10; 16:16; I Timothy 4:1-4; I John 4:1-6).

Vocal gifts—Inspirational Gifts

Prophecy. The benefit here is that the believer will supernaturally be made to reason with the divine and obtain information by way of the native tongue. It is a miracle of divine utterance that surpasses human thought, explanation or reasoning. Its purpose is to speak to men so as to exhort, comfort and ultimately edify them (I Corinthians 14:3; Acts 3:21; 11:28; 21:11; II Peter 1:21)

Diverse kinds of tongues. The vessel of God will be granted supernatural utterance in other languages which are otherwise unknown to them (Isaiah 28:11; Mark 16:17; Acts 2:4; 10:44-48; 19:1-7; I Corinthians 12:10, 28-31; 13:1-3; 14:2, 22, 26, 27-32).

Interpretation of tongues. Bearer of such a gift is entitled to supernaturally interpret in the native tongue what is proclaimed in other languages and which, otherwise, would be completely unknown to the one who interprets—sort of like being the mouth-piece of the Spirit (I Corinthians 12:10; 14:5, 13-15, 27-28)

Power gifts—Operational gifts

Faith. This gift is a subunit of the Spirit of the fear of the Lord. It involves the supernatural ability to believe in God beyond any human shred of doubt, unbelief and/or carnal thinking (Matthew 17:20; 21:22; Mark 9:23; 11:22-24; Hebrews 11:6; 12:1-3)

Healing gift. This is nothing but the God-given unction to heal all kinds of sickness without the interference of any scientific or modern methods of treatment known to man (Mark 16:18; John 14:12; I Corinthians 12:9)

The working of miracles. This involves, amongst other things, God's prerogative to alter the course of nature in ways utterly unknown to mankind. That is to say, the supernatural power to intervene in the flow of natural events with a view to defying their authority and power, if need be (Matthew 17:20; Mark 9:23; 11:22-24; John 14:12; Hebrews 2:3-4; Psalm 107; Exodus 7:10-14:21; II Kings 4:1-44; 6:1-7).

AN EPILOGUE TO THE TRILOGY: TOWARD A CHRISTIAN COMMUNION

With The Holy Spirit To Birth Jesus, The Christ In Us (I Corinthians 12; Romans 12; John 17)

Lest we forget, Oh, precious one of the Most High! Thus, says the Lord: *"For my thoughts are not your thoughts, neither are your ways my ways…"* (Isaiah 55:8) which is suggestive of the fact His thoughts are sacred, and His ways, a secret. They are a mystery to the natural or secular world, and superior to the mundane: *"For as the heavens are higher than the earth, so are my ways higher than your ways, and my thoughts than your thoughts."* (Isaiah 55:9). Jesus anchored: *"And he said unto them, Ye are from beneath; I am from above: ye are of this world; I am not of this world."* Therefore, higher or above means divine, holy or superior, while beneath means devilish, mundane or earthly and that is why His ways or ethical values rank supreme to those of the world: *"For as the rain cometh down from heaven, and returneth not tither, but watereth the earth, and maketh it bring forth and bud, that it may give seed to the sower, and bread to the eater."* (Isaiah 55:10). Hence, His purposes are infallible, and are for the general good (Romans 8:28; Job 5:8-16): God is not partial or bias in His dispensation. He is the Righteous Judge (1 Peter 2:23). The song writer could not have been more right: *"You are too beautiful for description,…"* Beloved in the Most High: no song, nor verse; no poetry, nor music; no preaching, nor teaching; no representation, nor revelation can ever manage to capture the full range of His love, mercy and goodness onto us! Knowing His ways equips the saints with an invaluable asset—the kingdom standard which is sanctioned by the Holy Ghost (Isaiah 59:19). The Bible tells us that God's Perfect Law (His Word) is more to be desired than gold, and sweeter than honey, and in keeping His judgments and righteousness there is great reward (Psalm 19:10-11; James 1:25): *"I have more understanding than all my teachers: for thy testimonies are my meditation. I understand more than the ancients, because I keep thy precepts"* (Psalm 119:99-100). "With my whole heart have I sought thee: O let me not wonder from thy commandments" (Psalm 119:10). In life you keep secret anything you highly treasure, which is revealed only to those closest to your heart. That is why Christians are called upon to hear the Word, believe it, and keep it. To keep here, means to act on it through declaration and implementation, as the Spirit works up your faith to maturity. For all children of God, it is important to understand why we must praise and worship Him. First and foremost, He saved us; He called us with an holy calling; the Lord blessed us by His purpose and grace to be fruitful and subdue the earth, and finally it should be recalled that Jehovah planned for us before the world began, and the plan is of good and not of evil, so that we can have an enjoyable stay here on earth. His Son, Jesus also deserves our praise and worship. Jesus embodies His Father's blessings by His personal appearance (Immanuel) on earth; the same abolished death; He brought life through the Gospel, and also made available immortality to all mankind through His precious Gospel. That is why, Paul the Apostle of Jesus Christ, says in Romans 12: 3 *"I beseech you therefore, brethren, by the mercies of God, that ye present your bodies a living sacrifice, holy, acceptable unto God, which is your reasonable service."* Friend, herein lies the secret that is sacred. In the realities of this transient world, it is top secret! It is a privilege, even an honour to be privy to the things of God (Philippians 1:21; 4:4). Thus, Jesus had to declare the oracles of God to His chosen, only through parables, as from the thirteenth chapter of the book of Matthew so they may understand the value of their privileged position going forward:

> *"But blessed are your eyes, for they see: and your ears, for they hear. For verily I say unto you, That many prophets and righteous men have desired to see those things which ye see, and have not seen them; and to hear those things which ye hear, and have not heard them"* (Matthew 13:16-17).

An Epilogue To The Trilogy: Toward A Christian Communion

Consequently, as heirs of God, and within this current dispensation of grace, I vouchsafe right here that Jesus is that secret place prepared for us even before the world began. (Exodus 33:21; Psalm 91:1;Matthew 7:7-11; John 14:12-15; 15:5-7; Ephesians 1:3; 2:5-6, 10; 6:10-18; I Peter 1:3-5). To prove our case, however, we will have to look at the powerful mysteries wrought in both the Old and the New Testaments. In subsequent publications, to demonstrate the superiority of this current dispensation of the Spirit ,we will have to show the contained state of divine power before the first advent of the Messiah. We shall initiate a comparative study of Jesus' three-and-the half-year ministry and its overall impact on Christian life as a whole. But first of all, let us strike the key note, brethren. I reckon it would be appropriate to round up this maiden volume of the Production Bible with this verse taken from the book of James, the half-brother of our Lord:

> *"And the prayer of faith shall save the sick, and the Lord shall raise him up; and if he have committed sins, they shall be forgiven him. Confess your faults one to another, and pray one for another, that ye may be healed. The effectual fervent prayer of a righteous man availeth much. Elias was a man subject to like passions as we are, and he prayed earnestly that it might not rain: and it rained not on the earth by the space of three years and six months. And he prayed again, and the heaven gave rain, and the earth brought forth her fruit"* (James 5:15-18).

Friend, God delights in developing and keeping a relationship with each and everyone of us on a personal basis. This is evident right from the beginning (Genesis 2:19). That is why Jesus always prayed alone! The Father cherishes this candid intimacy to be without external influences: the prayer should be genuine and pure—straight from the heart (Proverbs 4:23; Leviticus 6:13). God delights in reaching out to His own. Jehovah adores fellowship. As a matter of fact, it is the only correction He made after His perfect acts in the process of world creation (Genesis 2:18-25). Adam needed company: someone to touch and feel, so He created Eve.

Nevertheless, once Adam undertook to operate in his sinful career, his acts and words were a total transgression of the truth which could no longer be condoned by the Spirit of God—Custodian of His Kingdom. Remember the Spirit of God upholds the standards of the Kingdom (Isaiah 59:19; Romans 14:17). That is when Adam 'lost touch' with his Maker (Genesis 3:7-11), to redeem him and restore the relationship, nonetheless, the Lord God had to sacrifice His only begotten Son to come down to earth so as to tabernacle, heal, save and reconcile through forgiveness of sins (Genesis 3:15; John 3:16; Philippians 2:5-8). Being a man, and having opted to pick up residence amongst His own (John 1:9-13): in a world bereft of holiness—even a cursed earth (Genesis 3:17-19). And given the manifold snares of the devil, Jesus could not have accomplished His task without the instrument of prayer. Like the lady with the issue of blood, we are healed and revived by touching our God in prayer (Matthew 26:41; Philippians 4:6).

The inability to initiate prayers on an individual basis is one of the shortcomings of the old dispensation. In the Old Testament church, every spiritual ritual was undertaken by group leaders, or spiritual chieftains: Prophets, Chief priests, Pharisees. Scribes or Sanhedrins. In short, worship back in the days was too elitist and/or impersonal and bureaucratic. This contributed in no small way, in alienating the people (II Corinthians 3:7,13-17). In Christ, however, we have a high Priest who knows our problems and has given us access to the secret place of God through His own life experiences:

> *"No man hath seen God at any time; the only begotten Son, which is in the bosom of the Father, he hath declared him"* (John 1:18).

> *"And no man hath ascended up to heaven, but he that came down from heaven, even the Son of man which is in heaven"* (John 3:13).

> *Neither pray I for these alone, but for them also which shall believe on me through their word; That they all may be one; as thou, Father, art in me, and I in thee, that they also may be one in us: that the world may believe that thou hast sent me. And the glory which thou gavest me I have given them; that they may be one, even as we are one: I in them, and thou in me, that they may be made perfect; and that the world may know that thou hast sent me, and hast loved me"* (John 17:20-23).

Now, notice that the Scripture uses present tense—reality, to talk about Christ's union with His Dad. That is what is expected of the born again Christian. For we are not only the temple of God, but also His royal priesthood; His chosen generation; and a peculiar people made ambassadors of Christ through the Holy Spirit anointing and power that has also crowned us with glory and made us an army that has might, even more than conquerors! Beloved, the singular challenge of today's church of Jesus Christ; to be able to win the hearts and minds of folks, the world over, is to emulate this union that Jesus demonstrated with the Father to show the world that their calling is of God, and that, it is what the early apostles were able to replicate again and again, in their ministration of the Word (Acts 1:14; 2:1, 46; 4:24, 32; 5:12). Today, alas, the church has fallen prey to the syndrome of disunity mentioned in the book of James:

> *"For where envying and strife is, there is confusion and every evil work"* (James 3:16).

Nonetheless, spirit-filled prayers also explain why old time warriors like Moses, king David, Solomon or Daniel, enjoyed divine favour so massively. They constantly sought the face of God in prayer from the secret place (Psalm 27:4; 42:1).

Brethren, like the song-writer rightly states, *"prayer is the key…"*, which means without prayer, there can be no invocation of divine grace by faith. The scriptures tell us that without faith it is impossible to please God (Hebrews 11:6). Therefore, a man of faith is, to all intents and purposes, a man of prayer. What heals the sick, as clearly stated in the circumstances of the above verses is when the prayer of faith is prayed and the name of Jesus invoked, the Spirit of the Lord initiates a fusion of your spirit with that of God to birth Christ in you, to the glory of God the Father Almighty. The Lord, then, shall raise up the sick and forgive him if he has sinned (v 15). The healing, forgiveness and deliverance power which is symmetrically linked to the power of resurrection in the Gospel of Jesus Christ is promised to all true believers, not only the elders of the church (Matthew 17:20; 21:22; Mark 9:23; 11:22-24; 16:15-20; John 14:12-15; 15:7. 16; 16:23-26). And oh, Lovely one in Christ, the secret place is sacred, and that is why any manifestation of the power from on high: whether healing or otherwise, is invariably intertwined with forgiveness, which stands for the reverence and purity in love of divine essence. Hence, fraternal love is evoked here to leverage the twofold condition for bodily healing:

1. Confess your fault one to another
2. Pray one for another, that you may be healed (Matthew 18:19; 21:22; Mark 11:24).

Putting individuals in the spotlight as we have experienced in the book of James is a tradition of the New Testament. This already speaks volumes of the influence of Christ upon the church. It is the New Testament church. The individual church. Just you and Jesus:

> *"There is one body, and one Spirit, even as ye are called in one hope of your calling; One Lord, one faith, one baptism, One God and Father of all, who is above all, and through all, and in you all"* (Ephesians 4:4-6).

Amen.

Other publications from the publisher

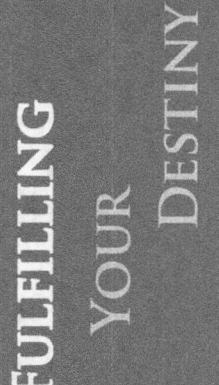

Other publications from the publisher

www.ingramcontent.com/pod-product-compliance
Lightning Source LLC
Chambersburg PA
CBHW071606080526
44588CB00010B/1042